TOURISM AND THE BRANDED CITY

New Directions in Tourism Analysis

Series Editor: Dimitri Ioannides, Missouri State University

Although tourism is becoming increasingly popular as both a taught subject and an area for empirical investigation, the theoretical underpinnings of many approaches have tended to be eclectic and somewhat underdeveloped. However, recent developments indicate that the field of tourism studies is beginning to develop in a more theoretically informed manner, but this has not yet been matched by current publications.

The aim of this series is to fill this gap with high quality monographs or edited collections that seek to develop tourism analysis at both theoretical and substantive levels using approaches which are broadly derived from allied social science disciplines such as Sociology, Social Anthropology, Human and Social Geography, and Cultural Studies. As tourism studies covers a wide range of activities and sub fields, certain areas such as Hospitality Management and Business, which are already well provided for, would be excluded. The series will therefore fill a gap in the current overall pattern of publication.

Suggested themes to be covered by the series, either singly or in combination, include – consumption; cultural change; development; gender; globalisation; political economy; social theory; sustainability.

160101

Tourism and the Branded City
Film and Identity on the Pacific Rim

STEPHANIE HEMELRYK DONALD
Institute for International Studies,
University of Technology, Sydney

JOHN G. GAMMACK
Griffith University, Queensland

ASHGATE

Published by
Ashgate Publishing Limited
Gower House
Croft Road
Aldershot
Hampshire GU11 3HR
England

Ashgate Publishing Company
Suite 420
101 Cherry Street
Burlington, VT 05401-4405
USA

Ashgate website: http://www.ashgate.com

British Library Cataloguing in Publication Data
Donald, Stephanie Hemelryk
    Tourism and the branded city : film and identity on the
    Pacific Rim. - (New directions in tourism analysis)
    1. Tourism - Pacific Area 2. City promotion - Pacific Area
    3. Cities and towns in motion pictures 4. Tourism - Pacific
    Area - Case studies 5. City promotion - Pacific Area - Case
    studies 6. Cities and towns in motion pictures - Case
    studies
    I. Title II. Gammack, John G.
    338.4'791

Library of Congress Cataloging-in-Publication Data
Donald, Stephanie.
    Tourism and the branded city : film and identity on the Pacific Rim / by Stephanie
    Hemelryk Donald and John G. Gammack.
        p. cm. -- (New directions in tourism analysis)
    Includes bibliographical references and index.
    ISBN 978-0-7546-4829-1
    1. Tourism--Social aspects--China--Hong Kong. 2. Tourism--Social aspects--
China--Shanghai. 3. Tourism--Social aspects--Australia--Sydney (N.S.W.)
    4. Tourism--Marketing--China--Hong Kong. 5. Tourism--Marketing--China--Shanghai.
    6. Tourism--Marketing--Australia--Sydney (N.S.W.) 7. Motion pictures--Social
aspects--China--Hong Kong. 8. Motion pictures--Social aspects--China--Shanghai.
    9. Motion pictures--Social aspects--Australia--Sydney (N.S.W.)
    I. Gammack, John G. II. Title.

    G155.C55D66 2007
    910.68'8--dc22
                                                                            2007009694
ISBN 978-0-7546-4829-1

Printed and bound in Great Britain by MPG Books Ltd, Bodmin, Cornwall.

Contents

List of Figures and Plates

Figures

Colour Plates

Frontispiece: Tsimshatsui Clock Tower, Hong Kong (photo: John Gammack)

Acknowledgements

Our primary thanks are due to the Australian Research Council, which supported this project for three years. We also thank our institutional homes over that period and in the two years running up to funding: University of Technology Sydney, Griffith University, University of Melbourne, Queensland University of Technology and Murdoch University. We have worked with many people, including some excellent research assistants and graduate students: Ming Liang, Sandy Ng, Jeannie Wong, Ling Yan, Leicia Petersen, Oli Mould (Visiting Postgraduate Fellow) and Damien Spry. All have moved on to greater things and we hope that their stint on 'Branding' helped define some skills and ideas for their brilliant careers. We are grateful to the many respondents who took part in our surveys and interviews, particularly the busy people in the film and tourism industries who were so generous with their time. We have had support from institutions in China and Hong Kong, including the Hong Kong Film Archive, the City University of Hong Kong and the Hong Kong Baptist University. The Transforming Cultures Research Centre at UTS was a great support in 2004-2005, as were other UTS researchers in related fields, particularly Martin Kornberger. Amazing help and hospitality came from Ian Aitken and Philippa Kelly in China, and Fiona and Norman Fowler in London. We also thank Catherine Kevin for assisting us so superbly in organising a final conference at the Australian Menzies Centre in London, Australia House for allowing us to hold that event in such spacious grandeur, and to Middlesex University and Eleonore Kofman for their important engagement with that conference. Our ensuing collaborations have created a beginning rather than an end.

We owe thanks also to John Golder, our Sydney editor, whose patience, ability to see the wood through thick trees, and grammatical exactitude are inspiring. As ever, we owe special and heartfelt gratitude to our families, intellectual friends, and loved ones. Stephi thanks James, Morag and Ellen. John thanks Paula, Val and Diarmuid.

*   *   *

Some of the chapters of this book contain ideas and arguments that have been previously tested in earlier publications. We acknowledge and thank those editors for allowing us to explore the subject of this research in their collections, and hope that they appreciate the considerable revisions in sections of the following:

Donald, S.H. (2004), 'Love, Patriotism and the City: Hong Kong's New Regime', in D. Verhoeven and B. Morris (eds), *Passionate City: An International Symposium,* held at RMIT, 27 August 2004. Refereed paper in Online proceedings, at <http://www.informit.com.au/library/default.asp?t=coverpageandr=L_PASCITSYM>.

Donald, S.H. (2006), 'The Idea of Hong Kong, Structures of Attention in the City of Life', in C. Lindner (ed.), *Urban Space and Cityscapes* (London: Routledge), pp. 63–74.

Donald, S.H. and Gammack, J.G. (2004), 'Branding Cities: A Case Study of Collaborative Methodologies in Cultural, Film and Marketing Research', *Everyday Transformations: The Twenty-First Century Quotidian*, CSAA Annual Conference, 9–11 December 2004. Refereed paper in Online proceedings at http://wwwmcc.murdoch.edu.au/cfel/csaa_proceedings.htm.

Donald, S.H. and Gammack, J.G. (2005), 'Drawing Sydney: Flatlands, Chromatics and the Cinematic Contours of a World's Global City', *SCAN: Journal of Media Arts Culture* 2:1, at www.scan.net.au/scan/journal/0405/refereed.php.

Donald, S.H. and Gammack, J.G. (2007), 'Competing Regions: The Chromatics of the Urban Fix', in G. Marchetti and T.S. Kam (eds), *Hong Kong Film, Hollywood and New Global Cinema: No Film is An Island* (London: Routledge), pp. 193–205.

Gammack, J.G. and Donald, S.H. (2004), 'Establishing Identity: Collaborative Methodologies in Film and Tourism'. Proceeding of the *International Tourism and Media Conference*, held at LaTrobe University, 26–28 November 2004. Extended abstract, at http://www.ertr.tamu.edu/conferenceabstracts.cfm.

Gammack, J.G. and Donald, S.H. (2006), 'Collaborative Methods in Researching City Branding: Studies from Hong Kong, Shanghai and Sydney', *Tourism, Culture and Communication* 6:3, 171–80.

Introduction

An Argument for the Cinematic City

This book provides an interdisciplinary theoretical basis for understanding and critiquing *city branding* as a cultural and political phenomenon, while also setting out an introduction to the practice itself. It approaches the question of branding through critical interpretations of cinematic cities, and is reliant on the discursive prism of cultural research for its tone and declared interests. We should emphasize from the outset, however, that it is not a manual for those who would brand cities or, indeed, any other destination or investment opportunity. Such texts exist (e.g. Olins 2004; Anholt 2005). There is also a burgeoning field in tourism studies on the subject of place branding (e.g. Morgan et al. 2004), defined as a strategy in which the industry and the education sector need to become fluent. Similarly, there is interest in place branding in the creative industries paradigm. There the focus is on the intersection of digital and visual media, and the creation of hotspots, cultural corridors, quarters or precincts. These are not areas which we avoid, but which we take as a policy-oriented part of a complex background to our underlying questions. These may be broadly summarized as: how do residents and visitors experience cities, and what part might cultural representations play in that experience? Do the concept and practice of branding have political dimensions? What does branding contribute to a city's imaginary structure, or, more simply perhaps, how does one live in a 'branded city'?

A very obvious vector of modern urban experience, which transects all the approaches to place branding, is in the invention of tradition and the deliberate connection of tradition to locale. Festivals are created by tourism authorities, and the subsequent visualisation and dissemination of these events attract domestic and international visitors. In 1998 the Hong Kong Tourism Commission listed sixteen districts, aimed at a mobile population of six million people. The task was to induce them to look at their own city afresh, to 'see' it as a place of variety and to 'use' it as a leisure destination. The idea came from the then Hong Kong Tourism Commissioner, Rebecca Lai, who lamented that whenever international visitors came to Hong Kong to shop on major holidays, Hong Kongers themselves would go over the Mainland border to Shenzhen to get a better deal. Now, it was not that Hong Kong was 'shut' when tourists arrived, but rather that Lai recognized that she needed to initiate brand identities for individual areas. In trying to sell the city as a whole, she had to describe a fragmented city that locals would recognize, and even authenticate, by their support. By 2006 there were eighteen districts listed on the website, each with their own logo, historic credentials and 'fun' attraction. Sha Tin is a populous area well off the beaten track for Hong Kong Island tourists, and best known for its shopping mall. Its temple life revolves around kinship and agricultural associations, and has not previously been promoted as a phenomenon of special significance, but simply accepted – like the bus station next door – as an ordinary aspect of daily life. Sha Tin is now a tourism district, with attractions that include the Heritage Museum, the Che Kung Temple and Snoopy's World – something for everyone.

Another way of administering difference is through film. When we started this research in the late 1990s, and began talking to tourism managers, film critics and filmmakers in Hong Kong, the link between the marketed city and the film industry was assumed rather than explicit. By 2006 the scale and power of Hong Kong's cinematic identity had been seriously put to use as an attraction for visitors. At moments of hubris we wonder whether our questions might have helped bring about this massive shift! Brand Hong Kong and the Hong Kong Tourism Board have released joint brochures naming films and linking them to their various locations. They promise 'cinematic contrasts' as you wander around a trail of place and image, carefully selected to get you right across the island, up the Peak and into the islands and New Territories. The third part of *Infernal Affairs* (*Mou gaan dou*, dir. Wai Keung Lau and Sui Fai Mak, 2002) takes you to Lantau Island's Big Buddha. It's a gangster/police thriller, but the brochure is not concerned with genre, preferring to encourage you to look at the film's Hong Kong landscape, to sit in the tranquillity of Buddha's surrounding countryside, and to relax. Peter Chan's film about history, motherhood and prostitution, *Golden Chicken* (*Gam gai*, dir. Leung Chun 'Samson' Chiu, 2002) is set in Jordan, which is close to Mong Kok, the red-light district on Kowloon. Once enticed there, the tourist is encouraged simply to shop: the brochure passes politely over the location's most obvious link to the film, sex with Mainland (or, in the case of *Golden Chicken*, local) prostitutes in the nearby street markets.

The Hong Kong cinematic tour is part of a wider strategy of bringing cinema and location together for the purposes of tourism. The tie-in between enhanced film locations (Beeton 2005) and national tourism campaigns offers a perfect commercial and creative synergy between the digital media, the film industry and the tourism agencies. *The Lord of the Rings* trilogy (2001–2003) illustrate the point: the digital landscapes created by director Peter Jackson to match Tolkien's mythic narratives and New Zealand's aggressive promotion of the country's natural beauties throughout 2003–2005 proved to be of enormous mutual profit. However, while it is useful and pragmatically convincing to describe what happens when industries converge, or how a particular marketing mechanism works, it is probably not quite enough to simply state the fact. Just as a film is more than the sum of its locations, so a city is more than the sum of its brands. Indeed, cities are rapidly becoming the main locus for humanity's future. By the end of 2010, approximately 60 per cent of the world's population will live in cities. In Australia, where we are writing this book, that figure will be 80 per cent. In China the figure may be close to 50 per cent (UPI 2006), which might well translate into more than 1.5 billion people. How people live in these urban centres will depend on the centres' physical resources, as well as various aspects of their infrastructure, both imaginary and actual. Transport, affordable housing, access to water, sustainable energy, adequate jobs, cultural possibilities and education are the assets generally proposed when considering a city's future. We would like to think about them alongside consideration of two kinds of emotional relationship to a city, that of someone who *loves* it and that of someone who *belongs* there.

The question 'how' then requires an *affective* answer, and one which notes that urban infrastructure must be as much a set of emotional and cultural resources as pragmatic ones. *How* will people imagine their cities and those of other people and other nations? *How* will they understand the place in which they live? What will it mean to be where they are? What effect will the perceptions of others have on their own experience of everyday life in a city? In the following chapters we shall look at these questions through the prisms of branding and cinema. The seemingly disparate formations of cultural knowledge are, we suggest, both essential to the ways in which cities become visualized, known and inhabited. Brand designers aim to manufacture *how* we experience a product or a place through their affective use of narrative and image. This is not always successful, nor is it necessarily possible, given the complexity of some forms of lifestyle and urban engagement, particularly if we can describe living in a city as an act of consumption. Nevertheless, the idea of branding is highly suggestive of an infrastructure of symbolic and emotional capital. Certain key features are captured and promoted, others are disdained or re-narrativized, in order that a more desirable sense of self/place may emerge. The cinema also affords insights into how a city tells its own stories, and thereby builds its self-perception and the perceptions of others. New Yorkers are loud, self-obsessed, funny, clever and urbane. Londoners are either suave and class-conscious or edgy and disposed to crime. At least, that is what we learn from films. And, as we shall suggest, Sydneysiders stand for Australians in general, and the Sydney locations used in films are legible as such only to locals. Do these (mis)representations matter? If so, how might we use our theoretical tools of analysis to make of them meaningful commentaries on the urban condition?

Our discussions are supported throughout by reference to case studies on the West Pacific Rim: Shanghai, Hong Kong and Sydney. The geographical choice is pertinent to our core thesis, which is that *narrative*, whether realized through 'pure' text or in image and sound, is fundamental to the organization of space and place on local and global scales of imagination and practice. The West Pacific Rim, in which we include Australia, China, Japan and the Pacific Islands – although we focus on Chinese and Australian cities – is our deliberate regional bias. The Rim is a globally significant geo-political area that encompasses Greater China, Japan, SE Asia and Australasia. It is differentiated in our argument from the more widely discussed 'Pacific Rim', which, of course, includes the west-coast cities of North America. There are two main reasons for this distinction.

First, it separates first-world preconceptions of the Austral-Asian region from a regional understanding of place. In discussions of the global or world city there is a tendency to place Australian experience inside a so-called Western US-oriented paradigm within the Pacific Rim discourse (Tse 1999; Sassen 2002), and thus to undermine its strong historical and current links to the West Pacific Rim, to Asia and, particularly, to China. A recent example of this dichotomized and geographically illogical thinking is apparent in an otherwise thorough coverage of the Rim in terms of property markets, which yet explicitly divides the book editorially into east and west, and places Sydney and Melbourne in the 'west' (Berry and McGreal 1999). The refusal to allow even the possibility of a liminal Austral-Asian perspective panders to a political expectation that in matters of policy, population and (free) trade Australia should belong to the West. This tendency also encompasses Hong Kong by feeding a caricature of the city as a required gateway to China coming from a disassociated 'West', rather than an Asian city on the West Pacific Rim that has responded creatively to colonialism and global commerce. West Pacific cities are better seen as negotiators in the historical and contemporary relationship between China and the Western world (Chow 1998; Lo 2001). As such, the Rim is a region in which a city such as Hong Kong has a distinct but connective personality in relation to its neighbours. Hong Kong is entrepreneurial in collaboration with its competitors in Southern China, particularly in Guangzhou, and in competition with Shanghai (Jessop and Sum 2000), while Shanghai is itself self-promotional, addicted to development and hungry for ascendancy within the Chinese urban sphere (Wu 2000).

These partly economic, partly socio-cultural characteristics infuse the cities as places to be, places to watch and places to visit – but also as places that compete with one another for very similar cachet. Secondly, in cinematic terms, the mythological and imaginary power of the US cities on the Rim is extremely well understood and, indeed, has had global cultural purchase for a century. Shanghai audiences were watching the American city on film in the 1920s (Fu 2003). We wonder therefore about the cinematic counter-purchase of cities on the Western Rim, where, although films have been made and consumed, it is doubtful that they have achieved a global imaginary impact, equivalent to that of downtown USA.

It is, of course, no secret that the global narratives of cinematic affect and urban resonance are rooted in the pre-eminence of American and European cities. This is due in part to the academic and popular publishing power in those regions and also, need it be said, to the phenomenal success of American film export over the past century. Everyone who sees films knows, or thinks they do, what a US city looks like. New York, San Francisco, Chicago and LA are embedded in cinematic consciousness, thanks to the many versions of those cities that populate the Hollywood screen. Even specific locations (the easterly view over the Hudson River, the running path by the basketball courts in Central Park) are recognizable to viewers who have never set foot in the United States. Europe also has its cinematic cities: Berlin, London, Paris and Rome, and a number of scholars have dealt with the impact of these cinemas on the formation and character of the cities in question (see Shiel 2006; Lindner 2006; Tallack 2005; Marcus 2007). European cities are also powerfully evoked in literature and have reached way beyond the confines of their national and regional origins. Readers, especially those in postcolonial zones of South and South-East Asia and with access to the colonial canon, will surely have a sense of 'London' as a textual space which dominates their perceptions and disappointments of the city as an actual place. In her 2004 novel, *Small Island*, Andrea Levy describes in painful detail the shortfall between the imagined London and the life lived on arrival. But even in so writing she regenerates the image of the city that inspired the originary hope. An affective brand is hard to dispel. How many readers sharing a postcolonial history will know the London of Woolf, Dickens, Wordsworth, Austen, or even Hogarth's Gin Lane, as well as a Londoner quoting the Tube map? Indeed, how many Chinese intellectuals remember reading, as part of their revolutionary education, Lao She's story about living in a rented room in London? The ironies and reversals in the imperial system of text and image are revealed and countered in the works of many literary critics. (Rey Chow's work (1998a and b) on Hong Kong is particularly significant.) The present book does not take on that important engagement in the same way, but it does proceed from an acknowledgement of the uneven modernities within which we inhabit and consume urban culture, and the degree to which those hierarchies of knowledge and space regenerate themselves through such consumption. We need to counter received versions of the city by insisting on other modernities, different spatial limits and regionally relevant definitions of boundaries. So, here we provoke an alternative spatiality by refusing the European and American examples of urban affect, accessing instead a regional narrative of achievement, belonging and imagining.

Hong Kong is a place that exemplifies the break between colonial and postcolonial belonging. Only recently returned to Chinese sovereignty, its residents are torn between competing patriotic duties: they bear actual and symbolic allegiance to both the People's Republic of China and to Hong Kong itself. Both nodes of belonging are essential to what it means to be patriotic, and both are heavily involved in producing the meaning of the city, as a cinematic centre of production, as a place brand and as a place to live and have an impact. China is the centre of Chineseness in the region and across the world. It is an undeniable political force with growing authority over its neighbouring states. It is also a multi-social, multi-ethnic and multi-lingual identity structure, within which Hong Kong is but one set of iterations. To be Chinese is not therefore a homogenizing tendency, but a broadly understood political and social responsibility. Likewise, to be a Chinese city is not to be the same as all other Chinese cities (although this happens), but to recognize one's position in the state's hierarchy of economic and political functions. Where local structures exist comfortably and without undue friction alongside that standard requirement, a Chinese city can be both culturally discrete but also sufficiently 'national' to support the agenda of the Party-State. A status quo is thus achieved. Many Hong Kong residents are first- or second-generation Mainland migrants with an emotional stake in the Mainland, while others are finding that caring about China's development and prosperity is a reasonable and workable way of negotiating their new responsibilities in being Chinese. But, as we shall argue later, there is a local sense of belonging that is particular to Hong Kong and which makes narrating the city-as-brand a delicate task. When this narrative exercise is tested against the work of filmmakers, arguably the strongest voices in Hong Kong's cultural world, it emerges that the competing patriotisms are not invariably commensurable.

Sydney is also a postcolonial city, though it has, of course, been separated for far longer from the colonial power. Unlike Hong Kong, however, Sydney has not completely severed its political links with Britain. The British Queen is still the monarch, although her representative, the Governor-General, is nominated by the Australian Government and anyway impinges only minimally on the average Australian's consciousness. The narrative that Sydney tourism leaders promote is one of pleasure, beauty and diversity. Its soft focus is on the topography of land and people. It is an extraordinarily attractive place in which to spend time, and its visual character somehow smooths its rough history of deportation, settlers' struggle, crime, inter-racial destruction, and boom-or-bust development policies.

A recent 'vox pop' poll of rich ex-pats and new rich (*xin gui*) in Beijing's gated villa suburbs found that most people there dreamed of living in Sydney rather than where they were. Arguably, this softening is a boon for the city as a tourist and residential location, but a problem for it as a film location. The 'edge' of Sydney does not translate easily to cinema. On the other hand, that may simply be cinema responding to the city's pathology, where the edginess and the placidity of the city contest Sydney's character across historical matrices of old and new expectations. When we suggested to a group of ex-pat intellectuals from China that Sydney had 'gone flat', one very fluently countered that of course it was flat, that was why people lived there. They *wanted* flat, having had more than enough bumps in their previous places of residence or origin.

Shanghai is compared to Sydney by those of its residents who know both countries. It also has a sweep of topographic elegance, traces of colonial architecture and a predisposition to a relaxed life-style that runs counter to the madcap urge to succeed at all costs. Like Sydney, it has the reputation of being an international city, but in many ways enjoys the character of a much smaller, more parochial place. Intimate circles of power and influence run both cities. The place of the parochial in informing a large city's depth and variety (indeed, what tourism officers would term their 'districts') is evident everywhere. But, arguably, in Sydney and Shanghai, these largely benevolent parochialisms are close to the surface. And, finally, they share a history of peripheral acceleration. Just as Sydney did in the mid-twentieth century, so Shanghai is currently going through a phase of rapid development, which is altering the landscape dramatically. Historic sites are disappearing under concrete, fewer than 1000 buildings across the city are heritage-listed, and where it was once said that by visiting Shanghai you could see 'a hundred years of China's history', now it is more a case of only seeing the last twenty years of the country's development. The wholesale destruction of Sydney's old quarters stopped at The Rocks, but there is a great deal of concern that in Shanghai it may already be too late to apply any such restraints.

Unlike Sydney, however, Shanghai has a distinguished cinematic past, with films – especially those of the 1930s – that defined Chinese cinema of the pre-Liberation period. Indeed, many of the stylistic aspects of these films *still* define Shanghai's image of itself. This is ironic when set against the disregard for the buildings that populate, and grace, the films in question. So, Shanghai offers an excellent case study of a brand that is bifurcated along temporal lines. Whereas Shanghai the international city is excessively and obsessively postmodern, Shanghai the cosmopolitan treaty port and metropolitan lodestone is lodged in a 1930s modernity which simply cannot endure the weight of development it is currently undergoing in its new guise as an international centre of finance. Nostalgia thus competes with the aesthetic of the *brand new*, the *globally scaled*. But it also complements and contributes to its perverse attraction. As the older buildings and laneways (*lilong*) disappear, so their very absence becomes potent and piquant to the city's brand promise. Similarly, the idealization of the beauty and clever energy of Shanghai's women, memorialized in films as well as in novels, continues. The modern woman (*modeng nuxing*) of the 1930s was elegant but tragic – Ruan Lingyu, the suicidal filmstar-model for the modern woman, is iconic – and even in recent publications women are exhorted to re-discover that kind of cosmopolitan femininity (Donald and Zheng 2008). Yet, today Shanghai women are mainly known for their ability to succeed in commerce, their political savvy and their high level of education. So Shanghai presents an outrageous face to the world. The city defines herself as a modern woman, with a quaint and racy historical past; a show-stopping beauty making her way in the world with a flair for business, fashion, and self-regard.

The cities on the Rim each manifest specific temporal orientations to city identity and character. By way of an opening gambit we shall suggest that Sydney is oriented to the present, with a past that is neither denied nor confirmed in its brand. Historic Sydney is lauded mainly for its commercial offerings and its everyday hedonism, shopping, eating and drinking latte. Shanghai is oriented towards the future. It has, however, a vertiginous, postmodern approach to the past, whereby one period – the 1930s – ignores several decades of civil war and revolutionary leadership in order to provide a ghostly backdrop to the glamour of internationalization. In Hong Kong the past and present are better integrated. Colonial rule has left traces, and the current political system is powerful, but it is the people themselves who provide a continuum in the image of a city that has often been mistaken for a quintessential global city, as opposed to a Chinese city with strong cosmopolitan experience.

We hope that these city narratives will allow a number of different disciplinary perspectives to suggest themselves as complementary ways of thinking about urban belonging, spatial organization and the globalization of place. We come from different academic traditions – one from film and area studies, the other from psychology and business informatics – and our aim here is to write for our peers across a number of disciplines. We are particularly anxious, however, to interest younger scholars, whose habits of perception are as yet open to the challenge of equivalence across disciplinary boundaries.

As we noted above, the aim of our contribution to existing scholarship and expertise is to extend the idea of branding to cultural research, cinema and media studies. At the same time we critique the concept in so far as it ignores some of the deepest human responses to place, and the political contexts in which those occur. In short, we offer a fresh approach to reviewing the standard and emerging literature in these fields, and report primary research findings that include textual analyses, interview data and politically nuanced reflections on current situations and experience. The book is also careful to include the perceptions, aspirations and ethics that are important to residents, as well as the needs and expectations of tourists, business visitors and financial investors in the city's economy. Taken as a whole, this work supports our macro-thesis that, in an ideal world, a city brand should contribute to the widest possible discussion on development, identity, and sustainable economic well-being.

'The Image of the City'

In 1960 Kevin Lynch published a short, but inspiring book, entitled *The Image of the City*, in which he presented his research on how people understood urban space on a quotidian basis. Half a century later, we discuss our own findings on how urban space is experienced, extending the 'image of the city' to include cinematic and commercial considerations. We take Lynch's central point, that people make meaning out of space by moving through it in daily life and by finding their way as they go. We extend the point by arguing that filmic renditions of certain cities are also crucial to the experience of urban life and visitation. Similarly, we suggest that commercial, marketized, versions of the city can be both profoundly revealing and constitutive of the ways in which a city is understood by those who live in it. The idea of the city is not limited only to its physicality, and neither are its inhabitants its only stakeholders. These claims lead us inexorably to consider the contemporary phenomenon of 'place branding', and the ways in which this phase in urban developmental policy might inform a wider conceptual approach to the image of the city in social science and cultural theory.

The 'place brand' – or 'city brand', the phenomenon we specifically address here – is a concerted attempt to pull attractive and distinctive features of a city into a manageable, imagined alignment. It is a constructed personality of place, which is designed to allow people to build and maintain an ongoing relationship to a particular urban location. The branded city is presented as either touristic or 'touris*ted*' (Cartier 2005), as a desirable economic location for investment and as a metonym for the nation. Film is often crucial to branding strategies, particularly where a city is known for and by its cinema.

Lynch's work was concerned with American cities, but his approach has informed urban planning the world over. Our three core cities are all located on the West Pacific Rim and are regionally highly significant. Nonetheless, despite the rise of China, these international cities are not yet in the same global league as those at the heart of American and European influence: Paris, London, New York and Los Angeles. Part of the appeal and power of those cities is, we argue, their cinematic presence and their concomitant appeal to branding strategists. Can we see similar potential realized on the Rim? Is it feasible to argue that the filmic image of Rim cities can challenge the depth of cinematic attention demanded by New York and Paris? And, if so, how might the activity of branding and the pull of the image come together in a deep structure of international consciousness?

Hong Kong SAR (Special Administrative Region) is the most obvious case in point here. Film is a major export and asset of the city, and the genres are well known and well documented (Chu 2003; Yau 2001). A wider range of film styles and histories is described in the publications of the Hong Kong Film Archive (e.g. Wong 2003), reminding us not only of the martial arts (*wuxi*), sentimental love stories, gangsters, police dramas and ghost stories, but also of the literary adaptations, Cantonese social dramas, and strange tales (*liaozhai*) that have been part of a long history of translocal film in the southern part of China (including Hong Kong). As these historical perspectives remind us, Chinese language film (*huayu dianying*) has been a translocal, and even transnational, phenomenon for most of the last century, with producers (such as the Shaw Brothers), directors and actors moving across and between shifting borders of identity and political belonging. The Shaw family was originally from Ningbo, the children were educated in Shanghai, and the film business stretched and shifted between Singapore, Shanghai and, eventually, Hong Kong. One of the present author's first contacts with Hong Kong film occurred in

1981 in Taiwan, where she met Jackie Chan. He was shooting a film set in pre-modern China, for the Hong Kong and diasporic Chinese-language (*huayu*) market. To her shame, she had no idea 'who' he was, only that he was clearly famous and quite fun to socialise with. His status as the emerging 'King of Comedy Action' was fulfilled when, four years later, he made *Police Story*, possibly the film that most powerfully, and amusingly, captured the strangeness of British colonialism (and withdrawal) in the 1980s. Today Chan is an icon, a symbol of Hong Kong, but his film popularity has decreased markedly amongst young Hong Kongers. Irony and local love of place have not disappeared, however. The McDull cartoon series (*My Life as McDull* (dir.Toe Yuen, 2001), *McDull, Prince de la Bun* (dir. Toe Yuen, 2004) and *McDull, The Alumni* (dir. Leung Chun 'Samson' Chiu, 2006)) tells disarming tales about a small pig called McDull, who represents all that is hopeful and hopeless about contemporary Hong Kong culture. This pig was the film character that we singled out in 2003 as a phenomenon speaking eloquently about the *un*branded aspects of Hong Kong. Now, in 2006, McDull has been incorporated into the tourism lexicon. Short clips are even shown on welcome monitors as one arrives at Hong Kong international airport, with segments specially animated in order to teach children and parents such things as safety procedures and correct airport behaviour. Such a congruence of scholarly and commercial thinking makes the subject of this book powerfully topical. It is appropriate, then, that we move from the American sites of Lynch's book to an Asian-Australian thematic. The image of the city is mobile, and increasingly so.

Lynch's 'image of the city' is the starting point, but certainly not the sole categorization of the relationship between people and the urban/e spaces they create and inhabit. James Donald's 'idea of the city' (1999) makes the point that city space is also cinematic, literary and musical space, accommodated in the minds of those who have read, seen and heard the sights of the city in mediated forms. This is not to argue that the idea of the city is the same thing as experience, but to acknowledge that the imaginative potential of renditions of the city have the ability to inform and enable imaginative responses to actual place. In film and cultural theory, the 'visual city' is an important descriptive category for understanding modern urban life, the built environment, and the fantasies and cultural mores that sustain both. Thus, the image of the city exceeds the schematic and emotional mapping of its literal geographical and environmental features, and combines at an imaginative level with the artistic, cinematic, sonic and literary expressions of its sensuality, its tough – or perhaps exotic – beauty and glamour.

So, this book argues that the city, humanity's most complex built achievement, has always been a text for mapping the spatial ambitions, productive possibilities and mobility, or constraint of human beings. The city constitutes an image, an idea, a vision, a musical score or a sound-scape. It is all of these and more than the sum of its possibilities. Thus, people know a city as they know a particularly dear or complicated friend, but it is also a place they use: material, traversable, liveable. The idea of a city that exists beyond its solid self is crucial in a project that aims to open up the idea of city branding to historical trajectories, to the interpretative world of film and to the various mapping projects that are logical extensions of ways of understanding the city over time. The most recent iteration of urban mapping is the trend for creative cities and knowledge economies. These part-economic, part-governmental notions have triumphed as orienting themes for development in post-industrial society. The creative mapping of cities is concerned with making a qualitative, economically-oriented statement about how much revenue certain 'creative' activities produce, and the degree to which, especially, digital futures provide a foundation for employment and wealth in modern urban settings. This research, exemplified in the work on the knowledge economy (into which film and branding is categorized) by the Creative Industries Centre in QUT (Keane 2007) and by Simon Roodhouse in the UK (Roodhouse 2006) fits into a longer context of visualizing the city in the present or past in order to understand it in the present or future.

Creative mapping is one way of addressing how a city lives as a dynamic sensorium of human occupation and activity. Historical mapping is another crucial pathway to understanding how a city has developed its sense of self, its personality and its engagement with the people who make it work. The idea that one must map the past in order to gain access to the present is the very foundation of the discipline of history. Arguably, then, maps of the city are forerunners, not merely of modern orientation maps, nor of the creative cities with their clusters and hotspots of economic activity, but of the idea of the city in film, the image of the city in modern urban planning, the city as a 'hub' in creative policy, the city as a brand, and the visual city of cultural criticism.

Cities on Paper

In Peter Whitfield's *Cities of the World: A History in Maps* (2005), the world is not configured along the West Pacific Rim. Nor, on the other hand, is it particularly biased towards the current world order of global cities. Whitfield's maps, drawn from the British Library collection, are interested in the very idea of a drawn city, and what the drawing itself tells us about the world in which that map made meaning. The collection does not deal with either Hong Kong or Shanghai, but it does look at Sydney, a world city with a relatively recent international profile and a strong brand, based on sun, sky and relaxation. Sydney is also now a centre for digital imaging for films, a contemporary fact that sits strangely with the haphazard city of the nineteenth-century map, where one gets a decidedly vertiginous sense of a semi-planned economy of space that cannot quite overcome the tyranny of the terrain, the, now prized, spits of land that project into the ocean. Whitfield's book also contains a map of another, much older city that was founded as a repository of learning in an early iteration of the 'knowledge economy' of the élites of Europe, Oxford. The Oxford map is a good starting-point for this backdrop to the branded and cinematic city. First, the map is an encounter with a spatially realized ideal of knowledge concentration, what might nowadays be considered a 'cluster'. The meaning of Oxford is highly controlled in this image. Each college, library and University building is noted in a detailed aerial view 'as if seen from some non-existent hilltop east of the Cherwell' (Whitfield 2005, p. 139). The map is an engraving of a place in which people (and very few are depicted) are representative of the scholars and travellers who populate the city, but are secondary in importance to the place itself, to the 'cluster' that these august buildings create, and to an idealized and curtailed idea of the city that would in contemporary parlance be dubbed a 'place brand' or 'brand identity'. There is nothing on the map that does not relate to the ideal of learning as embedded in an architectural form, designed to house knowledge and to inspire the minds of those who come to study and teach. This not only suggests that the city's identity has been established by its spatial proportions and the way in which they map onto an ideal of knowledge accumulation, but also that the visual proportions of the city are bounded by that expectation rather than by any more realistic view of Oxford's heterogeneous nature (a city of erstwhile car manufacture, deprivation, fights between 'town and gown'). From this we might speculate that creative clusters, which are vital to much of the developmental and research work in the branding paradigm of urban development, are not unlike the imagined collegial spaces of knowledge in the quintessential Oxford. They exist, and can be shown to exist, through the activities of mapping and visualization, but they offer – as, arguably, does all mapping – no more than a partial view. For instance, the digital industries which 'characterize' Sydney, Vienna and London congregate either due to active seeding in urban regeneration projects or educational development programs, or as an unplanned, but organic clustering in relatively cheap areas where start-ups can thrive and personnel can live close to the workplace. Simon Roodhouse (2006) has argued that this leads eventually to inflated housing costs and the gentrification of areas which succeed, thus enshrining particular high-cost clusters but restricting access to new start-ups. It is not a huge move to suggest that the halls of Oxford also spent many years as a prohibitively guarded institution for the children of the rich and just a few scholars from the lower-middle and working classes. In other words, the creative clusters model is inherently a class-based vision of development, whereby artisans lend cultural value to place, but are themselves inevitably replaced by richer members of the bourgeoisie, the middle classes or the global élites.

One might argue from the start therefore that branded, clustered versions of creativity are threatened by their own success. Knowledge economies attract a different sort of life-style investor, as they are supposed to do, once the creative workers and entrepreneurs have got something moving. Or, the creative cluster promotes affluence for some, but sits amidst a wider world of disadvantage. The challenge, then, is to manage a knowledge economy to have more porous boundaries in its spatial incarnation – not at all like the walls of Oxford, which were built in the late eleventh century, at a time when the settlement developed from being a farming and religious community into a centre of learning and religious élitism.

The brand image is also a contemporary factor in this reading of creative clusters against the management of knowledge in Oxford. Oxford has become, as *Brewer's Dictionary* nicely puts it: 'a neatly packaged heritage product that attracts very large numbers of tourists from around the world' (Room 2005, p. 843). The point for academic approaches to branding as a disciplinary focus is that this 'heritage product' was set in train eight centuries ago with the walling of the city and the creation of buildings that were at once real and affective. The relationship between urban development, historical trajectories of power and (something like) knowledge economies understood over time, rather than in a bubble of contemporary economics, allows us to see very clearly how place identity is forged.

Sydney is represented by a nineteenth-century map in Whitfield's book and this offers us lessons in how the spatial imagination can give us metaphorical access to the past and the future. The Sydney map is less figurative than that of Oxford of the same period. Its aim is to describe the broader pattern of spatial organisation rather than the features of heritage buildings with inspiring contours and contained collegial histories. There is no sense of clusters, but rather of flows between the land and the sea. As Whitfield points out, the city has not at this stage claimed back the land that is now part of the harbour side. Nor has the city yet gained an identity that can be willingly shared as a branded entity with 'neatly packaged' outcomes for its economy. The reality of the city's nineteenth-century grimy (and plague-ridden) streets is deliberately hidden by a schematic attempt to record its emerging urban shape. Clearly, the latent brand of Sydney has not emerged. This is not yet a map of a place known for its sun, sea and generally relaxed approach to life, although its parallel ambition as a capital city (still obvious to those who live there, but never achieved) is apparent in its adoption of Empire-derived street names and statues. Today, in the twenty-first century, Sydney is a veritable hub of the creative economy in Australia, and it is also the centrepiece of 'Brand Australia' (identified by the Anholt-GMI Nation Brands Index (Anholt 2005) as the world's top national brand). Yet it still resists mapping as a series of discrete and identifiable clusters. Personnel in the digital industries associated with filmmaking are instead networked at subtle levels of social and personal horizontal integration (Mould 2007). In other words, this is not a clean set of clusters and architecturally imaginable entities, but rather a viral and interest-based skein of connections and friendships and favours. Again, looking at the nineteenth-century map – or, indeed, at the current and complicated Sydney rail map, which opens up another set of possibilities (and takes us to a second map book, John Clark's *Remarkable Maps* (2005)) – it is arguable that the topographical image of Sydney manages to both obscure and inadvertently reveal that productive complexity which characterizes the city's identity.

Clark proffers the story of the London tube map (p. 76) as evidence of a visualization that undoes unnecessary conceptual complexity, while enabling a workable directional understanding of a major city that grew through several centuries of power, commerce, religion and knowledge and is suitably convoluted as a result. For Sydney, that complexity has not yet been tamed, nor, indeed, might it ever be: there is no teleological imperative that all cities have the same propensity for visual management as the package that is Oxford or the commonly imagined nodes of London travel which are based entirely (we would contend) on four generations of the Tube Map, designed by Harry Beck in 1932.[1] The tube map uses spatial relationships, and colour to mark the nodes, edges and lines of the city above, giving 'the impression that the Underground was the outcome of a conscious, unified, intelligent design – which it certainly was not' (Whitfield 2006: p 185) Tragically, the location of the London bus and tube attacks of July 2005 were mapped onto our consciousness because of the tube map: anyone who has

---

1   Without the Central Line, who would connect St Paul's and Tottenham Court Road? And what histories have been created by these haphazard connectivities?

visited London for any length of time knew exactly where Aldgate East, Russell Square and King's Cross stations sat in relation to each other.

There is, of course, an undoubted brand identity attached to the modern Sydney, one that emphasizes its coastal blue and yellow beauty, its sandstone heritage, its playful hedonism and its villages of culture and, crucially, food. We will explore the chromatic and emotional, tasty side of this brand in later chapters. There is very little in its brand value, however, about its contribution to the knowledge economy of the state, the nation or, indeed, the world. The underplaying of Sydney's digital brand value appears almost as a self-directed collusion. A Beijing-based film and digital content manager acknowledged to the research team that Sydney was 'pretty good' at post-production, but that it 'wasn't Hollywood'. What might we learn from these small slights? Perhaps we see simply that the cartography of a city is accurate to the extent that the shape of urban space is indicative of the way in which topography and the nature of settlement occur/develop. In Sydney's case this was always random, anti-élite (except in the case of those few who were sent out as rulers) and always dominated by people who were either forced out of England, Wales, Scotland and Ireland or else came of their own free will, in search of an alternative set of life chances. There were also Russians, Dutch and French, and, prior to the White Australia policy after Federation in 1901, there were many Chinese who came to Sydney to (literally) set up shop. The visual city of the European and particularly the British imagination probably did not match what was actually occurring on the streets of Sydney, where the Asian and European settlers, together with Indigenous workers, toiled in an attempt to make the city a going concern. This untidy diversity is not mapped.

Visualizing the city over time and branding the city in the contemporary moment are linked narratives. The one tells us something of a city's desired self, and the other tells us what aspect of that sells to tourism and investment clients. Neither does more than hint at the experience of a city on the ground, but those hints are visible if we use maps as a guide to what is hidden as much as to what is on display. In terms of the cinematic present and digital futures, the maps of the past will reveal the ways in which networks and patterns of human activity have been embedded as a spatial characteristic of a specific place.

Looking at the more banal examples of the mapping industry, such as tourism brochures or council web-pages, we may feel that urban cartography has gone backwards, losing much of its structural and draughtsmanlike quality. Indeed, we might go so far as to suggest that the city of brochures and websites has taken over from the city on paper. Yet, the combined sophistication and integration of visual media – outdoor screens, cinema, advertising and online commerce – truly bear witness to the world of attractions (Crary 1999) through which we understand ourselves and our daily lives as city dwellers. The screen does not take us away from the content of a city's history, commercial strengths and cultural mores. Rather, the importance of narrative is closely tied to the convergence of screen conventions with other modes of public discourse. Thus, a wise brand designer will seek to discover the stories which thrive in a particular location, and which underwrite how people imagine and regulate their lives on a symbolic level.

In Hong Kong in 2003–2004 the city brand team ran competitions in which local residents were invited to submit stories about Hong Kong as a place, inventively combining shared history and personal memory. The resulting submissions married mythology to local detail, and suggested a rising patriotism in the post-SARS era. And memories of sheltering under a Song Dynasty stele during the Japanese invasion of the territory made Hong Kong's further reaches, up into Sha Tin and areas known for years as the *New* Territories, appear as though they had always been part of the Hong Kong imagination and spatial ontology. 'Off the map' for the Hong Kong islanders, Sha Tin is now on the map for visitors who take up the invitation and narrative enticements of these kinds of initiative. Such stretching of the spatial dynamic is more problematic in Sydney, where the concentration on the iconic centre – that rushing down to the sea of the original maps – is unchallenged in all but the most local of print and televisual media stories and is mainly characterised by inter-suburban rivalry at the most banal level. But the point is common to both these cities and arguably all others. However heavily mediatised and digitised a city may appear, it has no shape beyond the scope of its narrated local and international identity.

The visual city of cinema, which reached its premature apogee in the 1920s films of Germany and the Soviet Union, and its postmodern apotheosis in the 'Tokyo-like city' of *Blade Runner* (dir. Ridley Scott, 1982) has moved into a new phase. Over the last twenty years, students of design, cultural studies and media have moved from universities to the professional world, taking with them a canny and assured understanding of the visual field. In the late 1990s, the postmodern city of cinema became utterly familiar, not through film but through its repetitions in other media: through clever ads, the multiplication of those ads on screens in urban space, and within the convergence of style and identity, commercial and aesthetic taste, use and superfluity which essentialize urban living on film. Stasis and transition have been used in concert as elements of design, indicators of ludic elegance and, cumulatively, as a dialectic of cultural change which eschews a political agenda.

Situate this argument in the cities on the West Pacific Rim, and the visual city opens up a multitude of pertinent political questions of belonging, transition politics and development issues. We might ask how China, a nation increasingly obsessed by national branding, is drawing on its visual heritage and its contemporary attractions to build on stasis in a period of transition. What are the national characteristics that are encouraged, cultivated and encapsulated to sell China to itself and to its neighbours? How do cities with national and international status position themselves in China as a whole? And, what is the nature of competition in the context of a regime which wants to devolve regional responsibilities across its territory, but which assumes centralised control of the national agenda? We might also ask how Australia, in a close trading relationship with China, and increasingly aware of Chinese strategic pre-eminence, seeks to differentiate itself as a multicultural outcrop of West Pacific identity, with specific urbanities and aspirations at its core?

The Cinematic Visual City

Elsewhere in this book we argue that place identity has an effect on the status and affect of local cinemas, where cinema and brands converge to either make or break local film cultures (also Donald 2006 and 2007). The ways in which one measures this effect must be quantitative, qualitative but, finally, intuitive. America is the ultimate case in point. Many films are set in New York, Chicago and San Francisco. Those films sell all over the American international film market, which is one of the two largest such markets in the world. Those same cities are hyper-brands: everyone would claim to know a little about all three – an accent, the weather, an icon, or just a way of being. At the same time Bombay (Mumbai) is the urban centre of the other global film player; India. Its genres, stars and music are exported all over Asia and Europe. But Bombay has no place brand, and very little popular recognition as an urban entity outside of its immediate Indian population and diaspora. This anomaly is partly due to the way in which US films have been used as spearheads of international trade and cultural diplomacy over the century of cinema. The export and consumption of US cinema linked the film industry to the branding phenomenon. The US recognised early that the cinema offered them not just export dollars but also a cultural stalking-horse in the post-war Cold War era. Of course, the Soviet bloc and the CCP also used film for ideological purposes, but, frankly, the US did it much better and more effectively, perhaps because film was seen first and foremost as an entertainment export. Perhaps the US ideology allowed a diversity of narratives and fantasy structures that created a familiarity based on location rather than solely on typologies or narrative. Perhaps the US was selling its belief in itself as a geopolitical and social destination, more than it was underscoring the ideological means to achieve that. Perhaps its advanced modernity simply suited the rush of film, giving its major European landing-stage more energy and more sensation, all of which could be shown to great advantage in cinematic genres (Tallack 2005).

Principally, however, while American film travels, America's cinematic brand lies anchored in the glamour and despair of its cities back home. San Francisco has Alcatraz; Sydney has Cockatoo Island. Both were prison islands, but which is the better known and why? Moreover, US filmmakers have a domestic audience as well as an international one. Their films are both parochial and attentive to global desires. Indeed, it is arguable that their local bias makes their international appeal stronger, precisely because of its demands on the international imagination. An American cinematic city becomes *the* cinematic city, setting a standard that other cinemas must consciously ape or eschew. The effect is that, in national cinemas other than that of the US, cities are *by default* exotic, other, or – and this is often a problem for Sydney – unrecognizable as cities at all.

The normalization of US cities as the default urban space on film is a remarkable American achievement. In the terms of Michael Billig's paradigm of nationalist banality (1995), the US has cultivated a banal nationalist branding mechanism through cinema. It is banal, or 'cool', in so far as there is no necessary vigour or danger to the patriotic tendency maintained through such cultural strategies of the national brand. Only in times of war or recovery from war (as in the quotas imposed on the export of US film specified in the Marshall Plan following World War Two might this banal narrative of US supremacy burn hot and shift location outside the US. *Rambo* (dir. Ted Kotcheff, 1982), *Apocalypse Now* (dir. Francis Ford Coppola, 1979) and *The Deer Hunter* (dir. Michael Cimino, 1978), for example, are all icons of hot US nationalism after war's end, and the motivation in each of their narratives is to get people home, or away from a madness offshore. While variously critiquing the impact of war on individuals, such films never waiver from the assumption of US subjectivity as the continuing factor in narrative interest and closure. To watch these riveting films is to be confronted with American values, and understand them spatially as much as intellectually. Now, two or three decades later – specifically since Americans flew their flags at home in grief at 9/11, and then overseas in the ensuing war against terror – Billig's cool or banal flag-waving has of course shifted entirely to a hot national temper of the times.

The third film exporter is Hong Kong. Although the SAR film industry has experienced difficulties since reunification with China (Pang 2002 and 2005) film is still a crucial element in the city's life. The place is still strongly branded through its films, actors and famous genres: martial arts, cops and gangsters, Wong Kar-wai urban romance, with a touch of Cantonese social realism for the locals. The brand requires the idea of film, and the various strategies that support the brand in tourism and investment marketing use film as a vital component of their content. Arguably, without film Hong Kong doesn't really 'work'.

The 'City of Bits'

A different conceptualisation of cities based on informatics concepts and their transformative potential has been emerging in recent years. In 1989 Manuel Castells (1989 and 1999) described 'the informational city' and new urban forms where tertiary economy flows coexist with devalued social groups and spaces. Coward and Salingaros (2004) view cities as complex interacting systems of flows that can be analysed using concepts of information architecture appropriate to evolving, dynamic forms. Their focus on functional rather than structural path-making allows everyday journeys to be conceptually modelled to provide insight into urban connectivity. Effective plans can then focus on ensuring effective and adaptable information exchanges rather than the urban 'violence' of thoughtless road-widening and high rise apartment blocks. These may look neat and efficient, but they ignore the complexity of human spatiality. Tall buildings are not necessarily ugly, but they contribute to the destruction of sustainable urban life, together with its local paths and connections.

Online communities, whose functions, temporary structures and adaptive shapes are designed by the users themselves, imply different conceptions of distance, time and presence, and suggest new planning models for live or mediated experience (Churchill and Bly 2000). This is particularly important in countries such as Australia, where large distances, even within metropolitan areas, mean social interaction is often dispersed and mediated. Simon Mackay, based in Melbourne, first proposed the concept of an Internet city in 1999. He designed a virtual reality experience of 'walking' through specialized precincts. The walker makes electronic purchases and enjoys various entertainments. Plots of land on the walk are sold for real money through estate agents.[2] Mackay thereby attempts to usher the capitalism

---

2   The city was called e-Estate. See 'City Life Beckons on Net', *Sunday Times* (Perth), 12 December 1999.

at large in virtual space onto a comprehensible city pathway. His city walk reduces the commercial information from millions of unorganized web pages to a navigable model familiar from everyday life. Another Australian, MIT's William Mitchell (1995 and 1999) proposed the 'city of bits' hypothesis: a new economy of presence, in which choices among combinations of physical presence and telepresence, synchronous and asynchronous modes of interaction in space and time, become possible. He subsequently developed this idea into an expanded understanding of architecture and urban design infrastructure that took into account the ways in which communication, work and community life are enacted in the digital, as well as the physical, environment. Both dystopias and utopias can be predicated on these possibilities, although community life may well reproduce itself in traditional ways whose temporarily stabilised forms overlap and intersect with the virtual and the physical. Mitchell, a technology enthusiast, suggests a new and adaptable urban typology, in a global urban system that is more rhizomic than hierarchical in character. Such ideas extend both the visuality and functionality of the city to its transmission and mediation through Internet channels, and also to proximal electronic possibilities of the built environment.

Ken Goldberg's collection of essays (2001) reminds us of the powerful dialectic between the garden and the machine as the objective of progress, and this tension increasingly informs the city as idea and realisation. World-wide 'digital city' projects are blending the physical with a virtual, informational experience of the city and introducing digital modes of citizenship and identity formation. While this is not a new aesthetic, it is more widely realisable than ever before, thanks to telepresence and virtual reality. The 'enchanted circle' of eighteenth-century panoramic tourist rotundas and the 'automaton in the metropolis' are both mythic tropes that are now being reproduced as civic life becomes mediated (Grau 2001).

Even in understanding the physical city, Lynch's base concept of 'place legibility' refers essentially, as he well knew, to an information space: its aim is to help people understand 'where they are and what is going on'. Large cities are traditionally characterised by strong paths, distinctive, clearly-visible landmarks, and areas in which tall buildings dominate. However, despite the regularity of their topography, they often require representational signage, which is not always helpful and merely adds to visual pollution and clutter. Hong Kong and Sydney are two such cities. On strategic street corners, both have maps or signs indicating significant landmarks, but which are not always visible among tall buildings and only of use to pedestrians.

Walking is surprisingly important in place legibility, even in a world city. The Legible London project aims to make London a world-class, walking-friendly city, by simplifying confusing signage and 'giving people the confidence to walk in the capital is an important milestone for [its] continued success' (New London Architecture 2007). An elementary form of the (everyday) experience of the city (see De Certeau 1984), walkability is important for residents, and also for visitors, not just to get a sense of scale and feel for the place, but to explore the shops, parks, eating and entertainment options, and other everyday but unfamiliar sights. Walking gives visitors direct experiences, allowing them to be thrillingly, but neither irretrievably nor unsafely, lost in spaces that reflect a particular way of life or history. One Sydney marketer we interviewed observed that it is '(unusual) to become lost in Sydney – Melbourne's city blocks are functionally easy to navigate, but Sydney's irregularities are part of the character'. Ironically, Tourism Victoria (Melbourne) ran a 2006 advert, gorgeously displaying its urban shapes and carrying the message 'It's easy to lose yourself in Melbourne'. Indeed, in recent years Melbourne has enacted policies that have revitalised its public life and desirability (City of Melbourne 2004). Meanwhile, this practice of everyday life in Hong Kong, whose central area is physically walkable, is oriented more towards business than pleasure. Hong Kong's business ethic is revealed by its long urban escalators through the mid-levels. These outside escalators are necessary to citizens who need to reach shops and homes on the steep slopes of the central island. The underlying expectation of these passages is that people want to travel swiftly to their destination, and so the technology directs citizens to unnatural speeds the 'movements [of which] are fully pathed according to the needs of [businessmen and politicians]' (Siu 1999, p. 668).

Any agora, especially a city, is a plexus of information and communicative interchange, but most information is now born digital, directly and variously communicable and recombinable, and this is radically changing ideas of urbanism. For example, Taipei, already among the world's most wired cities, has a development vision to enhance its competitiveness as a cybercity with unlimited, ubiquitous and accessible cyberspace. In Taiwan's tertiary education, long established technologies of distributed video-conferencing, networked meetings and interactive broadcasts are now so pervasive, affordable and useable that education models need no longer rely on either staff or students travelling to a physical university. Implementing policies which will increase Internet use in education and public life (Ma 2001), Taiwan has established information kiosks and community websites throughout the city, freeing up roads and overcoming the lack of physical space. It goes without saying that Hong Kong and Shanghai are also highly wired cities.[3]

In everyday city life, cameras record and track vehicles, calculating and billing tolls automatically, and beacons detecting bus positions in order to update electronic signs at bus stops are now common. In many cities, ubiquitous computing devices and communication technologies also allow parking meters and cars to communicate, traffic signals to coordinate their activity dynamically and visualisations to be projected on buildings. Local maps are able to be generated and displayed on demand. Such examples are a part of the contemporary city's emerging digital infrastructure, and technology's next generations can be expected to serve ever more applications as they are required.

What will be the expectations for a city of the future, familiar with telepresence and asynchronous interaction? With Shanghai a prominent and enthusiastic participant, a high-level forum on Urban Information in the Asia-Pacific Region has been held every year since 2000. Recognizing cities' information exchange function and seeing informatization as 'a new impetus for city development', the first of

---

3   This is starting to engender other social problems: apart from censorship issues, excessive internet use is blamed for student failures, with one in eight young Chinese net users reportedly addicted – i.e. online for more than 38 hours a week (Watts 2006). 'Half-way houses' have been set up in Shanghai and Hong Kong to support minors who would otherwise spend all night in Internet cafes.

these forums – 'Promoting City Informatization for a Better Future' – adopted the Shanghai Declaration, which stressed the promotion of mutual understanding and ICT cooperation among Asia-Pacific cities.[4] In its mundane aspects, informating the city provides an infrastructure that immediately allows different forms of citizen engagement with government, employment, education and transport, eliminating any need of a physical environment for the town hall, the university and the cinema, at least as far as their essential informational functionality is concerned. But this may become just the entry level of infrastructure for increasingly complex mediated experiences.

Virtually real cities allow safe and effortless traversal and engagement in cyber-shopping, cyber-tourist or cyber-social experiences and are not alien to the prosumer[5] successors of the playstation generation, who can expect to participate in designing their experience. Cyber communities are already common, extended networks of online friends who may never have met in the flesh, but who are changing concepts of sociality and community. And transfer from the virtual to the 'real' world is already possible. A generation that has grown up with games such as SimCity are now beginning to participate in 'alternate realities', lifestyle games in cyberspace that cross over to the physical world, where characters within the game space can phone, fax or email players in their physical homes and induce physical responses and social behaviours. These parallel universes, such as secondlife.com – used by one hotel chain to market test possible designs – and Habbo Hotel,[6] allow players to live imaginary, 'second' lives, in which they can conduct everyday activities or realise dreams. They are able to buy real estate, avail themselves of various services (including real currency transactions conducted on- and off-line), design city neighbourhoods (or anything else) and participate in all manner of events that mimic the historical development of cities – but without being tied to traditional social or physical structures. New land can be 'created' as required, and there is a currency exchange mechanism between virtual and 'real' US dollars. In July 2006 the Veronicas, a Brisbane-based pop duo, performed at the Habbo Hotel Australia (Habbo.com 2006), chatting with users of the online community, while other established media stars are morphing into cartoons, thereby avoiding the constraints of age and increasing their image manipulation possibilities.

McKenzie Wark's concept of the virtual republic is relevant to discussion of these new 'cities within cities', that are at once local and situated, yet unconnected. Wark suggests (1997, p. 11) that 'the virtual is that world of the potential ways of life of which the way things actually are is just an instance'.[7] Conversations,

---

4   The Shanghai Declaration 'responded enthusiastically' to UN resolution 231 (54th session). Informatization addresses globally imbalanced ICT development, and its principles for co-operation among cities to reduce the digital divide were subsequently adopted.

5   Described in Alvin Toffler's *Future Shock* (1970), the term is a contraction of 'producer' and 'consumer', and implies a close involvement in the production process by consumers themselves.

6   www.habbo.com.au/ is the address of Australian hotel in the chain.

7   Quantum computing theory suggests that this is how situations are actually realized.

particularly about identity, take place in the virtual space of media to produce 'our sense of the public thing': communication, once referring to transport, is now about information and the structures and possibilities it shapes, imposing a 'second nature' on the natural environment. These behaviours intimate an imagined environment that supports virtual communications. We contend that the imagined place is nonetheless predicated on the actual connected cities that make virtuality possible and fun.

Digital or cyber cities also promise a rapprochement allowing for recombinant urban design, governed by four principles of technology-enabled place-making: fluid locations, meaningful places, democratic designs and threshold connections (Horan 2000). These principles imply new activity patterns at what Manuel Castells calls 'the interface between places and flows' (1999, p. 41), along with an anchoring sense of physical place.

Hanne-Louise Johannessen (2004) describes a new sensibility of space as performative, user-oriented, information laden and based around immersive social flows and interactions. Marcos Novak's trans-architecture concepts, such as eversion, connote an invisible architecture in which the virtual becomes the physical experience and creates a 'habitable cinema' (Gullbring 2001). This allows an experience of a place that is not limited simply to its physical reality, but which is nonetheless emplaced. Both being of a place and yet separated by the fact of technology is also the condition under which cinema is to some degree mapped into its supposed locations.

Currently, the virtual is understood as a secondary reality, even in an immersive environment where a three-dimensional world is experienced.[8] Novak's 'digital places manifesto' augments physical reality towards an enlarged conception of place and its technology-enabled possibilities. His eversion concept complements immersivity to render and invisibly shape the physical world in synaesthetic concepts originally virtual, as traditional distinctions between interior and exterior blur and technology becomes ubiquitous. With new ambient qualities given by mutable colours, sounds and other synaesthetically designed electronic engagements, the experience of places becomes freed from the immediate restrictions of the built environment. This blurring of interior/exterior boundaries is also becoming realized in built forms, where shapes project into spaces to add dimensionality that is neither clearly inner nor outer (Benjamin 2006), echoing older, particularly Chinese, architectural forms. Similarly, the design of multifunctional but wired spaces permits communities to gather and shape the use of those spaces flexibly, as may be seen in the case of MIT's newer student laboratories and social spaces, which are designed to allow emergent forms of student interaction and engagement.[9] These various approaches

---

8   Architects already use immersive virtual reality in design processes: for example, in a study of the design of a toddler's rooftop playground and a helipad for Central, Hong Kong showed its value in communicating a possible realisation to users and professionals (Schnabel and Kvan 2001). Place-making, cognizant of symbolic associations, would thus increasingly involve a citizen-engaged design process, informed by Novak's trans-architectural pragmatism in organising and everting information in physical space.

9   The point was made by William J. Mitchell in a talk given at Queensland University of Technology in March 2004.

to the modern conception of place are, we would suggest, based on the knowledge of cinematic presence and urban experience that the modern world has gleaned since the 1900s. The speed at which we move through space – whether it is in Novak's imaginary worlds, or on a Hong Kong escalator – has already been prefigured to us by the speed of film (J. Donald 1999, p. 76). And, as we move through spaces with the rapidity of cultural technology or of engineering, we are also given access to the very places they traverse and represent.

The Ideal City

The ideal city has been theorized since Plato, through Leonardo and Thomas More, to the realized visions of architects such as Le Corbusier, social reformers such as Robert Owen, and many others. Since ancient times cities have emerged that are both organic and planned: Brasilia and Canberra are familiar recent examples of ideal city planning, cities that have been designed, rather than allowed to grow organically. Shanghai's satellite Lingang New City is a planned port city of 800,000 inhabitants, to be built around a circular lake with an 8-kilometre lakefront promenade and structured concentrically in a series of 'ripples'. Dongtan, also near Shanghai (on Chongming Island) is a planned eco-city, to be three-quarters the size of Manhattan, but designed for self-sustainability. China's Rim is not the only place where these adventures are taking place. Chengdu in Sichuan province has its own ideal cities, with a creative industries corridor to the south and gated communities such as Luxe Hills being built according to American models and design. In the latter case, according to the developer, branding is the 'next step'. Again, it has been acknowledged that infrastructure and functionality need to be connected to a narrative of place. In these new developments, that narrative is one of aspiration and sustainability. Whether that proves sufficient for places to succeed as 'places', what Lynch might term a 'true place', is yet to be seen.

Rhodri Windsor-Liscombe (2004) has recently brought the thematics of Ideal City thought together and produced a resource intended to engage young people in future city planning by means of interactive games and activities. Recognising that there can be no *one* ideal city, he redirects his attention from the built city to its 'creative conscience and critical measure' (p. 43), where aesthetic, technological and sociological perspectives dynamically come together in flexible processes. Technology, critically applied, will help optimize land and energy use, with ecological, cultural and social equity awareness in governance. He concludes that, in the design of future cities, themes of participatory debate, ongoing analysis and decision-making about urban community construction are likely to feature, informed by common values and changing conditions. This shifts planning ideologies from a centralized, command-and-control model towards one that is based on greater participation.

David Skrbina (2001) outlines an emerging participatory worldview, which he describes as holistic, spiritual, animated and co-creative, and which he believes needs to replace the mechanistic worldview that has characterized Western thought for 2500 years. He conjectures a philosophical basis for this worldview, which he calls hylonoism: the idea that organized structures bear an imprint that is dynamic, interactive and participatory, and from which higher-order structures emerge through interaction. He cites Plato's assertion that the city (*polis*) has a psyche analogous to the functional parts and characteristics of an individual, and assumes personality characteristics such as courage (2001, p. 297); in this view the city is a form of 'group mind'. Skrbina suggests that Plato intended a literal interpretation. If that is the case, then Plato's ideas prefigured contemporary thinking about the city as a branded entity! The branded city must indeed assume personality characteristics, and make every effort to represent those qualities as distinctive and essential to its stories, its art and its spatial dynamics.

The Cosmopolitan City

Cosmopolitanism is a reviving theme in social and cultural research, partly because of a recognition that the world needs a better (less aggressive) political model than the nation-state, and partly because the globalization debate needs an injection of philosophical optimism. Theories of cosmopolitanism are diverse, however, as what is or is not 'cosmopolitan' depends greatly on how *difference* is accounted and valorized in different national spaces. Fractures of class, economic status, ethnicity and rural and urban division inflect discussions and positions in profoundly political ways. Different sorts of cosmopolitans are equally passionate about their particular formation of the universalism, localism, grounded identity, migration politics, élite trans-national residencies and flows of capital which denote the cosmopolitan ideal in its several guises. Evaluations of competing cosmopolitan paradigms exist and so do profound challenges to the Eurocentric assumptions at their heart. When the cosmopolitan visitor is a migrant, and therefore will not perform the Kantian requirement to go 'home' – no matter whether that home is overseas, or across a provincial border, or even somewhere else in the same city, made invisible by deprivation and dispossession – then cosmopolitanism becomes hard to define and manage. An Albanian migrant to London in 2005, a Subei ren in Shanghai in 2006, a Koori in Sydney in 1845, a Mainlander in Hong Kong in 2003 – these are all people who give the lie to the idea of cosmopolitan cities as surely as they underpin those same cities' claims to cosmopolitan identity. Why this anomaly? We would argue that, just as the visualization of a city is subject to spatialized self-deception, so the diversity of a city can provoke parochial indifference or outright hostility on the part of locals, even as their urban character accrues cosmopolitan credentials. In our examination of Shanghai's film and touristic identity, for example, the nature of the city's cosmopolitan acceptances and denials must be called into question. This is a city where local accents have profound effects on the way in which people are treated in everyday encounters, and where rural migrants are still regarded as having insufficient quality (*suzhi*) to fully count in the new harmonious (*hexie*) society.

   In a cosmopolitan city, the power of place resides in the diversity of the individuals who live and work there, and in the possibility of mobility which attaches to them. In a global city, cosmopolitanism is not assumed but it is a desirable characteristic, which facilitates and is facilitated by networks of communication primarily established for commerce and trade. John Friedman's 'world cities' hypothesis (1986) identified the importance of cities as nodes for global capital, their capacity in particular business sectors and as migration destinations. Equally, Manuel Castells (1989) and Saskia Sassen (1991), and the auditors of global city status (Beaverstock et al. 1999 and 2000) that have followed in their wake emphasize that to be global a city has to be globally networked. The cities in the game are then ranked according to their reach, depth and financial influence. The GaWC index, which prioritizes these cities as alpha-, beta- or gamma-grade 'global cities', is something of a mantra for the places such as Tokyo, London and New York, that sit near the top of the list. Hong Kong, Shanghai and Sydney all aspire to be global cities and in a comparison of advanced services Hong Kong is a second-tier alpha city, Sydney a beta and Shanghai a gamma city (Beaverstock et al. 1999).

But a global city's depth goes beyond its capacity to provide international financial and other professional services, and media industries in particular are a prime driver of globalization processes (Krätke 2003). As a node in the culture industries network of global media firms, Sydney's 2003 classification was as a beta city, whereas Hong Kong was gamma-rated. Shanghai in 2003 was an 'Other centre of the global urban system' and neither a global media city nor a major node for business-services connectivity, whereas Hong Kong was third (behind London and New York) and Sydney thirteenth. Shanghai's positioning remains highly dynamic as continues to emerge as an information economy and a global city, but in terms of its creative industries it is far from being competitive with Tokyo, London and New York.[10]

In the following chapters we shall look at the ways in which these three cities thematically present physical and imaged propositions to their publics, what these mean for the brand of the city, and the purchase of such a brand on the world's imagination.

---

10 Creative-sector workers in these three world cities comprise about 12–15% of the workforce. In Shanghai they comprise 1% (see Zhang 2006).

Chapter 1

A Discussion of Method

Cities can and have been examined through a range of specific disciplinary lenses, but the resulting insights rarely cross silos to integrate and inform distinct modes of practice, or to inspire and enrich new lines of theorization. Traditionally, branding too has been narrowly equated with marketing, as we shall discuss in Chapter 2. However, especially in relation to entities as complex as a world city, it engages deeper questions far beyond that discipline's traditional scope. The journey of this book is to explore and demonstrate the possibilities offered by multidisciplinary and trans-disciplinary[1] research across, in particular, cultural studies, and film studies, marketing and psychology in the complex theoretical and applied problematic of 'branding the city'. Knowledge production, driven by wider social and economic agendas and accountability contexts, is increasingly characterized by heterogeneity, structural diversity and breadth of practical application beyond disciplines (see Gibbons et al. 1994).[2]

In this opening chapter, we shall discuss the modes of collection, evaluation and analysis of primary and secondary data from a series of studies and probes, noting both the benefits and challenges of working across quite different paradigms of thought, vocabulary and expected outcome. Our concern is to demonstrate the value of collaboration in cultural research, while at the same time acknowledging the problems of establishing a working and meaningful discursive field across disciplinary boundaries, interests and methodological habits. While a disciplinary focus implies competing, though equally valid, discursive objectives, collaboration is presented here as a continuum across researchers, team members and participants in the fieldwork. This gives a common focus relevant to both academic and practical constituencies, though their respective orientations to the outcomes will naturally differ. Partly mosaic, partly blurred and partly fused, our aim is to establish 'terms of reference' towards a working and systemic basis for appropriate consensus. This is a precursor to specific, context-bound studies that still need to be undertaken, such as when commercial decision-making needs specific market information, or to reliably establish a critical point. We present representative studies to indicate both pragmatic modes and disciplinary research

---

1   For appropriate definitions, see Tress et al. 2004.

2   Different forms of scholarship are appropriate for dealing with the type of subject matter that is of a higher organizational order, multi-perspectival, dynamic, interrelated, emergent, self-organizing, systemic, dissipative, environmentally open, and epistemologically fraught. Dynamic systems theory addresses material of this type. For example, Zev Naveh's work (e.g. 2001 and 2005) on multifunctional landscapes provides a model that may be transferable to cities.

directions, but these are best considered as sketches or essays suggesting designs and patterns in a larger composition.

The project from which this book developed, entitled 'Branding Cities on the West Pacific Rim', began life when an interdisciplinary 'technology and culture' research group responded to the call for academics to combine skills and expertise in addressing cross-disciplinary questions, and to seek seeding grants to fund their research. The 'technology and culture' grouping gave rise to dialogue between cultural theorists, new media theorists, psychologists and a research group specializing in electronic business and digital technologies. Perhaps an unlikely combination, but it did produce some understanding of how disciplines differ, why they *must* differ in order to answer the problems that they find in the world, and how occasional strategic partnerships help researchers to achieve intellectual and pragmatic growth. The questions asked and answered in such circumstances may be neither more nor less pressing than those asked within the bounds of accepted disciplinary structures, but the difficulties that arise oblige the researchers involved to re-examine their practices, differentiate their expectations and acknowledge their weaknesses.

In our case we discovered first that we were interested in the ways in which online transactions and marketing were capable of transforming everyday experience. In particular, we asked how the destination-image in tourism marketing addressed the affective sensibilities of a prospective tourist, and whether this was qualitatively different from the address of other powerful media which also use locations, for example film. Interviews with tourism officials in Hong Kong persuaded us that global cities – already a serious topic for filmmakers and film theorists – would provide the situated depth of visuality that we sought. These preliminary discussions were followed up with a presentation to the then HK Tourism Commissioner, Rebecca Lai, on the greening of Hong Kong. We emphasized the theoretical value of the 'idea of the city' in suggesting new versions of the urban experience – for instance, 'greening' – to the underlying structures of attention embedded in residents' experience of the place itself, and that should include a sensitivity to the cinematic image.

Given the triple focus at the core of the investigation (cinema and tourism and the branded city), this project required that we find ways of explaining our aims not only to ourselves and our research team, but also to a wide range of interviewees and focus-group participants. The methods that we chose in order to collect data often involved sharing various sorts of information with the participants, in a process of shared mental mapping. The model is similar to that used by art historian James Elkins, who uses intuitive maps in order to analyse the production of history. These 'unguarded and informal' maps (2002, p. 11) help him to elicit information from students and professional colleagues, who are asked to 'draw' the history of art and to represent themselves somewhere in the drawing. He does not claim that this technique produces a polished version of art history, but rather an 'insight ... into the necessity of thinking about the shape of your imagination' (p. 11). The maps that we have elicited from participants are verbal, free-form interviews that invite people with varying types of local expertise to enunciate *their idea of the city through a particular medium*, cinematic or touristic. Our role is to translate the 'shape of their imagination' into diagrammatic and discursive representations for dissemination to academics, students and the parties themselves.

The placing of the speaker in the mapping conversations, however, was no simple matter for us. Film professionals would talk about their own films and those of directors they admired, but then, by requiring that we also discuss our work and our perceptions of the city in which we were 'outsiders', they would oblige us to reveal ourselves as cast in the roles of incidental voyeurs and tourists. We used the suggestions of all film-oriented interviewees (professionals) to guide our selection of films for further analysis, and to select audience groups. The research team was thus collaborating at every stage of the work with participants as well as with one another, 'a way of listening to people and learning from them' (Morgan 1998, p. 9, quoted by Madriz 2000, p. 835). Tourism managers and urban planners also addressed us as potential tourists at some stage of the interview, advising us on routes and special activities that would allow us to 'see' the city, be it Sydney, Hong Kong or Shanghai, more effectively. In the case of Sydney, this was easily achieved, as the offices looked out over the Harbour! In Hong Kong, one of our interviewees (the Deputy Tourism Commissioner) became our interrogator, asking whether we had children, checking on our nationality, enquiring what purchases we needed to make before returning home, and whether we had good walking shoes and stamina! Only then did he deliver a suggested schedule for our free time. The same role reversal in potential interview situations took place with filmmakers and critics. In Hong Kong in 2003, an invitation to the Hong Kong Film Critics Society annual dinner turned into a conversation about contemporary Hong Kong and Australian films, hosted by HKFC and where we were expected to produce insider interpretations of recent Australian films, such as Philip Noyce's *Rabbit-Proof Fence* (2002).[3] Once again, we found ourselves both guests and interlocutors at that event. We were also fortunate to have access, both direct and indirect, to senior city marketers and branding teams in each of the three cities, all of whom were both candid and generous with their time. Although our academic responsibility implies that we shall have critical things to say, the common purpose was sympathetically understood. The normal process of settling an interviewee and establishing a commonality between interlocutors involved information-sharing and role assignment – as Esther Madriz writes, '[E]stablishing rapport with the participants is key to eliciting high quality information' (2000, p. 845) – but in many instances it was a more extensive practice, requiring the researchers themselves to be cast as tourists and observers by the interviewees. We have taken from these encounters a permission to enter ourselves as collaborators in the narratives that unfold in these conversations. We also take from this that there is a tendency amongst professionals to place us within the body of their work – the city – and urban representations in cinema. It also appears that they are taking a phenomenological approach to their work, which supports our hypothesis that

---

3 Particularly successful on DVD in Hong Kong as the cinematographer is Christopher Doyle, a well-known resident of the city and Director of Photography (DoP) star of Hong Kong and Asian cinema. Doyle cemented his role as a Hong Kong icon by taking the part of a fast-food shop owner in *McDull, The Alumni*.

the idea of the city is founded and maintained by means of structures of attention that are closely associated with many aspects of daily interaction with other people, and with media sources. This in turn supports the underlying questions, which derive from a phenomenological approach to cinematic reception: relating experience of a particular city to the experience of watching a specific film and the implications of this for other forms of city engagement, particularly, but not exclusively, touristic.

In structuring our meetings with respondents, we have, therefore, used textual, visual and cinematic elicitation (film extracts, stories and postcards); occupation-specific focus groups (cinematographers, urban planners, audience members, backpackers); extended administered questionnaires (senior strategists and directors), location-based surveys (street interviews), and we have backed this data up with image-based content and cluster analysis, participant observation and concept mapping.

The development of ideas throughout the life of the project derives in part from the need to translate disciplinary perspectives into a common language, and eventually to work towards a transferable discourse. We argue here that this attempt has two possible coterminous effects. The deliberate transfer of ideas and terminologies across disciplines allows us to test the limits of familiar jargon, and to make vocabulary breach complex meanings. It also reduces the meaning of the ideas and the words used to something less useful in the disciplinary application. So, although we do produce some complex maps, using words and free drawing, we also try to codify associative talk by means of diagrams adapted from data-modelling systems used in information systems. Although often the activity of modelling produces insight but the model itself is superfluous, one of the hardest parts of this kind of data collection is judging whether simplicity or reduction, development or bastardization is in play, and at what point of the collaboration.

In exploring collaborative discourse, this chapter discusses and illustrates some of the methodological ideas that we have employed in researching this book, focussing mainly on the first case study, Hong Kong. We first give a brief summary of our findings, expressed in terms that we hope are intelligible across disciplines. We then introduce the parameters of data analysis and design that have been drawn directly from disciplines other than cultural research. We test these models with reference to results that we understand as cultural and historical *insights*, rather than as proven quantitative *information*. Finally, we return to the source of our enquiry, the cinematic phenomenology of touristic experience in the city, to evaluate what we have learned and what ways of expressing that knowledge have become available to us through collaboration.

Branding History

One of our first core findings is that local historical memory and the cultural narratives that sustain such remembrance are of interest to tourism strategists. In Hong Kong, there are place-histories which may come closer to retrieving the character of the city in the long term than either the outworn tag of 'East meets West' or the ambitious claims of 'Asia's Global City'. In 2003 we found that interviewees were anxious to articulate, on film and in theatre, but also in conversation, a history of Hong Kong which would remember its Chineseness without forgetting its radicalism, its internationalism and its suffering. So, in 2003, and in the wake of the SARS epidemic, the *1:99* series of short films, which had been sponsored by the Tourism Commission and the Hong Kong Film Directors Association, memorialized the bravery of Hong Kong residents in the context of a series of challenges stretching from the Japanese invasion (1941), through Typhoon Wanda (1962), the demonstrations of 1968, cholera, drought and SARS. In these films, the history of Hong Kong is removed from external interests, the discussion of British or Chinese sovereignty, and reinstated as an experiential trajectory for residents. Also in 2003, there were retrospectives of key early-twentieth-century Cantonese filmmakers Law Dun and Lai Man-Wai, and a theatre production extolling Lai (1893–1953) as the (Cantonese) father of Chinese film. Born in Guangdong, Lai studied in Hong Kong and moved frequently between the two centres in response to the vagaries of war in the first half of the last century. In so doing he became part of the establishment of Hong Kong as an alternative filmmaking space for Chinese talent. The same exodus occurred after 1949, when many Shanghai-based filmmakers migrated south. The 110th-anniversary production is a celebration of Lai himself, but also indicative of Hong Kong in 2003 as a place with a will to control its historical narrative.

We question, however, whether these 'thick' histories are sufficiently respected and communicated both to the residents and the visitors by tourism initiatives, and we suggest that 1990s brand identity might be better served in the twenty-first century by a pluralistic approach to urban identity on the Rim. For the brand designers, branding the city encompasses an articulation of corporate identity, in which urban space performs place as though it were an extremely large and complex company interest. A strategic brand platform has five core aims: an immediate recognition by the market, an attractive proposition for the market, a statement of sustainable difference from other products (here, places), long-term viability, and positive susceptibility to various aspects of development (Temporal 2000, p. 51). Translating those strategies to place branding, we can argue that historical depth is crucial. Places are differentiated not only by their physical forms and architectures, but also by the contexts of their construction and development, by the known experiences of usage and by the currency of the memories which attach to them. Arguably, the maintenance of cultural memory will sustain and transfigure the tests of the present by re-appropriating the spaces created by 'aspects of development' for use by residents. Thus, while 'East meets West' might have been immediately recognizable up until 1997 as a brand for Hong Kong the ex-British colony, now the city has to be 'pitched' to Mainland Chinese visitors as 'China meets the World' – even though neither slogan fully captures the complexity of emotions with which Hong Kong residents negotiate their Chinese and Hong Kong identities. Such complexity is occasionally captured on film. In Stanley Kwan's *Rouge* (1987), Anita Mui and Leslie Cheung play two lovers, Fleur and the 12th Master, who find themselves trapped in sediments of time by the betrayal of the 12th Master, when he fails to honour a joint suicide pact they have made in the 1930s. The film follows Fleur, as, 50 years later and now a ghost, she searches for her past in the morass of modern development that has stifled its memory. When she finally meets the now aged 12th Master, he is a great disappointment, a man who has failed to live up to the romantic and nostalgic standards of pre-war glamour. This is a text in which Hong Kong is succinctly summarized as a cluttered space, where histories jostle for physical expression and where the present literally topples the sites of the past. Although generically a ghost film, by presenting the past as a walking inhabitant in the present, *Rouge* also presents its audience with their own everyday experience of Hong Kong. Kwan's achievement challenges the filmmaker; as it does the researcher and the branding expert, to capture the layered histories of the city, as a space, a destination and a location, and as immanent in the experience of those who work and live there. Above all, it is vital that the film itself not disappoint, but rather present disappointment as itself a poignancy of maturity. Mui and Cheung both died tragically in 2004, while we were researching this book, she of cancer and he by his own hand. Kwan's film immediately became even more of a palimpsest of the city it portrays.

Research Models in Translation

From several literatures outside those of cultural studies it is clear that methods, and the results to which those methods lead, have different values, objectives and interpretations, even when using similar categories and constructs.[4] For example, the intellectual origins of marketing derive largely from mid-twentieth-century US empiricist psychology and it remains strongly associated with a pragmatic ethos of quantified measurement categories and definition-seeking. Tourism, too, is often viewed as a market-focussed application area, or else an instrument for economic development. While a weighty critical literature may be found in both these disciplines, their pragmatic, particularly economic, imperatives still dominate research motivations and trajectories. Since branding is viewed as a strategic equity, and our current understanding of city competition is largely predicated on business models derived from corporates, these disciplines supply numerous methods whereby we can access the knowledge structures that reflect rational appreciations of propositional aspects.

Cognitive mapping, concept mapping or conceptual mapping is a term used in various literatures to describe formal ways of modelling knowledge or informational structures.[5] Broadly, the term refers to attempts to visualize relationships among concepts, using a diagrammatic representation for convenience. The nature of the diagrams, the scope and focus of the representation, and the semantics of the

---

4   In 'scientific' psychology, personality and 'mental illness' are often viewed as specific traits or characteristics of the individual. In 'social' psychology, however, situational aspects such as cultural or family determinants are the focus. Different educational and social policies follow from the different interpretations.

5   For example, the literatures of cognitive science, management science, information systems, cognitive linguistics, artificial intelligence and psychology, to name just a few.

relationships' structure all vary across the formalisms used, and according to the purpose of the map. We like to describe our approach to the term 'map' as a bridge between on the one hand those disciplines and on the other the present work in cultural research.

Maps range from the individually designed and generated, to representations of group processes, to outcomes abstracted from other sources. They also vary according to the degree of formality they embody, from simply descriptive with nominal and subjectively meaningful associations, through to graph structures with mathematical properties, such as directional and/or numerically weighted links, and with identified dimensionality.

What they tend to have in common is a structure in which concepts (or, in the terminology of various specific literatures, *entities, things, nodes, points or vertices*) are associated by relationships (or *arcs, links, edges*) with the assumption that this represents a meaningful organization of material. The meaning will depend on the purpose of the representation, and the semantics may be subjective only, formally sanctioned, or a selective abstraction from evidence. The maps may be considered as a literal representation of an externally organized reality, or as a convenient and communicable impression of, or insight into, some constructed understanding. Cognitive mapping, in the literal sense of mental cartography (Downs and Stea 1973), not only involves psychological transformations of acquisition, coding, recall and decoding of information about the everyday spatial environment, but also non-spatial (e.g. kinaesthetic and auditory) cues. This provides a selective, but topographically analogous, information structure relevant to subjective uses and specific saliencies. More abstractly, mental structures also represent associations with no physical analogue. While in principle any concept may have a relationship to any other, generally some selection process will apply in explicating understanding, bringing some relationships into relatively greater focus, and conferring a meaning conditioned by the theory brought to bear in the selection.

Some techniques require no training and are used to explore or visualize ideas and associations; for example, the family of spray-diagram techniques also known as *spider diagrams* or *mind maps*, as popularised in the commercial work of Buzan (1974). Claims made for this technique include the ability to provide an overview of an area, to gather and hold large amounts of data, and to aid in organizing and memorising notes and similar material. The visual aspect allows patterns to be detected or shaped, and communicated, using attributes of visual languages, including colour, size, spacing, shading, symbolization and emphasis. The map is organized around a central topic, with branches leading off it on all sides, and sub-branches and leaves giving details. The semantics of such maps are subjective, and a typical context is organizing notes from texts or from brainstorming sessions. The colours (not reproduced) and shaping are chosen to be personally meaningful, and this helps memorization. The process of engagement with the material helps insight, and any map that results should not necessarily be seen as a definitive product. An indicative mind map for the branding cities project is reproduced below and illustrates a simple understanding of the topic 'Pacific Rim city icons'.

Tourism and the Branded City

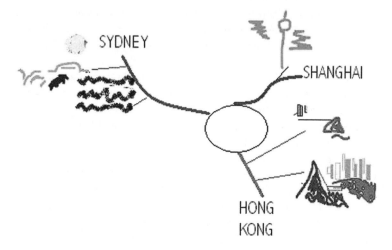

Figure 1.1   Spray diagram representing a subjective understanding of relevant city icons

Concept mapping, a specific technique developed in education theory (Novak 1991), assumes that human memory has an associative structure that assimilates new concepts and that meaningful learning occurs through structuring and restructuring concepts. Building new ideas on old provides a constructivist, revisable and evolutionary (but paradigmatic) basis for mapping the traces of knowledge and learning. Concepts are perceived regularities that warrant identification, labelling or naming and are connected into meaningful propositional statements to both enable and constrain particular forms of organisation.

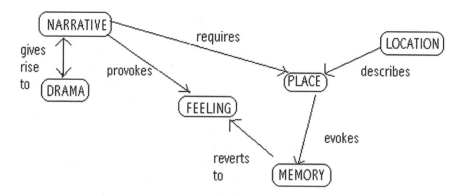

Figure 1.2   Concept map showing some elementary concepts and their semantic relationships

Conceptual modelling aims to 'capture the meaning of an application domain as perceived by someone' (Wand, Storey and Weber 1999, p. 494) and is an approach closely associated with data modelling and information systems more generally. It operates at a notational level, relating structures understood in the social world to precise and specific design and implementation commitments. Although interpretivism, critical realism and pluralism are all well established in information-systems thinking, the typical pragmatic requirement to commit to a particular model of a situation for active implementation necessitates a single coherent view and definition, whether consensual or shaped by a dominant stakeholder (Chen 1976).

The essence of the conceptual modelling literature is best seen as evolution of Peter Chen's entity-relationship-attribute formalism, or E-R diagram. These forms begin to impose some formal semantics on a propositional statement. Although the terms are nuanced and have specific meanings within ontological frameworks, broadly, this approach identifies *entities* (things, concepts), their *attributes* (which may also be concepts and are sometimes known as weak entities or properties) and defines relationships among these, which may be mandatory or optional and which have cardinality, i.e. may be *one to one*, *one to many* or *many to many*. These concepts may be readily seen in Figure 1.3. Their use lies in reminding us how people (respondents or target markets alike) think, and thus how they might make connections between cultural forms and experiences.

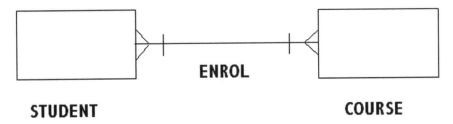

Figure 1.3a

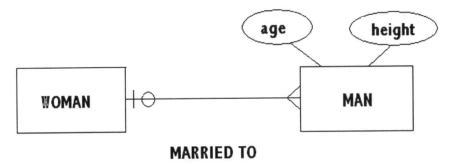

Figure 1.3b

Figures 1.3a and 1.3b   Examples of entity-relationship notation

Other sophisticated techniques use map representations for complex situation modelling and identifying stakeholder agreement or otherwise. Colin Eden and his colleagues' *cognitive mapping* technique (Eden, Jones and Sims 1979; Ackerman and Eden 2001) represents personal or group thinking on a topic or problematic issue. The links have direction; implying causality between concepts and 'cause maps' is a synonymous term. They are explicitly distinguished (Eden 2004) from mind maps and from the similar influence diagrams (Schachter 1986). Following a key idea of George Kelly's (1955), their nodes embody constructive contrasts on an issue. These are not simple dimensions, but rather the cognitive structures within which conceptualization occurs. In addition, the maps are generally larger, have a management strategy and operation focus and have more properties amenable to formal analysis and modelling. They embody both hierarchical and linked organization, allow for detection of feedback loops in the structure and are suited to surfacing and structuring complex issues for discussion and consideration with a view towards action. Particularly in the sort of 'wicked problems' that are characteristic of social planning (Rittel and Webber 1973), in which many stakeholders require input but may have different objectives, understandings and even problem definitions, it is especially important to be able to model argument structures, antecedents to, and consequences of, choices and to visualize impacts. Branding cities is one such problem: consultative and accountable implementations are required, and all stakeholder perceptions must be elicited and considered.

Other individual or group workshop methods complement more formal 'problem structuring' techniques, but do not impose the requirement for agreement leading towards specific action. This is appropriate both in exploring stakeholder views of complex or unknown areas without imposing constraints too early, but also in identifying that categories derived from prior theory are meaningfully understood and have a suitable range of convenience. Specific studies may then follow on a grounded theory basis, whether prior theory is admitted or not.[6] In our research we opted to run focus groups in which researchers and research assistants took extensive notes on discussions between individuals in the same professional group. In most cases these people knew each other and had perhaps encouraged one another to attend the meeting. The conversation was given a certain structure by a questionnaire, but the conversation was frequently allowed to linger on themes about which the participants felt most passionate or informed. Within the wider conceptualization this allowed specific parameters to become identified, without premature structuring or evaluation.

The 'structures of attention' which inform the design of our project are 'nostalgia', 'everyday life' and 'aspiration'. Our model has been developed from the work of Raymond Williams and Jonathan Crary and will be described in greater detail in the next chapter, in relation to Hong Kong's response to SARS. In discussing methodological choices drawn from psychology and marketing, as we do here, it is important simply to note that structures of attention must be hypothesized, tested and interpreted at every stage of a research itinerary. They are, if you like, the hierarchical

---

6   Theory grounded in its subject matter is appropriate in theory building where none exists. There are differing schools of thought on the extent to which prior categories should apply.

elements of the conversations in a focus group and in individual interviews. All respondents are asked directly to think about those structures of attention at the beginning and towards the end of the meetings. This is the main mode of researcher intervention and management of their responses to the 'idea of the city'.

A focus group held in Brisbane in June 2003 brought together production designers, cinematographers and theorists to discuss Sydney as a film location. However, given that all of the participants were at that time based in Queensland (although none considered themselves 'Queenslanders') the conversation quickly turned into a comparative discussion of Brisbane and Sydney as cinematic sites in the Australian film industry:

> Brisbane tries to imitate Sydney in terms of raising its profile through events, but hasn't got the marketing side of things down like Sydney has. Sydney is a large financial centre that can draw cash from around the world.
>
> (MR, Respondent 1)
>
> …
>
> Sydney has views everywhere, whilst Brisbane has just the view of the river.
>
> (NM, Respondent 2)
>
> …
>
> [On nostalgia] Twenty-five years in Sydney and Melbourne couldn't really feel nostalgia embedded. Nostalgia can go wrong. It's a new adventure to move from Melbourne to Queensland. Coming to Queensland feels like coming to Australia, to discover Australia and Aussie, in Gold Coast, people drive wheels, surfing, a beach culture.
>
> (NM, Respondent 2)
>
> Sydney is a place where young people go to find themselves, like New York, London … [On aspiration] Sometimes it is a city of broken dreams, people brought success, but interestingly, in Sydney you see old people but in Brisbane only see young people, very young people city. When young people all go to Sydney, why they will be here?
>
> (A, Respondent 3)
>
> [On nostalgia] The harbour is very nostalgic, particularly that sense of ancients, you can see history, whilst Brisbane is larger and more alive.
>
> (A, Respondent 3)

The conversation, only fragments of which are transcribed here, shifts from describing the cities as locations to articulating the experience of living in them as personal narrative. It might also be significant that respondents 1 and 3 – both of whom had been born in Australia – kept 'returning' in their conversation to the ultimate qualities of the place they had left (Sydney). The three (long-term) migrants in the group were more able to transfer their loyalties from one city to another, and could not identify nostalgia in a particular place, but preferred to emphasize the everyday life and aspirational qualities of all the cities they knew (Brisbane, Sydney and Melbourne). The cognitive constructs that this suggests relate to the emergence of personal place-histories as an organizing concept in formulating a professional version of the city as a location. This links to the experience of researchers that they were themselves 'placed' as experiential subjects when in conversation with filmmakers and tourism strategists. Given that these speakers were all in the film business, trained as cinematographers, directors of photography (DoPs) and art directors, it is worth noting that the eye of filmmaking (*das Kino-Eye*) is as likely to be inflected by very personal place loyalty as it is by style and professionalism. This observation was backed up by interviews in Hong Kong, where filmmakers spoke of *location* in terms of their personal memories. Thus Fruit Chan emphasized Hong Kong's harbour, by referring to his own office-window view. He was speaking from a sense of fulfilled aspiration. Mabel Cheung focussed on the University of Hong Kong, where she was herself a student, as though that site summed up the value of pre-1997 sophistication amidst the indignities of colonialism.

In the branding research we have results that suggest that our three structures of attention (nostalgia, aspiration and everyday life) can feature separately in an audience reading of several different films, or else all three may occur in just one title. *Ordinary Heroes* (*Qian yan wan yu*, dir. Ann Hui, 1999) tells the story of political struggles in Hong Kong in the 1970s and 1980s, and deals particularly with the struggle by Hakka Mainland workers for on-land residency and family rights. It is made in Hui's signature style of ficto-documentary and contains period detail as well as accounts of the ordinary harshness of everyday life. The activist workers are the 'ordinary heroes' of the title, the 'voices of many'. And, to the extent that the narrative follows, in flashback, the characters' struggles to live as good a life as that enjoyed by Hong Kong residents it is a film about aspiration. The film is coded by respondents and by the researchers as nostalgic, aspirational and a film about everyday life. In a conceptual model, the reading might look like this:

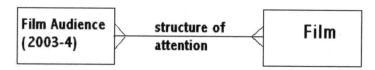

Figure 1.4a   Structures of attention model using entity relationship notation

The crow's feet indicate a plurality of view-points and several points of entry into interpretations of a film within the scope of the research project. Specific attributes can be added, by convention using ovals, as shown in Figure 1.4 (b). Similar relationships between a city and its audience might be modelled in a similar way.

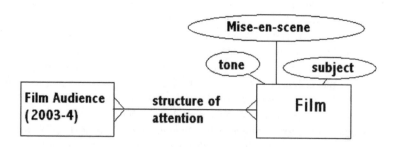

Figure 1.4b   Structures of attention model, with some attributes shown

The original applications for conceptual models were concerned with relationships that target a computational outcome. Figure 1.4 is essentially a reductive model and as its stands it gives no details of any particular film. What it does do, however, is provide a simple starting-point for further discussions of the ways in which people understand film, and semantics. It streamlines the cognitive approach, as the structures of attention already assume a complex network of experience, understanding and definition. Also, while it does not stress a phenomenological take on the link between lived experience and the body of the film, such a link is already implicit in the basic idea of structures of attention. The model does not deny the complexities that it contains, but rather seeks to communicate one finding, namely that multiple structures of attention are likely to be in play in the reception of certain films. In so doing it suggests further avenues for discussion, or the way in which particular relationship structures that might emerge could be represented.

So, while in much of this book we attempt to describe these analytical findings in words, we argue that there may be additional value in giving a conceptual form to the findings. This is partly the value of conceptual description at an introductory but at the same time inherently sophisticated level, and partly the value that arises from a visualization, which forces questions by virtue of the difficulty of imagining and creating a visual representation of something that is as yet poorly understood. In Hong Kong in late 2003, at one focus group held with audience members at the Hong Kong Film Archive, eight respondents were asked to give a numerical value (from 1 to 5) to the posited structures of attention. They did so as the summation of a series of conversations about Cantonese film, the visual characteristics of Hong Kong city (cinematic and actual), the relationship of the city to its residents, and the tone and feeling of Hong Kong as a lived experience. The numerical value that they gave to one or more structures of attention was indicative of how they experienced the city, but, beyond that, *proved* nothing at all. We did note that the numbers were uniformly high (3 and above), suggesting that the structures of attention we proposed made some sense to the respondents and that – however they chose to express it – they all had a strong engagement with the city.

The group was representative of an audience for a retrospective screening of the films of Cantonese director and comic actor Lao Dun. Except for one Singaporean, all the members of the group were both born and raised in Hong Kong and were of Chinese ethnicity, but described their nationalities variously as British (1), Hong Kong (3), Chinese (3). A content analysis of the findings was unnecessary given the scale of the information, but nonetheless a number of observations could be made that relied on trends and frequency of responses. The respondents aged 40 and above (50 per cent) talked about Hong Kong as a place with which they had a deep affinity, and in describing it used words such as 'love', belonging' and 'motherland'. This group very quickly understood the tenor of our question when we asked them to describe the 'character' of the city. They offered reasonably complex character analyses, which, when collated, would read: 'cohesive and energetic, hilarious, cold, pragmatic, passive, selfish because it's a family not a nation, materialistic, vigorous, adaptable and optimistic' To 'nostalgia' and 'everyday life' they gave high scores of between 3 and 5, but nonetheless coded 'aspiration' into their discursive descriptions of the city. These responses were echoed by Hong Kong-based filmmakers who, when pressed to give us the key narrative of Hong Kong, across all genres and periods of filmmaking, resolved that the city's story is one of 'making something out of nothing against the odds'. We might code that as 'aspirational', but our direct questions to audiences suggest that it is a way of telling the city's story that is so familiar that it is understood as 'nostalgic'.

By contrast, in Sydney, the same question put to a visiting filmmaker and tourism strategists produced a definite bias towards 'aspiration'. A reading of Kate Woods's *Looking for Alibrandi* (2000) that was offered by one subject, Phil Lewis, an American documentarist briefly based in Brisbane but usually located in Hungary, was that the film was outstandingly successful as an aspirational tale about Sydney. He argued that aspiration was best summed up in the case of Sydney as an ongoing narrative of the city as a place of contrasts, and where peace can only be achieved by putting one's aspirations aside (as happens in the film), or by re-tuning them to non-mainstream values. *Alibrandi*, it should be noted, uses a few carefully placed shots of the Harbour to narratively locate privilege. The fictional school in the film is actually Kambala, a very exclusive Catholic girls' school in Vaucluse, with a Harbour view 'to die for' and buildings which are almost regal in their command of the bay below. Cinematically it also recalls the school in *Walkabout* (dir. Nicolas Roeg, 1970) from which Jenny Agutter is plucked for her walkabout in the NSW hinterland.

Of the aspiring protagonists of these Sydney films, none are privy to the view of the Harbour (Bridge, Opera House, boats and water). The view is always a visual depiction of the habitus of very rich Eastern Suburbs residents. This solitary status symbol is an underlying theme in all the films. But it is interesting to note that the extremely aspirational Muriel (in *Muriel's Wedding* (dir. P. J. Hogan, 1994), is not satisfied with simply the view and wishes for more from Sydney, 'the city of brides', as Phil Lewis called it. Her wish is played out across Sydney's wharfs on Saturday and Sunday mornings in the summer, when numerous bridal couples turn up to stand against the backdrop of the Opera House and the Bridge in order to capture and preserve their small moment of 'the view' (Plate 1, Boy at Circular Quay). Their collective moments are thus cinematic, populist and answerable to the brand identity of a city that offers the view as a hallmark of its beauty.

Phil Lewis was selected to work on the project in the capacity of a subject-researcher. He was invited to devote focussed time to the Sydney film aspect of the work and he was fully informed of the structures of attention which we were attempting to map. His judgements of *Alibrandi* and *Muriel's Wedding* were based on twenty years of professional filmmaking, a brief to watch over fifty films set in Sydney and archived at the Sydney-based Australian Film, Television and Radio School, and a stay of four complete days in the city itself. Lewis was a subject who was capable of making highly informed choices based on his professional expertise, but who only knew the city as a short-stop tourism destination. Lewis was a naive professional in respect of Sydney: he watched films which are more or less well known to Australian filmmakers and audiences, but which were previously unknown to him. In other words, his 'idea of the city' was developed in situ through cinematic engagement and an immediate touristic experience. For all these reasons, Lewis's input to our research was invaluable.

In the light of the salient attributes and the implied structures arising from our conversations and interviews, we also used a psychological technique that allows various forms of *construct elicitation* and conceptual mapping, theories attributable to George Kelly (1955). Informed by an underpinning constructivist philosophy and a cohesive psychological theory, the *repertory grid* approach has affinities with many of the other methods described, and has a long history of practical use in several fields. Often used outside their original theoretical contexts, conceptual domains are unrestricted in nature; examples from fields as disparate as tourism, urban design, political imagery and product differentiation may be found throughout the literature (see J.T. Coshall 2000; Gammack and Young 1984; Gordon and Tan 2002; Anderson 1990 and Ruiz 2000). The repertory grid technique has a range of application that potentially connects the presence of deep, unverbalized and complex psychological structures (at both individual and social levels) with the potential for ultimate representation of these in quantified and computable models. This makes it directly applicable to understanding and reifying the structures of attention by means of which psychological sense is made and experiences meaningfully organized within a conceptual domain. *Elements* in a domain of focal interest (such as a particular set of films or destinations) become organized along conceptual lines, or *constructs*, identifying an underlying conceptualization that both differentiates and integrates experience that is true for a person. This experience might also be more widely shared or recognizable by a group or community, but does not otherwise impose a requirement to be verifiably true against an 'objective' standard.

Olivia Jenkins (1999) argues that in destination imaging, for example, construct elicitation must precede any more structured study with a specific population of interest, otherwise important attributes may be missed, while unimportant ones are included. Maps, photographs and other pictorial material, as well as verbal terms, are suitable elements for construct elicitation, which can be done individually, in focus groups, or in a variety of other ways. Arthur Stamps III's meta-analysis (1990) found a very high correlation between preferences found in situ and those obtained from photographs, with clear implications for destination image studies, and the reduction of problems due to language translation.

The concepts can be elicited and mapped at different levels of abstraction, either to provide the basis for further discussion and refinement, or as a suggestive representation of themes in a focal area. In this case the technique can be applied to the thick data collected by means of the modelling methods described above, which have been applied in the context of focus groups and interviews. The conceptual structures elicited formed the basis of computable decision rules for these systems. They may also be combined across respondents in various ways to allow (nonparametric) multidimensional, cluster or factor analysis. Thus, the approach has the power to extend from the mapping of a construction to a basis for modelling and action.

Considerable work has been done on the development of a suitable repertory grid-based approach, which has several variations in its application. Some of the conceptual mapping representations described above may follow from its use on a single interviewee or on a group of interviewees. Often, theoretically suggested elements or constructs will be supplied by the researcher, elicited by other means than from the current respondents, though the meaning of these will normally be clearly grounded in the social and established in the practical context. Normally, a principled sampling technique in relation to an identified population of interest should apply, and the elements should be theoretically referenced.

We may illustrate its conjectured application with reference to film analysis, by using three methods of selection for the films. First, the non-film-oriented researcher uses the method most likely to be used by an average tourist, that of searching out 'something to watch' from a movie database on the web. This would be deliberately straightforward, using our search terms: Hong Kong, Sydney, nostalgia / aspiration / everyday. These searches throw up titles such as *Looking for Alibrandi*, *Walkabout* and *Once upon a Time in Shanghai* (dir. Xiaolian Peng, 1998). Secondly, we take up titles suggested by contemporary filmmakers in conversation about the same terms, or structures of attention. Thirdly, we look at films that are 'insistent' or 'spontaneous' in that we encounter them through the process of research. The *1:99* post-SARS series of films comes into this category. Once the sample is collected, a random internal sample (in which each film is termed an 'element') is taken for illustrative comparison. Applying the method of triads, three *constructs* are used to differentiate and relate the qualities and affinities pertinent to each film. We have already indicated that our 'structures of attention' can be used as the constructs by means of which a film can build its conceptual profile. Each film is scored on each construct, and eventually a unique profile emerges: a repertory grid.

Figure 1.5 shows what might result when the method is applied to a set of films as naively analysed by a non-film-oriented researcher (Gammack). In the first phase, a search of the Internet Movie Database (imdb.com), filtered by plot and using the keyword 'nostalgia', might yield twelve titles. Being largely unfamiliar with the material, the naive analyst might consider *Rock Around the Clock*; *The Wedding Singer* and *Cockroach Hotel* and suggest that *Rock Around the Clock* and *The Wedding Singer* had 'music' in common, but that the 'nostalgic' element of *Cockroach Hotel* was not based on its musical content. The construct 'music-non-music' as a way of differentiating the nostalgic content of films would then become the first column of the developing repertory grid.[7]

Each of the twelve films would then be given personal ratings from 1 to 5, depending on the strength or relevance of the 'music' theme. Repeating the exercise for three other films (e.g. *Symphony of Silence*, *Jagadakeer* and *Soccer Dog, The Movie*) the analyst might identify nostalgic content related to a 'location' (e.g.

---

7   Purists might say that 'non-music' is only a dimensional contrast, not a real organizing mental construct, and that a score of 3 might reflect irrelevance as much as a median value. Although such a criticism is valid, depending on the types of analysis and conclusions of the study, insight, rather than quantitative analysis, is our intent here.

CONSTRUCTS

ELEMENTS	NON-MUSIC (1)- MUSIC (5)	LOCATION (1) - UNIVERSAL (5)	CHILDHOOD (1) - ERA (5)
American Dreams	2	1	5
Cockroach Hotel	1	2	5
Heaven on Earth	1	1	5
Jagadakeer	1	1	5
Maestro	5	4	5
Making of "Beatlemania"	5	3	5
Rock Around the Clock	5	4	5
Soccer dog: the movie	2	4	1
Symphony of Silence	3	1	1
That Championship Season	2	4	1
Tribute	5	4	3
The Wedding Singer	5	3	4

Figure 1.5   A partial repertory grid for a naive viewer of 'nostalgic' films

Armenia), or connote a more 'universal' theme applicable to any location. A third iteration might identify 'childhood' associations as the key differentiating idea, as opposed to nostalgia associated with a particular period (the 1950s). A grid is thus built up and analytic implications can follow: someone who liked *Heaven on Earth* might also like *Jagadakeer,* which has the same profile (1,1,5), though usually the constructs give a basis for discussion in relevant terms rather than implying that the statistical properties are the main result.

The technique's flexibility is useful in obtaining insight and the potential to surface different constructions of the same material. Film theorists would have richer, more sophisticated and more specifically understood categories used in reading these films intelligently. Moreover, as one theorist in Hong Kong pointed out when the naive grid was (knowingly) proffered, their construct system might look quite different. One of the present authors (Donald) would argue, for instance, that film tropes and coincidences of meaning or thematic are fairly meaning-thin without the information contained in the visual text itself, which must also be read in light of its viewership, its context and its aesthetic tradition. But it is a corollary of Kelly's theory that the naive construct system partially represented in Figure 1.5 may also be construed and comprehended by others who do not necessarily anticipate the world in that way themselves, but who can socially relate to those who do, and thus help change their thinking. At last, a systematic way for film theory to change the world – albeit by submitting to naivety!

There are several ways of developing the input of a grid. Material may be freely elicited, questionnaires drawn up or interviews of various sorts arranged. Or, when specific comparisons or respondent demographics are of particular interest, previously established theoretical categories and element sets may be used. Support for use of the instrument is also widely available, where undifferentiated ideas are highlighted, new elements are added as required, hierarchical forms are targeted and iterations between data gathering and instrument development are pursued. Originally designed to surface unarticulated worldviews in clinical psychology settings in any interpretative field where perceptions determine choices and behaviour, the technique's ability to provide insights that can be explored towards computation or towards empathy positions it as a central method for our study.

We cross-referenced the *constructs* on our grids in order to assist us, as researchers and writers, to gain access to the idea of the city evinced by respondents, and to give comparative value to aesthetic choices in films. Attention was drawn to Sydney's aspirational, harbour-hugging profile by respondents in two quite different ways. Films such as *The Matrix* (dir. Andy and Larry Wachowski, 1999), which was filmed and post-produced in Sydney, but does not advertise the fact within the diegesis – in fact, it is implied throughout that we are in post-Apocalypse American urban space – match the Sydney grid admirably, because the city is situated as both central to the international (US) urban aesthetic, and devolved from it by the obliteration of cultural power. Sydney in the grid emerges as a world city that nonetheless has a distinctly regional character. Likewise, smaller Sydney films and *moments in films*, Nona's walk in the Kings Cross streets in *Radiance* (dir. Rachel Perkins, 1998), for example, testify both to Sydney liveliness and energy, but also to its local, Australian specificity and distance from Euro-American foci of cultural might. This could perhaps be termed an aesthetic of 'momentary glimpses', a term that is suitably descriptive, since it immediately recalls for any visitor or resident of Sydney the glimpses of water (rivers as well as the Harbour itself) and the Bridge, which arguably constitute the visual organization of real estate, and a common spatiality for Sydneysiders.

Glimpses of the Harbour Bridge also indicate a sense of time: a glimpse in the penultimate scene of Nicolas Roeg's *Walkabout* confirms that we are now in contemporary, everyday Sydney (Plate 2, Sydney CBD, 1970s) in striking contrast to the timelessness of the bush, and, in Donald Crombie's film version (1986) of Ruth Park's novel *Playing Beatie Bow*, the return from the Sydney Rocks of a hundred years earlier to the Sydney of the 1980s is signalled by the appearance of the Bridge in the scene. As a reassuring icon understood by both Abigail, the film's protagonist, and the audience, it is a marker around which a shared interpretation can be organized. For any mapping exercise it is mandatory that such markers be identified: discourse in any community requires agreement as to which elements are appropriately involved, regardless of how they may be valorized. Their roles and associations within a construct system may then be explored, at individual or group levels.

Chapter 5, which deals with chromatics, suggests a further way of bringing material and emotional choices into a legible relationship. The colour of cities is evocative of complex ideas of place, some of which relate to fairly universal responses to hue (red always denotes some measure of extreme, for instance), but also of an iconic, or practical filmic approach to capturing light. Blue blocs of solid colour are used as markers of the everyday (a strong feature of Sydney locations, for example), while night-shots, fast cutting, and red tones might indicate the nostalgic edge of a haunted city (Hong Kong, say). We might also suggest that film locations which concentrate on iconic views (in Hong Kong the Harbour and the Peak; in Sydney the Harbour and the Opera House) are coded as nostalgic pending other locational juxtapositions and associations established during the course of the film. The use of (database) conceptual modelling in a 'structures of attention' model is radical to both of the disciplinary areas involved and provocative to our general thesis of convergent visual fields. Here we are merely anxious to illustrate our methods in unfamiliar contexts, without needing to depend on the theoretical context of our enquiry prior to using them on the actual project data, where issues of theoretically informed choice and sample are addressed.

The Phenomenological City-Respondent

The modelling techniques outlined above are the means to an end of collaboration through disciplinary translation. The collaboration is itself an extension of the negotiation between different ways of articulating sensory experience. Studying film and tourism communications is also, then, a translation between intellectual and phenomenological engagement with visual and aural information, and as such the experience of film is, in part, a phenomenological engagement with place. Location and its treatment by the camera and editing team are essential, not only to the development of the narrative but also to the emotional impact that the narrative is to have on an audience. In the two-hour traffic of a film there is a great deal to convey, and this tends to be achieved through the *story*, which relies on genre, typology, and location to bring depth and breadth to the treatment of the *plot*. It seems plausible to suggest, therefore, that place value in film could act upon the place value of a tourism destination, and that the two might play off one another in supporting an idea of the city in the minds of residents and visitors. This hypothesis relies on an understanding of lived experience, which links intellectual understanding, cultural and sensual memory, sophisticated habits of spectatorship and consumption to the development and growth of place identity. Our research techniques also draw on these factors in eliciting an idea of the city from those who use it and whose lives are embedded in its actual, and represented in its cultural and commercial, worlds.

Cross-disciplinary techniques allow both film and business-oriented researchers to pose questions in mutually decipherable ways, and to present them to each other and to a wider audience. One advantage of collaboration of this kind is that it builds a visual vocabulary, which we can use in describing complex discipline-specific ideas to professionals from outside the academy, while giving ourselves the means to transcribe their equally complicated relationships with the city into meaningful notations for our purposes. Secondly, we conclude that the richest idea of a city resounds in its *phenomenological access* to its own historical trajectory. This is allied to the idea of 'structures of attention'. Finally, the elicitation techniques to which we have referred also remind us of disciplinary boundaries and of the internal strengths of cultural research. The cross-disciplinary discussion between psychology, marketing and interpretative cultural theory emerges as a field peculiarly able to combine empirical data with philosophical reflection, and interpersonal interaction with social description. Likewise, there is some value in reminding a brand manager, through diagrams they can take away in their portfolio, that locally supported notions of history should not be forgotten in the search for a new logo. We would contend, however, that the real worth of cultural research which takes on the methods and motions of data management is that it puts us in a position to begin to address the structures of attention that we *share* as city dwellers, professionals, and professional thinkers. As a result, we might be able to take each other seriously as political and cultural actors in a social world that is organized by both the market and the sensorium of everyday aspirations, emotional needs and values of a city's people.

Chapter 2

Branding the City

This chapter explores the conceptual background of branding; the motivations, origins and development of the practice, as well as academic explorations and deployments of the term. It discusses how the city as marketplace, in which branded goods have had a long history, has evolved into the city as product. It shows how this transformation has brought into focus the competing claims of the city as a place for everyday life, as an imaginative site of extraordinary fantasy, and as a focus of aspiration, nostalgia and political power.

Branding a city is both a rational and an emotional engagement with place, aesthetics and everyday life. If the idea of the visual city is central to cultural debates on the nature of modern life, then we would argue that branding has entered those debates in an attempt to capture and shape the city as a product and knowable entity for residents and visitors. While brand creation and brand maintenance for goods and services have become an immensely sophisticated industry and set of practices, 'destination' and – especially – 'city' branding pose a yet more complex layer of challenge, identifications, and contradiction.

Place branding is now well understood, at least as an activity, if not through its principles and best practice. Place branding's origins in product development and sales are both a sine qua non and an important starting-point for any redeployment of the theory across academic boundaries. In this chapter, therefore, we briefly visit the meaning of the term 'branding', in order to introduce the various considerations – historical, psychological, aesthetic, pragmatic and cultural – that apply in branding any product. We are particularly interested in issues specific to branding in Asia, and critiques of branding in global markets and of the current thinking of practitioners and researchers. We describe the evolution of place branding from the functional destination branding of the tourism brochure, to the 'state and trait' manufacture of dreams – which may or may not be sustainable in place over time –, to brand evolution in the nation-state, where way of life, political agendas, financial futures and social programs interact and jostle for position. We survey the ways in which national positioning is pursued through branding mechanisms, even to the extent of branded wars and claims on intellectual, cultural and organic property made through territorial rhetoric. We examine claims made by international branding experts regarding a convergence of national identity and brand, noting the validity of their position, but at the same time questioning the circularity of arguments that excise the complexity and contingency of experience from the emergence of narratives of the nation. The final section of the chapter locates these phenomena in a specifically Asian context, in order to demonstrate the intersection of globally dominant brands with locally produced and respected brands, and their potential for wider export and global position.

History of Branding

The idea of a mark signifying a reputation is an old one: China traditionally tattooed criminals (Turner 1999), and families, merchants and places have always 'traded on their good name'. Place branding and identification is no less time-honoured: heraldic coats of arms representing specific symbolic or natural features in official colours have been developed for families and municipalities throughout Europe and beyond since at least the Middle Ages. Edinburgh, for example, has long been symbolized by its castle and the rock on which it stands. Mottos reflecting a city's nature, values or aspiration are both traditional and widespread, predating the brand concepts of logos and slogans. Trade-marking allows brand protection: the names of sixteenth-century whisky distillers were burned into their barrels, guaranteeing quality, and the analogous cattle-ranching practice of burning a unique symbol into the animals' hides to identify proprietary stock popularized the term 'branding'. This function was emulated by manufacturers and came to connote specific product quality attributes. A brand describes names, designs, symbols, or other identifying features that distinguish one offer from others.[1] Applicable to services, products and product families, classic brands also imply a certain reputation, and associated ownership.

A brand functions as a sign or a symbol and, having served originally to distinguish and identify, began to assume fetishistic qualities of image and power as advertisers crafted associations, attributes and characterizations designed to induce a psychological response to the point where '[David] Ogilvy didn't believe consumers could distinguish between products were it not for their images' (Rushkoff 2003).

The image began to acquire its own economic value: brand equity refers to the perceived financial or competitive value of a brand and its components, and its ability to meet or exceed consumer expectations. Brand name can add value to the basic product: brand equity measures this extra utility, and this provides differentiation that goes beyond price competition (Aaker 1991). D.A. Aaker's proposal that brand equity creates value for both customer and supplier has been well-supported: as well as increasing consumer preference and willingness to pay a premium, brand equity has been shown to influence stock-market perceptions, merger and acquisition decisions, and marketing communication effectiveness.

Brand equity is seen as a multidimensional concept by various researchers,[2] themes of brand awareness, loyalty, perceived quality, strong brand image and associations all recurring in leading brand equity models. There are different schools of thought regarding the extent to which a brand's value is determined by what exists in the minds of consumers, in terms of their experiences, thoughts and feelings,

---

1 A widely used definition of 'brand' is from the American Marketing Association: 'A name, term, design, symbol, or any other feature that identifies one seller's goods or services as distinct from those of other sellers. The legal term for brand is trademark. A brand may identify one item, a family of items, or all items of the seller.' Lisa Wood (2000) discusses this and other relevant definitions and the constructs and measures implied in each case.

2 E.g., Aaker and Joachimsthaler 2000; Shocker and Weitz 1988 and Keller 1993.

and the extent to which market effects such as perceived added value, salience and preference over generic brands contribute as measurable or financially identifiable aspects.

'Co-branding' refers to a situation in which two or more products form a short- or long-term alliance, thereby allowing the transfer of certain aspects of image from one to the other/s (Rao and Ruekert 1994). In certain markets, rum-and-cola is more appealing than either on its own, and an alliance can open up new markets for a product. Product-place co-branding, in which products associated with a place help establish terms that have a public meaning (e.g. Cornish pasties, Peking duck) is a sort of place branding, even if the association is no longer unique to that place, as in the case of Parma ham (Kavaratzis and Ashworth 2005). Brand equity is ideally increased for both, as has been the case, for example, for the Olympics Games and Sydney, each of which has done the other a lot of good. Olympic cities are not chosen lightly, nor would either brand wish to risk its reputation publicly by a poor decision or subsequent delivery. Australia's strong reputation in sport has synergies with the Olympic brand values: co-branding theory predicts that transfer of image will occur through brand association and this has indeed been shown for destinations hosting sports events (Xing and Chalip 2006). Each successful Olympic Games strengthens the Olympic brand, and for a brief period of time the showcased city is provided with a global platform upon which to stand and establish or promote its image.

Brand image is shaped by marketing programs that make strong, positive and memorable associations, but also by direct experience, by word of mouth and by identification with particular events, people or places etc. (Keller 2003). Sydney's Olympics, Shanghai's Expo and Hong Kong's Rugby Sevens are specific examples of such associations. Brand image requires both brand awareness and meaningful associations linked in memory. Strong brand associations, ideas linked to remembered episodes and instances gives a cognitive knowledge structure that is reinforced with repeated exposure (Faircloth, Capella and Alford 2001). Brand attitude is an evaluative association, an overall feeling that colours the brand image, giving an emotional as well as a rational engagement with the brand. These associations are often interdependent in the individual's mind, where the strength and meaning of associations may or may not be shared across different people, and where evaluations and even the salient descriptors may not be agreed upon.

Brand awareness and salience are known to positively affect choice among competing products and destinations. Major broadcast events can increase a host city's salience and, while cities may have little direct control over the choice of images presented, nonetheless unique architectural or natural features,[3] or place names help to build and reinforce a salient image. Both the frequency of its media exposure and the manner of its representation affect the way in which a city is perceived. Indeed, the identity of a public event's host city may not always be clear from what is shown in a television broadcast. During the 2006 FIFA World Cup, Nuremberg's Schöner Brunnen (Beautiful Fountain) was temporarily enclosed within a 'double-helix of 780 chairs removed from Berlin's Olympic Stadium' (Wilson 2006). This caused

---

3   Including flora and wildlife; see Hill, Arthurson and Chalip 2001, quoted by Green 2002.

considerable community opposition, since a characteristic and historic landmark was now unavailable for televised city promotion and visitors. Asking whether the city is a distinct character or merely a backdrop, Christine Green (2002) describes how host cities without obviously identifying cityscape features can still benefit by using iconography to anchor an association in memory. She discusses a San Antonio sports event which was held at a venue named after the Alamo and whose logo associated the city's name with its landmark Alamo image. With frequent exposure through televised images logos associating the event with a local icon, particularly one with a strong visual component, designed icons can effectively represent the city and increase its perceptual salience.

A dishwashing liquid made from a demonstrably superior scientific formula may fail in the market because its colour is considered to be inappropriate: it is a sales cliché that 'marketing is not a battle of products, but a battle of perceptions'. When a brand, and its messages, has a wide range of users who bring their own associations and personal meanings to it, a simple consensus on brand image may be unachievable, especially when the brand itself is complex and multifaceted. Commercial research often uses propositional statements associating a quality with a brand (e.g. low cost, Western, modern, good for Australia), but these are often ambiguous in meaning (Wild West / Western Sydney), and this is methodologically and pragmatically problematic within currently dominant modes of branding research (Bock et al. 2001).

'Personality' is one category of statement associating a brand (Volvo, for example) with a quality (solid, secure), and it is theorized by Jennifer Aaker – who defines 'brand personality' as 'the set of human characteristics associated with a brand' (Aaker 1997, p. 347) – in terms of the 'Big Five' dimensions of human personality (sincerity, excitement, competence, sophistication and ruggedness). Literature and introspection suggest it is easy both to anthropomorphize brands and for consumers to imbue brands with associations. A strong, distinctive brand personality can also provide a meaning to which consumers can relate emotionally. As we argue in later chapters, cities lend themselves to anthropomorphic identification, but the depth and scale of a city's personality and the ways in which that personality emerges or is disguised, or understated, in branding and in film, hint at both the potential and limitations of the brand concept.

Personality associations and personal qualities may become established not only through brand ambassadors and spokespersons but also the ordinary people helping shape a distinctive brand identity. The rugged image projected by the Marlboro Man may have been manufactured, but Paul Hogan's believable character in Australian Tourism adverts was consistent with Australia's now well-established persona of a fun and relaxed place, with rugged nature and honest, sincere people. Moreover, since many ordinary Australians also presented this character aspect, trust in the brand was reinforced by the underlying honesty of the proposition. However, Tim Bock and his colleagues (2001) observe that many of Aaker's descriptors do not correspond to the psychology literature, are more sociological in their nature and are ambiguous in interpretation and application to brands. In short, they agree with Gian Vittorio Caprara, Claudio Barbaranelli and Gianluigi Guido (2001) in suggesting that the metaphor of the Big Five dimensions of human personality may become stretched for branding more complex entities.

The 2004 Brand Australia television commercials attempted to broaden the image, understanding and appeal of Australia by showing the country in 'a different light'. They used famous Australians such as singer Delta Goodrem, cricket legend Richie Benaud, poet Les Murray and Aboriginal artist Barbara Weir to highlight aspects of the culture, particularly food and wine and the arts, not previously well-known to overseas visitors. But, as some of these personalities were not recognizable outside of narrow demographics, a year later the campaign was replaced by the invitation 'So Where The Bloody Hell Are You?', a campaign that exchanged 'real people' for celebrities and targeted the psychographics[4] of potential visitors to sustain associations while simultaneously deepening the image. Brief video clips show experiences that appeal to travellers' various motivations and common needs. Safety, for example, is implied in the voice-over comment 'We've got the sharks out of the pool'. Other images and commentary associate quality service with the Great Barrier Reef, a classy restaurant with Uluru, and Aboriginal dancers who 'have been rehearsing for over 40,000 years', addressing human motivations at both personal and higher levels.[5] Building a place brand can take many years (Curtis 2001) and both these campaigns help to broaden Australia's brand image, drawing together familiar imagery and lesser-known aspects. At the same time, the flippancy of their 'rehearsing for over 40,000 years' betrays scant regard for Indigenous cultural history.

To manage brand equity over time both the sources of that equity and brand consistency should be maintained, paying appropriate attention to brand fortifying or leverage decisions and also to specific marketing support, including slogans, jingles and promotional events (Keller 2003). Leveraging involves strategic activities undertaken around the event, particularly for increasing investment, business and trade. Business Club Australia was a federal government initiative designed to leverage from the Sydney Olympics, recognizing that longer-term return on the unprecedented investment involved would go beyond sector-specific impacts (such as on local athletics) and visitation (O'Brien 2006). Extended for the Rugby World Cup of 2003 and Melbourne Commonwealth Games of 2006, the initiative provided consistent national branding and promotion, organized international networking and business matching activities, and targeted overseas business media to ensure positive promotion of Australian business. Longer-term impacts from leveraging may include boosts to city and country brand reputation, profits for associated organizations, sponsors and the city itself, civic pride, as well as to ongoing local and national tourism, although measuring such success factors is 'challenging' (Ratnatunga and Muthaly 2000).

While all its elements affect a brand's value, success relies on its consumers, their loyalty and sustained associations: brand building is all about the development

---

4 Psychographics addresses psychological characteristics and values e.g. venturesomeness, irreverence that can apply to any age or national demographic.

5 Based on Mark Goodman's analysis, using Abraham Maslow's (1954) hierarchy (personal communication).

of a sustainable offer and continuing relationship. A brand's perceived quality and its image will depend on the particular experiences and needs of the individual together with its identifiable mix of legally protectable elements, such as names, logos, spokespeople and jingles that help increase or decrease brand equity. Memorability, meaningfulness, adaptability as tastes changes, and appeal (sensory or otherwise) are criteria that help build and sustain brand equity (Keller 2003). Kevin Keller's Customer-Based Brand Equity model adopts a consumer perspective, assuming that a brand's power 'lies in what customers have learned, felt, seen and heard about the brand as a result of their experiences over time' (2003, p. 59). Differentiation arises both from brand awareness (brand recognition and recall) and brand image. Brand feelings and resonance (the emotional responses to, and identification with, the brand) are two of the six 'building-blocks' of the model, which also includes cognitive components addressing awareness and judgmental aspects. Resonance is the goal of brand building, where a loyal, intense relationship is developed.

While emotional engagement with brands has long been recognized, Kevin Roberts's (CEO of Saatchi and Saatchi) concept of *lovemarks* takes brand engagement to its extreme, making clear that brands are owned by those who use and love them. Lovemarks are products or places that inspire a loyalty and human connection beyond reason, a deep emotional resonance arising from mystery, sensuality and intimacy. Roberts sees stories as central to establishing this resonance, layers of personal narrative telling what people love, had loved, or could love, convincingly linking past present and future, and exhibiting the sincerity of this passion.

In 2001, Roberts said that Sydney was considered a lovemark (Roberts 2001). However, while five years later neither neither Shanghai nor Hong Kong had qualified as one, Shanghai Tang fashion had. The lovemarks site (www.lovemarks.com) lists people's stories about why they love something. Sydney has several entries, not only (and predictably) on the Opera House, but also on other Sydney locations and on the city itself. In 2006, the *Shanghai Business Review* identified the components of the lovemarks concept in relation to China's perceived comparative advantages: '5000 years of culture rich in philosophy, myth and story … the secrets of China's past and the excitement of its future have fantastic allure … China's wisdom, harmony balance … offer huge sensory advantage', and a Chinese TV station has since commissioned Roberts for a series on Lovemarks (Roberts 2006).

Lovemarks, stories and sensory appeal represent richer categories than the simple identifying marks of most product brands, and point towards an experiential engagement with brands through which a relationship and place in the public imagination may develop. Experiencing – in particular, hedonic – products through virtual interaction can evoke vivid imagery and memories, increasing both salience and favourable attitudes. In two independent studies looking at prospective web purchases, both Ann Schlosser (2003) (looking at Kodak cameras) and John Gammack and Christopher Hodkinson (2003) (an Australian coastal destination) found that direct interaction with objects in virtual worlds accessed through web browsers increased involvement, imagery and product engagement beyond equivalent (but passive) information-only sites. Memorability and purchase intentions were also affected and it is well known that imagining or virtually experiencing a scenario makes a purchase seem more likely to eventuate.

The advertising industry is beginning to respond to the Internet and its impact on the consumption of products, information and entertainment. In particular, models of advertising are changing from 'reach and awareness' to more sophisticated concepts of engagement, which are known to affect brand preference and loyalty. Engagement, which occurs when an idea or media experience with a brand leaves a positive impression, is now seen by the advertising industry as the construct relevant to understanding consumer involvement with brands at three levels of engagement with advertising messages (Advertising Research Foundation (ARF) 2006). These are engagement with the medium (active involvement versus merely present), engagement with the creative execution (sufficient viewer interest and involvement to impress the brand) and active 'engagement with the brand, creating identity, meaning, affinity and value'. The rhetoric of the ARF's definition implies a seduction: 'Engagement is turning on a prospect to a brand idea enhanced by the surrounding context' (ARF 2006), in which the richness of the 'media experience' is likely to dominate brand perception, and to involve emotional engagements as well as purely rational choices. Only relatively recently, however, has branding theory started to move beyond product models to the identification of constructs relevant to more complex branding.

Beyond Product Branding

With the emergence of corporate branding, the 1990s saw the beginning of a strategic focus towards branding more complex entities. Francisco Guzmán (2005) notes it is the core values of an organization that crucially inform brand building, whereas this is not the case with product branding. He cites, from Mary Jo Hatch and Majken Schultz (2003), six distinctions between product and corporate branding. These include corporate entities' greater reach and different societal exposure, their necessary relation to all stakeholders, not just customers, and their temporal dimensions of past and future. These, of course, apply to cities as well, and, once liberated from the constraints of a product model, services and other complex entities such as individuals and places also begin to be thought of as brands. Although product-based models remain dominant, long-established theories are now starting to be tested.

Leslie de Chernatony and Malcolm McDonald (1998) define a successful brand as 'an identifiable product, service, person or place, augmented in such a way that the buyer or user perceives relevant unique added values which match their needs most closely'. This seems to suggest that the branding of both a product and a place can be accommodated in a single, marketing-oriented conceptualization. For example, Philip Kotler, a leading marketing researcher, and David Gertner (2002) interpret a product-derived conceptualization as a direct response to the question 'Can a country be a brand?', and equate brand equity, image, slogans and other associations with country-specific examples. As the titles of books of which he has been the principal author indicate, Kotler has dealt at length with marketing both 'Asian places' and Latin America (2002 and 2006), and many followers of the 'Kotler et al.' product marketing model see no difficulty in transferring the concepts directly (Kavaratzis and Ashworth 2005, p. 513). By 2006, de Chernatony was more explicit about the differences between product and city branding, pointing to factors such as lack of control over the experience; a mutating target market, and the risk of confusion and brand dilution due to competing brand visions from the sheer variety of stakeholders and steerers (Virgo and de Chernatony 2006). Destination marketing remains a common practice in the tourism industry, and numerous examples may be cited of destinations whose product aspects have largely been mapped onto standard brand building models. Destination marketing exists at city, region and country level, as examples such as Bradford and Nottingham, Oregon and Western Australia, Wales and Spain readily attest (see Morgan, Pritchard and Pride 2004; Curtis 2001). Brands and sub-brands can be structured into an architecture in such a way that a family of related brands can be made to support and reinforce one another. Within an encompassing national brand architecture, regions and cities can both inherit and build equity while at the same time achieving mutually greater exposure.

The appropriateness of this type of model, when applied uncritically, is currently under question. Niall Caldwell and Joao Freire (2004) review literature that highlights how different attributes are more applicable to a country as a whole than to any specific part of that country. Additionally, smaller destinations imply more specific propositions than the complexity and fluidity inherent in a nation's image, whose own identity and image is also subject to volatility from temporal and political events. A branded product implies a consistent quality that will meet consumer expectations. Ireland's traditional image as the emerald isle with welcoming people and a relaxed life-style found itself seriously at odds with that of the Celtic Tiger, the widely-used metaphor for the Irish economic boom of the late-1990s and, accordingly, the country's ongoing image promotion needed to be reconsidered (O'Leary and Deegan 2003).

Not only is the product mutable, but the modes in which it is understood are also subject to variation. Graham Brown (1990) describes two competing models for tourism behaviour, both of which produce meaningful place identity. In one, tourists' interaction processes create emergent meaning, in the other a destination's symbolic character is used instrumentally by tourists with specific goals. 'Although the meaning associated with a particular place may be unique to the individual', Brown writes, 'a destination may embody shared meanings as a symbol endowed with cultural significance' (1990, p. 2). In Brown's study respondents typically mentioned places associated with their childhoods as most meaningful, a finding that suggested that formative childhood experiences may influence tourist destination choice. One of his respondents commented directly on Australia, feeling it to be 'meaningful as a "fantasy" destination … a big, mysterious, lovely place … If I go, I may never come back' (p. 101). Another found the redwood forests of northern California most meaningful, but knew of them only indirectly through books and television. (Presumably, the respondent who mentioned Australia was similarly influenced by the media.) Affective themes of nostalgia and fantasy, either personal or culturally symbolic, add yet other dimensions to the understanding and images of place, and such images may themselves be vicariously received or 'unrepresentative'.

Images of destinations also may change over time, whether they derive either from an actual visit or a purely mediated experience. Depending on whether they have been manipulated by marketing efforts, or are more documentary or organic in nature,[6] images seen on TV, the Internet and films may have positive or negative effects on destination perception. Books, travel literature and music are other elements of popular culture that also influence place perceptions, and which can translate into increased desire to visit and visitation itself. H. Kim and Scott Richardson (2003) describe the impact of films, citing the influence of Mel Gibson's *Braveheart* on tourists' decisions to visit the Stirling area of Scotland and showing that exposure to Richard Linklater's *Before Sunrise*, which was set in Vienna, increased interest in visiting the Austrian capital. Although a film may represent a destination literally, its imaginative possibilities differentiate it from a simply mundane rendering. In *Before Sunrise*, the everyday city was essentially a backdrop to a love story. However, the key landscape scenes in *Braveheart* were actually filmed in Ireland: there were no Stirling tourist locations in the film. One of us (Gammack) grew up in Stirling and immediately noticed that the green landscape of the opening scenes was not the green of that area, though a certain Celtic quality was successfully conveyed. The retreat from authenticity that all film – indeed, all representation – necessarily requires, is heightened by the expectations that cinema will somehow describe a true place, simply because it has to be filmed *somewhere*. But, as Chinese-language film exemplifies, films are trans-national, and filmmakers may go to Zhejiang Hengdian Studios to get a low-cost, high-impact set for just about any era and any aspect of 'Chinese heritage', while Hong Kong filmmakers increasingly shoot in Shanghai because permissions are easier to obtain, and post-production is more affordable than back in Hong Kong.

Based on a comprehensive literature review, a conceptual framework for understanding destination image has been proposed by Martina Gallarza and her colleagues (2002) that recognizes the complexity that all this involves. Place is mutable, imprecise, and subject to the narratives that sustain its representation. The tourism product's inherent multi-dimensionality, the mixing of images with subjective impressions of retailers, residents and other tourists, and the intangibility of access to pre-visit perceptions – all these make conceptualization and measurement difficult. Since destinations have different attributes and, indeed, different types of attributes and since markets have different functional and psychological needs, a model of destination image is required that admits of concepts susceptible to multiple interpretations, and which is at once relativistic and dynamic. In practice this means, amongst other things, that far-away destinations can be subject to a distorted and shallow perception, while residents' perceptions are naturally deeper and more meaningful, and it may be unrealistic to expect a collectively-held image that is not stereotypical. Nonetheless, as destination image is widely considered to affect market decisions and choices, attempts to theorize it continue.

Particular attributes are more relevant to some markets than others, and Sinéad O'Leary and Jim Deegan (2002) suggest that ideally attributes should stem from the participant's own perceptions rather than those of researchers. However, a destination may have a dominant perception in one market, excluding any broader appreciation of it in others. For example, despite being one of Australia's largest cities, Queensland's Gold Coast is generally thought of as a tourist resort, which

---

6 This distinction was originally drawn by Clare Gunn in 1972; see Gunn 1988.

potentially negatively impacts business and investor perception. At the same time, however, upscale residents may be attracted to the life-style of these coastal cities and bring in wealth or new businesses, while many existing residents take civic pride in a strong tourism proposition that differentiates their city. Australian coastal destinations have recently experienced significant resident influx, coincident with the broadcast in the 1980s of the ABC-TV series, *Seachange*. While the series attracted tourists to Barwon Heads, the Victorian coastal town where it was filmed, some residents were unhappy with ongoing impacts such as increased rental costs (Beeton 2004), which in turn caused more holistic and proactive city-planning to be undertaken. Asuncíon Beerli and Josefa Martin's (2004) analysis of the attributes used in a range of destination image scales identifies nine general dimensions, including natural environment, general and tourist infrastructure, political and economic factors, culture history and art, and general atmosphere. These classify various specific attributes that might be selected as appropriate to a particular destination and used in developing a model for determining the factors that influence image formation. Destination image is held to be formed from cognitive and affective images, informed by personal factors (e.g. motivations) and primary and secondary information sources (e.g. experience from an actual visit as opposed to an induced image from, say, a film). Affective dimensions, previously ignored in much destination-image literature, are directly relevant to the influence of films on destination image (Kim and Richardson 2003, p. 232), but emotional impacts related to this remain issues for further research and, indeed, film-induced tourism is now beginning to be theorized (see Beeton 2005) and related more generally to the marketing of places (Hudson and Ritchie 2006).

Destination is only one aspect of place, and beyond everyday tourism marketing, the activity of destination branding is also considered both new and under-researched.[7] Analysis by Carmen Blain, Stuart Levy and J. Brent Ritchie (2005) discovered both a narrow conceptualization and also selective application by practitioners, whose particular focus on logo design and development was based on destination marketers' belief that logos supported destination image, describing and differentiating the location. Unfortunately, however, many attributes – reflected in terms such as 'fun', 'historic' and 'vibrant' – are often overused and do not differentiate destinations. Blain and her colleagues offer an extended definition for destination branding which includes marketing activities over and above the development of graphics that identify and differentiate a destination. These include conveying the anticipation of a unique travel experience and reinforcing the emotional connection between visitor and destination, while reducing search costs and perceived risk in order to create a destination image that positively influences destination choice (p. 337). After being characterized for years by outdated images that have persisted in the public mind, cities such as Belfast, Glasgow and Pittsburgh have used a co-ordinated brand strategy to rebrand themselves so as to ensure a focussed message, particularly for tourists. Strong and sustained new messages are required to overturn negative perceptions and must be substantiated in ongoing experience for a considerable time

---

7   See, e.g., Kavaratzis 2004; Caldwell and Freire 2004; Blain, Levy and Ritchie 2005; Kerr 2006 and Virgo and de Chernatony 2006.

until they become firmly established. But focussing city brand messages is conflicted in ways not generally true for products: 'available cheap labour force' may be read as 'depressed industry and high unemployment' and, although targeting of a specific message is possible, often the public would already be familiar with a city's reputation. There is a risk of brand confusion across market segments when semi-autonomous agencies have different emphases or interpretations of 'the product'. But ignoring economic development imperatives, brand message and imaging designed for the tourist market is itself not straightforward. The work of Caldwell and Freire found both that different national consumer markets identify specifically different messages, and that the factors influencing tourist images at a national level differ from those at a more local level, suggesting that destination branding is not a unitary phenomenon, even when restricted to tourist markets.

Numerous as these complexities of place marketing on a product model may be, there are yet more layers of complexity to place branding, when it is considered in a wider context. Places are so unlike traditional brands that, according to traditional brand theory (Blichfeldt 2005), certain aspects of them are 'unmanageable'. Greg Kerr (2006) distinguishes destination branding from a more holistic location branding, implying a responsibility that goes beyond the tourism office. Brand steerers include those involved in promotion, but those in a position to manage the substance and appearance of the city are also required: if those managing housing, architecture, and transport connections are not co-ordinated, 'an attractive place to live and work' will fail as a message. As Ben Virgo and Leslie de Chernatony write, 'It's all very good for Hong Kong to have as its core values progressive, free, stable and place of opportunity, but, if the brand steerers do not concur about these values and operate in a manner which does not reinforce these, the chance for brand success are reduced' (2006, p. 381) Their work in Birmingham used Delphi, an iterative and convergent group decision-making process, to identify agreed core values among brand steerers, but they note that other stakeholders would also need to buy into the brand vision, if its validity was to be strengthened.

Brand Oregon's original strategy combined tourism with economic development, mandating a consistent image, but found that the fit between tourism and developer imperatives was sometimes awkward. Later, a focus on positioning local business products 'using Oregon's distinctiveness' was more successful, due to allowing greater flexibility in aligning products with Oregon's image when appropriate, rather than enforcing a branding program by means of top-down regulation. While such case studies offer practical lessons (as in the case of destination branding), place branding remains under-theorized (Kavaratzis 2004). Graham Hankinson (2004) notes that, other than product branding, there is no general theoretical framework to underpin place-brand development. He offers a conceptual model, proposing that branding requires investment in infrastructure to make brand promise a reality, selection of consistent markets matched to the local character, and a 'strong network of stakeholder relationships which all share a common vision of the core brand' (p. 116). Although this extends destination marketing beyond image towards inclusion of relationship concepts, it still assumes a unitary product and has no empirical validation. On the other hand, it also opens the door to the politics of place, residency and deeper meanings

– including those which challenge the principles of branding that might assume that a place brand's character is always enough to convey place-ness, or 'the idea of the city'. Mihalis Kavaratzis and Gregory Ashworth (2005) find evidence of both a confusion of guiding approaches and a recognizable gap between general principles and practitioner activity. Kavaratzis and Ashworth do not focus on product, but rather take a place management approach, which entails the qualities of identity and place-making with multiple stakeholders. Giving an experiential value that is 'uncopiable', this may involve, say, an urban renewal that 'creates an identity that touches upon structure, ... actions and activities that characterise the image of the city [and] the chemistry of the people who operate there' (Florian 2002, p. 24). Although many place marketers realize that their image depends on their people, this means extra complexity for image-makers and city managers.

A meaningful place identity will entail not only substantiating those aspects of the city-as-product that are relevant to the markets in which it is to compete, but also addressing the distribution channels for marketing the destination. As a means to this end, one-size-fits-all, mass-market messages about a place messages are being replaced increasingly by a mass customization that involves the active search via the Internet for particular experiences which engage with individuals (King 2002). A web site capable of automatically identifying a surfer's geographical location and offering language choices can begin to build a tailored profile: as already noted, the Hong Kong Tourism Board's site has for some time offered differentiated access through tailored front pages linked to the different interests of its key markets, and online retailers such as Amazon have many sophisticated profile mechanisms for engaging customers appropriately.

Can a city be a brand? This question has recently begun to receive considerable attention, both commercial and critical,[8] and, while most commentators agree that a city can indeed be a brand, all recognize that city branding involves layers and complexities that require conceptualization and theory beyond the models of product branding.

The issues underlying the apparently simple question, we suggest, require a critical analysis that goes beyond applying or even extending theory derived from product advertising, and that goes to the heart of questions of identity and social evolution. Something as complex as a city may be theorized, represented, imagined and experienced in ways infinitely more complex than those applicable to the products upon which branding theory was developed. Moreover, they embody particular histories and locations, depth of social capital and invested futures that promise or highlight certain specific possibilities, but at the same time deny or downplay others. Denmark's EU presidency in 2002 identified some critical issues for European cities and their urban identities in a global era, issues more widely applicable as local differentiations disappear or resurface to produce a distinctive (or a bland) identity. It has been suggested that some places have 'a distinct atmosphere', that some (but not others) are 'built out of layers of time' and that '[we] all agree that Venice is something other than Frankfurt, Helsinki or

---

8   See, e.g., Burson-Marsteller et al. 2001; Hanmin 2003; Trueman et al. 2004; Kavaratzis and Ashworth 2005 and Larsson and Wahlqvist 2006.

Brussels'.[9] So, considering how easily we move about the planet, eat the same fast food and watch the same films, does it really matter where we are? And if it *does* matter where we are (or choose to be), then *why* does it matter, and what are the factors that shape our choice?

That cities are in competition with one another is obvious, but the various stakeholders and markets, which are not necessarily either consistent or compatible, give extra complexity: residents' views may differ markedly from tourist or business attributions. The concept of a unique selling proposition hardly applies: many cities have, or can replicate, what others offer. A city is a dynamically changing entity that cannot be taken off the market or simply discontinued in adverse times, and it is a multifaceted entity, whose various propositions risk sending confused or contradictory messages to its markets.[10] A city such as Pisa may have little external reputation beyond its iconic leaning tower, and while tourists may have no other expectations of the place, all those investors, touring-events planners, academics and students, entrepreneurs, creatives, traders (or other potential stakeholders) may have little image of, and hence no view about, the brand and its distinctiveness.

In 2000 Hong Kong's government commissioned research on perceptions of its brand and competitive positioning. Business, government, media and community in Hong Kong and around the world were surveyed and interviewed in depth, using a proprietary brand instrument and a global database in which Hong Kong is included as a brand and with which benchmarking can occur, in this case against other autonomous economies (Burson-Marsteller et al. 2001). The development of a framework for Hong Kong's visual identity was a research goal, and many stakeholder-specific perceptions of the city's attributes were identified. Hong Kong is generally well-regarded, one of the pillars of brand equity. While we shall not discuss particular strengths and challenges until later in this book, clearly there is a high-level view – i.e. at the level of government – that a location can be treated as a brand, and this has significant policy implications. In Hong Kong's case a government unit was set up specifically to manage Brand Hong Kong.

Myfanwy Trueman, Mary Klemm and Axele Giroud (2003) discuss the conflicting objectives of various local stakeholders in the northern English city of Bradford, including residents and municipal representatives, employers, and community and sporting groups, and the way in which the perceived value of their city's brand lies in meeting their particular needs. A focus on culture may not be considered the appropriate focus for business. Indeed, there may not be general agreement regarding what is appropriate for a multicultural city: Bradford's failed bid to be the 2008 European Capital of Culture was apparently not 'grounded in stakeholder perceptions of reality or "social expectation"' (Trueman, Klemm and Giroud 2003). Changes in local political priorities and vision can make it difficult

---

9   See http://www.byplanlab.dk/English/europeancities_intro.html. Retrieved on 15 September 2006.

10   In films set in London, 'Richard Curtisland', with its lovable white eccentrics, co-exists with Guy Ritchie's East End of gangsters and geezers. Both are essentially bogus and not representative of the myriad other Londons that lie beyond the camera frame (Hari 2006).

to formulate clearly a city-brand message or to deliver on an aspiration. Moreover, different stakeholders may also understand the boundaries of a place differently, and so affect what precisely is being branded. City municipalities have obligations to their outlying areas. Bradford's attractive surrounding countryside is part of the metropolitan area, but this is ignored by the business community, whose visual image is of a blighted urban centre. Large cities are identified by their central areas, skylines or tourist icons, but they also have outer suburbs and natural boundaries with particular qualities that are part of their identity and that contribute to their overall substance and reputation. Boundary disputes also arise when lesser-known regions try to claim the brand cachet of popular neighbours and their specific attractions, seen as diluting or confusing the brand of the already successful region.

City brands are also less controllable than product brands: events, art, political or music movements, sporting teams, famous individuals, prosperity and tragedies all emerge, peak and decline, while the experience of the city relies essentially on its people, and the chance interactions that arise. Moreover, unlike products, cities are often works in progress – they have both an ongoing reality and an aspiration – but if the communicated brand image is dishonest (see Trueman, Klemm and Giroud 2004), and promise is not fulfilled in reality, then trust and reputation will be damaged.

Sports and other major events attract both visitation and media exposure and city marketers can leverage the increased awareness towards establishing a destination's longer-term economy (Green 2002). The 2000 Sydney Olympics was the first occasion on which a national tourism organization strategically leveraged the association prior to the opening of the event. A dedicated business unit of the Australian Tourist Commission (ATC) saw the development of 'Brand Australia' as a means of adding depth and dimension to customer expectations and awareness. The innovative model entailed working with Olympic sponsors and other non-traditional tourism partners in promotional strategies beyond tourism advertising, co-operating with partners who could also see opportunities to grow their businesses in Australia. Media and broadcast partnerships were also developed, with the ATC closely controlling the video footage and images of Australia made available for TV commercials. This ensured consistency of portrayal, in line with the Commission's promotional direction – to replace the Crocodile-Dundee stereotype with a more sophisticated culturally-complex image – and, integrating with the Olympics and its marketing, developing story ideas and associated images for use by the international media. The ATC was clear that it was Australia, not just Sydney, that was being promoted, and that the Olympics experience would apply to the 2002 Gay Games and other events, while also leveraging the experience for the post-Olympics meetings market (Chalip 2000).

The reputation of country-of-origin, or product-country, image also matters in the public imagination. Swiss precision, Italian style and many others have been shown to affect valuation and purchase decisions: German cars and French cuisine, as opposed to German cuisine and French cars. Although Chinese products are commonplace and even invisible in overseas markets, the brand 'Made in China' has not yet achieved the reputation that, say, Japanese and German manufacturing now have. Although trust in national brands can develop in time and their images may be multifaceted, the stereotyping or selective perception of attributes is possible for any given audience, with both positive and negative impacts on brand equity. All places come with some established reputation, which can be affected by media presentations.

In 2002, for example, Liechtenstein, a tiny country no bigger than some corporates, had a dubious, and unwanted, reputation as a tax haven. It sought actively to manage its own brand and reputation, hiring the consultancy Wolff Olins to rebrand the country. In order to do so, a new instrument for measuring country reputations, the Fombrun-RI Country Reputation Index (CRI) was developed. While noting differences between corporates and countries, this largely equated measures of corporate with those of country reputation and sought a quantitative measure that could be benchmarked and turned into activity (Passow, Fehlmann and Grahlow 2005). Financial appeal is one aspect of the CRI, along with emotional, physical, cultural and leadership appeal. Such scorecard models usually require complementary studies to enable a deeper understand to be reached, or to make it possible to disentangle the macro-political or other influences that affect aspects of reputation. For example, the instrument postdates a study that found that, due in large part to the 'one country, two systems' policy, Hong Kong's international business reputation has diminished since 1997 (Thompson 2004).

The branding of a country or any other global location also needs to take into account the various components of its proposition and their relative significance. A country seen primarily as a tourism location may not be widely thought of as a natural place for foreign direct investment. The choice of a location for foreign direct investment is rarely dependent upon the brand image of the country (or city) itself, but rather upon such factors as access to markets, low labour costs and tax incentives. While potential investors may share the dominant public image of the location, place marketing would be more specifically targeted, since even within a country, different regions and cities may have different taxation or regulatory regimes, and world cities, although a sub-national economy, can even compete with countries (Papadopoulos and Heslop 2002).

The country of origin of tourists also makes a difference to the way in which a brand is perceived. For example, while Spain's culture may appeal to the Portuguese, its beaches may be more attractive to Norwegians, and similar differences in brand perception have been shown in various studies (e.g. Richards 2002; Beerli and Martín 2004). Greg Richards (2002) examined foreigners' perceptions of the Splendid China cultural parks, with their scale models of famous landmarks such as the Great Wall and traditional temples, designed to create a destination image of China and ultimately to encourage visitation. The first of these parks, located in Shenzen, was followed by versions beside Disneyworld in Florida and subsequently in the Netherlands. Among the marketing issues involved in the establishment of these parks was the delicate question of which cultural symbols should be chosen to represent such a diversity of peoples. In the case of the Florida park this led to other cultural problems. The inclusion of Tibet's Potala Palace, amongst other landmarks, was seen as an attempt to legitimize Chinese Communist occupation of previously independent areas – and the whole enterprise was viewed as propagandist (Brown 2006). Moreover, American visitors were used to, and expected, rides and gaudy entertainments, rather than a place designed for contemplation and serenity. Not surprisingly, therefore, although a children's playground, side-shows and acrobats were introduced, the park closed in 2003. In Richard's study Dutch and Chinese participants, comprising subgroups, some of whom had visited China whilst others had not, were interviewed with a view to eliciting their views on authentic Chinese culture and its markers. Every one of them saw the Potala Palace as Tibetan, not Chinese, but while the Dutch felt that the Han Chinese had enough culture to fill the entire park, the Chinese believed that, since 'the park was about China', minorities should also be represented. There is an obvious, political dissonance here, as China's sense of self, at least from the perspective of the Party state and the Han majority, is that China's minorities are both exceptional and intrinsic to China as an encompassing and lasting world entity. One Dutch respondent commented on China's long history, but his experience in China was that what had been lost in the Cultural Revolution meant authenticity lay not so much in material culture – even though others remarked that much architecture remains – but rather in the people's way of life. A critique of his position would comment on his idealization of a certain aspect of Chinese culture and continuity. One might argue that a major Chinese concept of authentic Chinese culture stems from the family bond, and that bonds with place (*lao xiang*) and continuity with the past are maintained, not by the age of an original building, but by a wish to rebuild in the original style and location. These issues have implications for the way in which an identity is projected, and in which brand messages engage tourists and other potential visitors.

Beyond images and slogans, narratives are beginning to emerge as a construct relevant in branding particular industry sectors in relation to their country of origin. Erran Carmel and Jacob Eisenberg (2006) identify separate narratives for the software industry across six nations, Russia, Israel, Ireland, USA, India and Brazil, and these are argued to influence global capital decisions. Narratives are recognized as more complex than a story, and draw upon themes familiar in film and cultural studies. Mythic, historical and value-based constructs can be related to specific national and political identifications, and help sustain and build identity. Russia's 'hardship programming' narrative, for example, fostered efficiency and superiority in scientific programming. Israel's effectiveness and collectivism in achieving objectives is rooted in compulsory military experience, and individual heroes consuming pizza and cola while building the USA's current software hegemony connotes lone pioneers.

As '[i]mage and reputation [become] essential parts of the state's strategic equity', the concept of the 'brand state' is emerging where the outside world's ideas about a country are largely characterized by style rather than substance (Van Ham 2001). This is arguably true, not only of nation brands, but also of any autonomous economy – including corporates and superbrands – that competes globally. Peter van Ham argues that such branding is a positive political development, supplanting nationalism and contributing to (European) pacification by marginalizing chauvinistic conceptions of national identity. A simple analysis, however, may not be the most appropriate. An examination of English national symbols may reveal a 'generational' shift from historic symbols of authority such as parliament buildings and anthems towards contemporary sports and TV soaps. Nonetheless, an identity based on brand components not rooted in history, or its processes, will require something similarly compelling to produce narratives that are more than just amusements. In many places a brand is created by or emerges from the people, who also substantiate its continuing evolution.

This is one of the key differences between products and places: every citizen is an ambassador, and if they do not believe the hype, or fulfil the promise, any dishonest representation of the city will fail. A definite identity, a true place – however imperfect and impossible a concept that may be, but nonetheless honestly projected – is a *sine qua non* of brand believability. (The Czech Republic's great seafaring tradition could be fabricated, but it would not remain believable.[11]) Internally, too, the quality of life of a city is a major contributor to its image, affecting, among other things, reinvestment by its current business community (Glaser 1991). Brand image, together with its component quality-of-life indicators, is also important to residents and migrants, and Julia Winfield-Pfefferkorn (2005) proposes several factors relevant to an individual's decision to come and to remain in a city. These include employment and cost of living, good and affordable housing, reasonable climate and public transport, good schools and recreational attractions.

This chapter has laid out the trajectories along which brand capacity is built, and gives some sense of the aspirations and challenges of its extension to place branding. We suggest that place branding is a formidable tool for a city tourism agency. However, as we shall argue in the next chapter, the gap between brand personality and the shared idea of a city may be wide indeed.

---

11 Carmen and Eisenberg (2006) quote this example, from Schöpflin (2000).

Chapter 3

Structures of Attention and the 'City of Life' (Hong Kong)

In this chapter we explore Hong Kong and the concept of shared *structures of attention*, referred to in Chapter 1.[1] The idea of structures of attention is not a method per se, but rather an approach, a way of understanding and defining the predominant nuances by which the city is known to its various kinds of consumers, residents and guests. We also suggest that structures of attention are themselves characteristic of the visual response to the city seen in film and other visual culture. The following discussion of the relationship between lived experience and cinematic vision and response is based on case study material collected in Hong Kong from 2000 to 2004, with the major focus on that city in the period following the SARS (Severe Acute Respiratory Syndrome) epidemic. Our argument identifies where the cinematic idea of the city, the cityscape, is resonant with touristic strategies in peculiar local conditions. In Hong Kong at that time – and, arguably, still today – it was necessary to intuit and define structures of attention that were responsive to the political, social, and historical interests of residents and citizens at a time of crisis.

SARS made its first appearance in Hong Kong in February 2003. The disease was highly contagious, and therefore lethal in the densely populated, high-rise residential city. The effect on Hong Kong life was profound. The city was subdued, scared and intensely aware of its isolation. Most people wore masks outside, used gloves (or pens) to avoid touching public surfaces – lift buttons, train doors – and no longer dipped their chopsticks into the shared food servers in the middle of the dining table. Some janitors installed extra doormats saturated with antiseptic in the hallways of upmarket apartment blocks. The impact was complex, however. Fear flourished alongside other emotions, in particular an emergent pride in local heroes, in Hong Kong's historical resilience to suffering, and in the city's ability to fight back and take care of itself. The 'heroes' were those who died working as doctors, nurses and medical orderlies in the SARS wards. Their courage was likened to that of arriving migrants from Mainland China in the post-WWII period, and even to those who fought the Japanese during the War itself.

Although cinema and tourism were commercial casualties of the SARS months, it was cinema and tourism workers who took the lead in building and giving visual form to the positive emotions that the epidemic induced. In July-September 2003 the Tourism Commission and the Guild of Screen Directors produced a series of short films to celebrate the people of Hong Kong's response to the epidemic, and to

---

1 Earlier versions of this chapter have been published in Verhoeven and Morris (2004) and Lindner (2006).

promote the 'Recovery'. A group of filmmakers, led by Peter Chan, collaborated with the Hong Kong Tourism Commission to develop a sequence of short promo-films, each celebrating an aspect of the 'Recovery'. The series was entitled *1:99*, after the dilution ratio of bleach to water in the solution used to clean the city of infection. The *1:99* films comprised 19 short advertisements for local patriotism, each offering a bite-sized take on Hong Kong's attachment to itself. In Chan's own film, *Awakening Spring*, a man (played by the elegiac Tony Leung) in a long greatcoat walks alone through deserted city streets. The light is grey, the buildings are ominous and the ground is frozen. As he glances at the myriad windows, he sees a masked face staring out of each one. The city's skyscrapers have become elongated tombs for the living. Suddenly, a medical team rushes by with a patient on a stretcher. They slip and fall on the ice. There is a beat of despair, and then the orderlies and the man start hammering on the ground, at first in anger, then with determination. As they strike the asphalt, the city wakes up, the trees blossom, and the people in the buildings take off their masks. It is an image of spring, awakened by the city-dwellers; the response of the built and natural environment to their passionate attention. It is also an ideal cityscape, in which the urban character is negotiated from the natural, the built and the human. As the Tourism Commission would say, it's a 'City of Life'.

The term 'structures of attention' affords a description of how people produce and consume the idea of the city by paying emotional attention to it, as well as by the attention they pay through their professional practice. It is the job of tourism officials, filmmakers, urban planers and city politicians to understand the structures of attention which they can both deploy and respond to in the business of making a city mean something to those that live and visit it.

The cultural theorist Raymond Williams created the concept 'structures of feeling' to understand why people and communities think the way they do about place and social interaction:

> We are talking about characteristic elements of impulse, restraint, and tone; specifically affective elements of consciousness and relationships: not feeling against thought, but thought as felt and feeling as thought: practical consciousness of a present kind, in a living and inter-relating community (1977, p. 132).

This definition opens the possibility of dialogue between different aspects of everyday life. It refuses a dichotomy of thinking versus feeling, while still offering a structural approach to content and data. Williams is positive towards structures of feeling where they support communities of interest, and are in a fluid relationship with the pragmatics of community life. Our suggestion is that the concept is remade as 'structures of attention', taking up the implication of dialogue in Williams's concept as a positive analytical tool for looking across cultural, commercial products and responses as images and ideas that provoke, demand and inspire attention. 'Feeling' and 'thought', Williams says, are not in competition, but are dynamically engaged and 'inter-relating' in practice, even where that practice crosses commercial boundaries. The end-products of image making, whether it is a film, or a tourism brand or campaign, are coterminous with and dependent on emotional connectivity, if they are to contribute to building the 'idea of a city' as a coherent cityscape.

The art historian Jonathan Crary describes 'attention' as a condition of living in modernity. He explores regimes and codes of visuality, recording the travails of the human sciences, educational institutions, industrial manufacturers and government agencies to insist on attentiveness as a pre-requisite of secure, productive and organized modern living. He goes on to argues that an appearance of *inattention* is an equally necessary aspect of the 'delirious operation' of modernity (1999, p. 13), allowing – indeed, requiring – the modern subject to shift attention across an apparently endless stream of new ideas, new configurations of the world, and to simultaneously leave behind the obsolescent residues of progress and transformation, whatever their affective pull on the subject her/himself. Crary's argument dovetails usefully with Williams's earlier formulation of structures of feeling, in that it suggests a formation of the feeling subject, although it prioritizes the immediacy of individual attention and inattention above the long-term structures of feeling attributed to communities. Crary argues that the attentiveness of an individual is always susceptible to moments of disruption, to shifts, fragmentations and transformations. A structure of attention drawing on these contested regimes of phenomenological relationship with society therefore entails a paradigm of research that expects to see change, inconsistency and random incoherence, but which nonetheless clusters its findings around forms of attention which seem to prevail in modern urban environments.

The media beyond cinema pay a lot of attention to place, especially those that seek to address to a predominantly local audience. In May 2004, an online chat host, Kevin Sinclair 'On the Spot', for the *South China Morning Post* asked his readers to contribute some thoughts on their idea of Hong Kong. He asked specifically for positive rather than negative observations, but he was, basically, asking residents to pay *attention* to their city:

> Welcome, Chatmates. Today, I've challenged you to tell me some good things about Hong Kong. Give me examples of some of the things you love about our city. They don't have to be brilliant ideas or well-thought-out essays, just some thoughts about what aspects of Hong Kong attract you, make you smile, cause you to laugh, make you shake your head in wonder.[2]

The responses mentioned life-style, organization, access to technology, and an everyday engagement with iconic places, such as taking morning walks on the Peak, commuting on the Star Ferry, taking a slow beer by the Harbour and going to the races (see Plate 3). The comments encapsulated two of the structures of attention that we have identified in our observations in Hong Kong, *aspiration* and *everyday life*. Aspiration is connected to the idea of the city as a place in which dreams are manufactured and fulfilled. It is tied to social status, access to consumption and life-style choices, and to material self-fulfilment. It is also related to the predominant Hong Kong cinematic narrative of 'rags to riches through hard work', and is encapsulated visually in the manufactured and built beauty of an urban environment. Everyday life is closely related to aspiration in the attention to distraction, which Hong Kong respondents appear to value in their descriptions of the city. Everyday life is also

---

2   The authors are grateful to Kevin Sinclair for sending them a copy of this text.

very much part of the mediated modern world referred to in Crary's account of attention and inattention and in media theorists' descriptions of mundane media usage (Silverstone 1994). Paddy Scannell (1996) relates audience consumption to sincerity (a mis-recognition of nostalgia), but also to '*dailiness*', or '*everyday life*'. Dailiness is central to the chat-show host's invitation to pay attention to Hong Kong and, given the apparent life-style and socio-economic status of the *South China Morning Post* online readers, attracts *aspirational* forms of paying attention.

The third structure of attention in this study is *nostalgia*, manifested in different guises as people talk about their idea of the city. Nostalgia is commonly understood as a sense of loss, often in relation to childhood, or places of personal significance (Scannell 1996 and 2000). The phenomenon is also usefully glossed as a false description of the remembered past in order to displace traumas of the present. This usage captures the links running between all three structures of attention. Arjun Appadurai describes 'nostalgia for the present' as already a feature of mass marketing, a 'stylized presentation of the present as if it has already slipped away' (1996, pp. 77–8). Nostalgia underlies many of the contradictions in the consumption of post-colonial Hong Kong by Hong Kong residents who may be indigenous, European, or first-, second-, third-generation post-war migrants, and also by visitors, whether from the Mainland or outside Greater China:

From an indigenous university professor:
One [of my iconic places] is the China Bank, Shanghai Bank; one, of course, is the Clock Tower at Tsimshatsui – that's the landmark (see Frontispiece). When we are little, in primary schools or high schools, will meet friends at Tsimshatsui under the Clock Tower ... at the Five Flags, everybody knew it, you didn't have to describe, just tell them the name ...

[who continues ...]
In the old days, 10 to 30 years ago, they [the tourism industry] always used the fishermen village, Stanley, Aberdeen, because that showed the poor side of HK. It caught the foreigners' eye and that's how they saw Hong Kong: people in the boat make their living by catching fish, poor, just like 'San Pan' from Nancy Kwan's *Taipan*. It happens in Tsui Hark's films as well. They also used Stanley and Kowloon City, before they tore down the old buildings there were a lot of very unique kind of places, and they hid a lot of prostitution. Kowloon City is a public garden now, and new visitors just want to look at Chungking building, because of Wong Kar-wai [director of the film, *Chungking Express*].

From a British-HK tourism official and resident:
'Hello Kevin. Thanks for giving me the chance to set out some things I love about Hong Kong. It's a challenge. There's the efficiency of the place. There's the can-do spirit even in the worst of times (and, let's be honest, the reaction during the SARS crisis was nothing short of amazing, as groups such as Fearbusters showed). Great things? Watching my sons playing mini-rugby on a Sunday morning; watching my daughter in her school plays; the ride on the Star Ferry early on a weekday morning, one of the very best commutes in the world. If I ever had to leave Hong Kong, here's three things I would miss: the view over the Lamma Channel from my flat on a misty morning; the fact that Hong Kong is undoubtedly one of the safest places in the world for residents and visitors [and]

the convenience of living in one of the most vibrant, lively and well-organized cities in the world [and finally] the long-distance walks, with my personal favourite being from Stanley to Chai Wan along the Wilson Trail.

These opinions come from two professional men in their late forties, each with considerable knowledge of Hong Kong's image industries (film and tourism respectively) and each with a commitment to the city as their home. There is a difference, however, in their attention to the city. The university professor brings to mind the iconography of Hong Kong when he thinks back nostalgically to his youth and then looks disapprovingly at foreign (i.e. British) approaches to tourism in the 1970s and early '80s. The second respondent is upbeat about the life-style he currently enjoys, but his praise – both personal and professional, given his position as a senior official in the tourism industry – is couched in a nostalgic statement of predicted loss, 'nostalgia for the present': 'If I ever had to leave Hong Kong', he says. Presumably, there is a remote possibility that, as a British-born Hong Kong resident, he might one day be obliged to leave: Hong Kong residency is supposedly permanent, but there is no category of non-Chinese PRC citizenship, an anomaly which is open to concern. So, the attention paid to the city weaves together everyday life, memory and its nostalgic manifestation along with the determined aspirations of a global-city living. Nonetheless, what a Hong Kong-based Cultural Studies scholar described as 'very deep, very very deep, socio-political uncertainty' is also in evidence in the relationship to the past evinced here.[3] We shall see a similar formation of nostalgia in the Shanghai case study, which we discuss in Chapter 6. There we argue that the nostalgia is pragmatic. Here we perceive anxiety.

Structures of attention are scaled – indeed, they must be – if we are to capture the range of vision, perception and experience that inform and engross people in place. Taken beyond its local rags-to-riches narrative, Hong Kong's city-wide aspirations are focussed on being understood and consumed as a world city on the West Pacific Rim. In order for the city to compete successfully with other Chinese cities, a new challenge since the rise of reform and urban development on the Mainland, it has no alternative but to function on the Rim as well as in China itself. Thus Hong Kong's brand image is rightly focussed on investors as much as on tourists, who trust its brand values as a guarantee of regional best practice.

The cinema also plays a significant role in defining the idea of Hong Kong, and this definition has immense purchase beyond the region. The city's urban-specific cinematic imaginaries do not have the distributive reach of Hollywood, but nonetheless articulate a recognizable vision of the city that corresponds with the desires and perceptions of the permanent and visiting populations. This is the filmic equivalent of a brand campaign, and is highly effective over time. Visitors to Hong Kong come for its cosmopolitanism, its cool and its excitement. Arguably, the promise of all of these characteristics is implicit in the locations, actions and characters of major Hong Kong film genres and directorial signatures. How then can

---

3   Dr Stephen Chan, of Lingnan University, Hong Kong, in a seminar at the Centre for Cultural Research, University of Western Sydney, 4 August 2004.

we discern the structures of attention that organize film spectatorship? We argue that they are active in all aspects of film narration, and as such can tell us a great deal about city experience. In arguing this we encounter the problems faced by theorists of national cinema and will briefly deal with these before moving forward.

National cinema theory of the 1980s and 1990s posited a concept that was extremely useful in describing certain geo-political and cultural-social influences and characteristics in film, but at the same time very difficult to maintain as a logical category. There is no need here to rehearse the imperfections in the theory, which are well-known (see Chu 2002), but its power as a concept has persisted because it is both suggestive and useful (Berry and Farquhar 2006). The problems relate mainly to the way in which one conceives of place, belonging and ownership in a trans-national economy of filmmaking. First, is cinema categorized by its funders – in which case almost every production will be to some degree trans-national? Or, secondly, is cinema 'owned' by its creative personnel, or by its studio? If either of these is the case, then again, given the mobility of film professionals and film capital, there is likely to be an international component. Thirdly, is film to be named 'national' according to its filming location and its story? If the latter category outweighs the other two, how might we argue that the relationship between the story and location is understood or prioritized? If a script is conceived separately from place, then – once a national location is selected – how much emotional relevance can it have for the completed film? Finally, is it the nationality of the audience that should confer a film's national status on it? This last argument has an interesting effect, as America's huge domestic audience makes *Hollywood* films, (most of which are, at least in part, designed for export), *national* cinema. That the US audience experiences US film as 'American' is likely although further research would need to assess that claim, but it is also arguable that the national cinema tag is as useful for Hollywood viewed outside the US, as it is for, especially, the *transnational* productions coming out of other regions.[4] American film exports carry national (US) impact for international audiences because of their metonymic relationship to an extremely powerful global entity. We have suggested that films make the place, but that effect creates a two-way street. Given our global familiarity with the origins of narrative and narrational style in American film – and the emotional and political affect of the ideology and images that make up the idea of America – every audience watches US film with a sense of ownership. Even if international audiences do not understand the strategies and positions of American characters, politics and society in the ways that American audiences experience them, the status of American news and current affairs in the world is such that all audience opinions will be strongly held. National US cinema is such because it is viewed in a context where almost all audiences have some sense of the American nation. This counter-intuitive example demonstrates the contradictions that might exist between a film's origins and its motivations. Sometimes, more than one definition of national cinema must

---

4   The exception would be Chinese Mainland productions, such as Zhang Yimou's *Hero*, which involve strong ideological statements on the State that are most readily interpreted by Mainland audiences.

be invoked so as to allow sensible reflections on both a particular sector of the industry and the films in question. If a film is predominantly rooted in a culture and society that is recognizable *as such* to its audience, wherever they are located, and if it is predominantly made and financed by the economy and talent of that society, then it may properly be called national cinema. Likewise, if a film has a sizeable international audience and non-local stars – as is the case with Zhang Yimou's blockbuster, *Hero* (*Ying xiong*, 2002) which starred several Hong Kong and Japanese actors and attracted significant attention outside China (see Chiu 2005) – but it is nonetheless clearly an influential and successful film 'at home', then, once again, it may justifiably be categorized as national cinema. It is this kind of locally oriented, but internationally 'legible', cinema that captures the structures of attention with which we are concerned here. Qualifying the nature and origins of a particular film in terms of a national cinema rubric is not an exact art, but 'national cinema' is still a suggestive critical category, which allows us to interrogate the main aspects of cinematic narration.

Place is at the heart of narrational technique. For effective storytelling cinema requires identifiable and visually interesting locations. These are chosen in order to support the tone, the coherence and the affect of a particular narrative or genre. As the cinematic presence of a particular location builds over time and assumes a particular significance, it may become iconic and so provide filmmakers with a useful shortcut to desired meanings and responses. But, cities can borrow back their cinematic presence to re-invent and renew their urban identities (Enticknap, 2001). Alan Blum argues that the 'imaginative structure' of a city may be understood as a cultural invention, that it indeed may be 'nothing but a sign' (2003, p. 26); that cities are what they are due to the artistic and cultural self-representations that they produce. Yet, Blum goes on to argue, cities are also environments in which certain social functionalities must prevail (communications, transport, work, trade), and in which different contexts provoke different problem-solving responses from the collective city population (pp. 40–1). Blum describes this version of the development and maintenance of urban identity as a dialogue. In the complexity of a global city, and within the challenge of a regional dialectic, a dialogue may be better understood as a conversation between competing voices, interests, producers and consumers of a shared identity, one aspect of which is cinematic. The stories of cinema, in so far as they pay attention to the location, are powerful contributors to such a conversation. If we then interpret Blum's idea of a conversation within the notion of a structure of attention, we begin to imagine a highly mediated, visual field – cinema – in which people, ideas and images have sufficient imaginative space in which to pay attention one to another in particular locally defined ways (exemplified for us as nostalgic, aspirational, everyday).

The idea of the city is also explored in narratives, iconic structures, colour systems, local characters and dramatic tension. These stories epitomize particular cultural histories and contemporary social formations as much as they present images of beautiful and iconic locations. Jackie Chan, a trans-national kung-fu film star and official tourism ambassador for Hong Kong, is a world famous comic actor, with strong local credibility, particularly among the older generation. Described as the 'best side of the city', an actor who 'works hard ... is comedic and ... is really honest',[5] he was also the actor whose films, particularly the *Police Story* (*Ging chaat goo si*) series (dir. Jackie Chan, 1985–96), made the most humorous and ironic comments on Britain's 1984 agreement to leave the colony by 1997 (Chu 2002). One might contend therefore that, far from being the bland face of Hong Kong, Chan owes his enduring popularity amongst older Hong Kong residents and, indeed, his metonymic status as 'the best side of the city', not only to his skills as a performer but also to his previous, comedic attention to the idea of a post-colonial Hong Kong. In the 2006 HKTB tourism campaign Chan is shown making a film in the city, watched by a group of entranced young people. At one point he invites a young man to step up to the director's chair and take a look at the city through the camera's eye. The moment is a graphic epitome of Hong Kong's intention to be seen as a film set, a *location* for everyday life as much as for leisure and vacation.

The eye of the director is the eye of the camera, and the director's empathy with place offers a fast route to the structures of attention made possible by a film's address to place. When asked to describe the character of Hong Kong, the generation of filmmakers who emerged in the 1980s and 1990s – Mabel Cheung, Fruit Chan, Derek Yee, Ann Hui – tended to look back to the days of their youth, for some privileged days as a student at Hong Kong University in the late 1960s and for others tougher times working out an apprenticeship in the 1970s studio system. These memories re-emerge through the emotional intensities of narrative and visual forms in their films. Derek Yee's *C'est la vie, mon chérie* (1994) and Mabel Cheung's *City of Glass* (1998) both featured buildings that were due to be torn down shortly after shooting. In both cases the directors were articulating their grief at the apparent loss of tangible history and the severing of links with their colonial childhoods. As Yee admitted in 2003:

> [T]he inhabitants of the city are changing; the entire structure is changing too. So it's hard to work out what's happening. I was born in Hong Kong, I love this place, but sometimes I do feel disappointed; I don't feel as good as before. It was sad, but when we were still a colony, we would long to have our own people ruling in our own home, but now ... well, it's very paradoxical.[6]

Yee's paradox lies not only in the contradiction between autonomy and sovereignty, but also in the bitter realization that consuming the political present cannot replace the nostalgia of fighting for freedom as part of a shared youth and idealism. His perspective is peculiarly that of a forty-odd-year-old Hong Kong intellectual who demonstrated against the British in the late 1960s and again in the 1970s, but who has nonetheless been shaped by a Chinese past outside China.

At the same time, there are heterogeneous modes of attention occurring from film to film, and generation to generation of film-goers. The Hong Kong of fisher-folk and Cantonese opera is the source of the nostalgia and aspirations of the 1950s generation of mainland migrants. For them and for their icon, Jackie Chan, the Hong Kong Tourism Board (HKTB)'s red-junk logo, which combines references to the

---

    5   Critic Law Kar, programmer of the Hong Kong Film Archive, from an interview with the authors in 2003.

    6   Interview with the authors, Hong Kong, 15 September 2003.

Chinese mainland, to Hakka fisher-folk migration, and with a general rags-to-riches narrative, makes perfect nostalgic and historical sense. For cosmopolitan directors like Mabel Cheung, however, the junk is an inappropriate reference to colonialism. For her, Hong Kong resides in memories of the élite university and the steps up Victoria Peak, all of which are memorialized in *City of Glass*. So the films compete and merge over time as they give structure to the image-capture of a city that is moving yet again, and fast, towards something entirely different, perhaps an example of Crary's 'disintegration(s) of modernity'.

The distillation of everyday experience through the past and the future is a task that is common both to film narrative and tourism marketing, and is clearly seen in the making of place brands and cinematic locations. Everyday life is understood, by local tourism professionals in Hong Kong and Sydney, as a reference to authenticity and life-style. This again underlines the close relationship between the structures of attention mediating and maintaining the idea of Hong Kong. In tourism literature, however, everyday life is thought of as 'ordinariness' and, rather unfortunately, 'shallowness' (McKercher and Chow 2001). This academic reading better describes the supposedly anti-cultural interest that Hong Kong holds for Mainland Chinese arrivals. For them, the city represents shopping opportunities and a taste of something 'Chinese', although qualitatively different from the kinds of Chinese experience that Mainlanders derive from domestic experience within the Mainland PRC. During the 2003 Mid-Autumn Festival, the carriages of Hong Kong's MTR trains were full of Mainland tourists, taking advantage of the easing of visa requirements in China and the free time created for them by the inauguration, three years earlier, of the Golden Week holidays. Cantonese-speaking Hong Kongers fell quiet as loud, excited cries in *putonghua* (official Chinese, northern dialect, Mandarin) filled the air. The influx of these visitors from Beijing, Guangzhou and Tianjin suddenly altered the everyday acoustics. The immediate local reaction suggested that the everyday in Hong Kong is underpinned by nostalgia for a language identity that is feared lost, a nostalgia that is shared by Hong Kong's generations and class groups and, for all their heterogeneity, binds them together. The silence of young commuters was echoed in the thoughts of film professionals and audiences (generally older people), who remembered the intimacy of early Cantonese films and compared them with the 'shallowness' and escapism of Taiwanese and Korean soaps and multi-lingual films of the 1990s and 2000s.[7] Meanwhile, tourism marketeers make deliberate use of nostalgia to articulate the Chineseness of Hong Kong as a journey from fishing to finance, junk to skyscraper, indigenous village and shanty-town to 'Asia's only world city'. In Hong Kong in 2001–2003, the city fabricated a locational backdrop by keeping a 'real' junk in the Harbour when they decided to retain the red-junk logo for the Tourism Board. This is nostalgia with an aspirational edge. The contrast between the junk, a symbol of Hong Kong's poverty-stricken origins, on the one hand and the towering Bank of China, 'another big, modern building',[8] on the other tells the story of contemporary success as much as it reminds international visitors of

---

7   Interviews and vox-pops canvassed by the authors at the Hong Kong Film Archive, September-October 2003.
8   Fruit Chan, in an interview with the authors, Hong Kong, 16 September 2003.

the East-West dichotomy that they have come to savour as an aftertaste of European occupation.[9]

Among filmmakers, everyday life tends overall to be understood as social realism and domesticity. Fruit Chan and Ann Hui both consider that their work is about making the everyday available to audiences that either never see themselves represented on screen, or else choose not to be aware of the underside of Hong Kong life. These filmmakers mistrust nostalgia as a return to colonialism and an outdated and orientalist attachment to the underprivileged condition of indigenous (*bentu*) Hong Kong people. Nonetheless their social realism plays into an overall sense of Hong Kong as a place with its own distinctive past, rooted in a colonial experience that is neither shared nor understood by the Chinese Mainland.

Not only do films support the process of urban mythologization, but this in turn leads to films taking on a quasi-touristic quality, as people envisage a real place through the stories and the images to which cinema has given them access. Of course, there are differences between the imagined city and the lived city, and the structures of feeling and perception that support these ideas must be nuanced to allow for such distinctions. Urban 'pleasure' includes good services, impressive facilities and exciting, worthwhile activities, and – crucially for a world city – a sense of being at the centre of things. That may be the nostalgic centre of colonial loss, the centre of finance and everyday Chinese creativity, or the heart of the aspirational migrant. But wherever and however that centre is claimed, much of the emphasis in tourism place-building is a common focus on marketing and quality assurance, and, inevitably therefore, on the management of expectations. Visitors must be attracted to a destination, and they must not be disappointed once they reach it. The tourism industry and related government agencies have therefore attempted to promote their cities by condensing their unique appeal into a city brand (LePla and Parker 1999, Häussermann and Colomb 2003), and then by having that brand supported by planning, infrastructure and design initiatives. Cinema could arguably be both a help and a hindrance in this respect. For example, how might a film culture such as Hong Kong's – excellent at ghost stories, gangster thrillers and loony comedy – support the vision of an aspirational, nostalgic and everyday city that 'works' for residents, tourists and foreign investment? The idea of the city as expressed in these films is witty, sharp, tough and energetic. The branding campaigns in 1998–2003 have sought to reflect the same set of attributes: the 'City of Life', 'Hong Kong – Live it! Love it!' and 'Asia's World City'. But, the very fact that so many campaigns have been started and discarded over a short period also hints at a distracted attention to the city, and possibly a recognition that Hong Kong is not the kind of place that can be easily summed up for international or domestic consumption.

---

9   Tourism Commissioner Rebecca Lai, in an interview with the authors, Hong Kong, 2000. This and the earlier interviews were followed up with email correspondence from 2001 to 2003, supplemented with information drawn from an online survey of visitors to Hong Kong (HKTB website, 2001–2002). In September 2003, Jackie Chan made a post-SARS advertisement with the red junk, as part of the 'Hong Kong – Live it! Love it!' campaign (*South China Morning Post* (SCMP), 16 September 2003).

Paying attention to Hong Kong by smiting the frozen ground awakens the city and produces the perfect cityscape, where smiting is the originary act of that idealized spatial configuration of residents, buildings, trees and air. This is a sentimental but cinematically adroit address to the six million souls who may have watched it on their televisions. The idea of Hong Kong is of a city that is growing increasingly self-aware and learning to pay nostalgic but sharp attention to the minutiae of its character. The ideal cityscape is picture-perfect, not because its emotions are undeveloped or inelegant, but because it is so very composed, poised on a seemingly endless cusp of dramatic change. The city's long history of multiple colonizations and migrations give both the city and its residents a veneer of cosmopolitan sophistication. It is that which informs the elegiac beauty epitomized in Tony Leung's screen performances and his persona in general. But sophistication without power is not as politically effective as it is cinematically affective. Hong Kong is not a particularly strong force in negotiations between East and West over territory, trade and cultural priorities (Cheung 2000). Its political situation is fragile and loud opposition to the government has been voiced in street marches on July 1 of 2003 and 2004. These targeted, in particular, Basic Law Article 23, which was intended to permit the Hong Kong SAR to enact laws on its own to protect national security, but which was seen as a curb on civil liberties and a piece of media-gagging piece of legislation. Shelved since 1997, Article 23 was due to be passed in July 2003.[10] The response of the city government to the annual mass rallies was to refer to the 'City of Life' brand, suggesting that open demonstrations would lead Hong Kong to become a 'city of turmoil', just as it had been during China's Cultural Revolution.[11] This did nothing to convince residents and commentators that the government was ready to align public feelings with a collective re-assessment of the city's image and the state of its residents' nostalgic affiliation with the past – and, indeed, their nostalgic attention to the present – with their aspirations for everyday democratic practice.

Ackbar Abbas (1997) has famously argued that the cultural history of Hong Kong is premised on sedimented city development, and so is always prone to 'disappear'.

---

10 Further details on this struggle may be found in the archives of the *SCMP*, and also in the open letters of political activists such as Christine Loh. See, for example, her timeline:

9. 1 July 2003: More than 500,000 people protested at a march against Article 23 legislation. Weeks before, the government had anticipated between 30,000–70,000 people on various occasions. The week before, the organizers expected 150,000. Four days before, the number had risen to 250,000. Private polls showed that a very much larger number of people could show up.

10. 5 July 2003: Clearly stunned, the CE announced that he would give three concessions but not on passage on 9 July.

11. 7 July 2003: James Tien of the Liberal Party and minister without portfolio resigned from the Executive Council. This meant passage of the Bill could not be assured without the party's eight votes. The party called for delaying passage. The CE had no choice but to withdraw the Bill.

12. Postscript: Since then, there were protests on the 9/7 and 13/7; two ministers resigned and the CE travelled to Beijing so that Beijing could show that he still had their support. He promised to consult more widely and to listen to the public [Newsletters, 16 and 20 July]. The government is now working on a new consultation document for release in the autumn.

11 Zou Zhekai, quoted in Lee and Leung, 'City of Turmoil', *SCMP*, 7 August 2003.

The structures of attention surfacing in film suggest that the idea of Hong Kong is not so much premised on disappearance as on negotiation. Nostalgia, aspiration and everyday life interweave to outline a city that knows itself very well, but which is aware that the future might possibly overwhelm the present.

'Banal Patriotism'

The present is a complicated place. Hong Kong dealt with SARS bravely, collectively, indeed, patriotically. We would not claim this patriotism as an example of Michael Billig's 'hot nationalism' (Billig 1995). It was a steadfast flame perhaps, but not a consuming furnace as is the 'war on terror'. Rather, Hong Kong demonstrated its integrity and its facility at bringing cultural practice and social needs together is an inspired and practised manner. The effect on Hong Kong's tourism strategy was part of this, the post-SARS Recovery. It became more cohesive, and more integrated with the city's character. Arriving in Hong Kong in 2006, one no longer meets with a confusion of city logos and competing colours. Nor, on the other hand, is there the stultifying uniformity which would undermine Hong Kong's energy at source. The brand regime is in place, but it is sufficiently mobile to acknowledge the kitsch sentimentalism of Hong Kong's patriotism, exemplified by the little pig, McDull (see Plate 4). As one anonymous blogger wrote in 2006, '*Maidougushi* (*The Story of McDull*) has brought a bit of warmth and affection into the lives of Hong Kong people and into the society as a whole … [T]his exciting fairytale has become one of the ten reasons for living in Hong Kong.'

The film *My Life as McDull* is rapidly becoming a classic animated drama in Hong Kong cinema, where it has captured a sense of local patriotism, self-aware humour, and the surprisingly sentimental importance of the Hong Kong urban landscape to its inhabitants. The film and its sequels, *McDull,Prince de la Bun* (*Maidou, Bolouyou de Wangzi*) and *McDull, The Alumni*, comprise a phenomenon of cult, cartoon and childhood fantasy. Both films grew out of children's animation and stories created by the animator, Mai Jiabi, and the writer, Xie Liwen. The second film plays heavily on the first's emerging status as a cross-genre classic. Both are immensely popular across age groups, with adults still writing about the film in blogs in 2006, five years after the first of the films was released, while children play with the associated marketing goods and eat their recess snacks from McDull lunchboxes.

What marks this film series for such attention? Is it the style that exerts such strong appeal, or the sense of place, or the explicit encoding of 'small potatoes' as heroes in a post-1997 Hong Kong and following the economic downturn? One blogger claims that McDull's mother, Mai Tai, with her instinct for survival, is a contender for a 'classic female character' in Hong Kong film, art and literature. Or, is it the aural sweetness of children's voices singing 'All things bright and beautiful' that captivated an exhausted a post-SARS population, and caused them to turn a children's show into a cult film classic? The cartooning styles are based on high-quality television animation (*Yellow Bus*), although with a blended childish and painterly quality that is reminiscent of the work of Shanghai masters such as Te Wei, particularly the ink-wash classic, *Little Tadpoles seek their Mama*. Perhaps it is

McDull's careful double in-scripting of child and adult sensibilities that commends itself to its enduring fan base? Whatever the source of its appeal, the film is a bold assault on the adult imagination, using the bittersweet perspectives of childhood to describe contemporary Hong Kong. First a children's film, then an adult fad and now a classic of the Hong Kong cityscape, *McDull* stands out because, as one fan, Wang Laifu, has recently written in his blog: '[T]he movies reflect a real Hong Kong as it is seen through the eyes of ordinary people' (www.tianya.com).

McDull, The Alumni is the latest in the series and is predominantly live-action, unlike the previous films, which were entirely animated except for a couple of short sequences. The new film is unashamedly aimed at an adult audience, and specifically a Hong Kong audience. The film is, at one and the same time, a knowing pastiche of serious social drama – the unfulfilled aspirations of young people in the depressed job market of the adult world – and a classic, high-energy, cops-and-robbers film (Yau 2001). The setting is Hong Kong Central and the overarching subject of the film is food. Its principal gag is that robbers holding up a generic 'company' are most concerned, as are their victims, to give the police take-away lunch orders from a local café. The process of choosing a dish and arguing about its quality with gunmen, as policemen relay the orders by mobile phone, is very funny. The structure of attention seems straightforward, a humorous take on the banality of everyday life, located in a strong sense of Hong Kongers' obsession with talking about food. The *McDull* films are also deeply nostalgic in the sense in which we have defined the term – that is, an emotional response to the present through appeal to an idealized past. McDull's 'alumni' are all fresh-faced young people looking for catering and clerical positions after graduation (from Mabel Cheung's beloved Hong Kong University). Their avatars in the past are the little animated animals from the earlier *McDull* films (set outside Central in the highly populated tower-block suburbs) and the *Yellow Bus* television and comic book series. Thus Hong Kongers are asked to recognize themselves as infantile, cute products of their media environment, and their actual childhood memories. To be able to respond to the film as an insider the spectator needs to be deeply embedded in local culture and to quickly recognize its everyday banalities, aspirations and sentimentality. It laughs with, rather than at, its subjects, and does so in an enclosed narration that refuses any incursion from trans-national cultural alternatives. The film, we suggest, is deeply patriotic in a post-SARS environment, and very much in the mode of Billig's 'banal nationalism'.

Hotter Nationalism

As Michael Billig has told us, the flag is the basic medium of nationalism, while patriotism is often the emotional characteristic by which residents and citizens are judged. The resulting confusion between a national project and a love of country strengthens the power of particular regimes and administrations. 'The central thesis of the present book', says Billig of his *Banal Nationalism*,

> is that, in the established nations, there is a continual 'flagging', or reminding, of nationhood. The established nations are those that have confidence in their own continuity, and, particularly, are part of what is conventionally described as 'the West'. The political

leaders of such nations – whether France, the USA, the United Kingdom or New Zealand – are not typically termed 'nationalists'. However, … nationhood provides a continual background for their political discourses, for cultural products, and even for the structuring of newspapers. In so many little ways, the citizenry are daily reminded of their national place in a world of nations. However, this reminding is so familiar, so continual, that it is not consciously registered as reminding. The metonymic mage of banal nationalism is not a flag, which is being consciously waved with fervent passion; *it is the flag hanging unnoticed on the public building* (1995, pp. 8–9, *our emphasis*).

Thus, as the world heads towards the Beijing Olympics – 'New Beijing, Great Olympics' is the motto – sporting nations are flexing their media muscles in an effort to associate images of sporting prowess with feelings of pride and love of country, but they are likely also to be building a case for patriotism by means of metonymic example and association. The Olympic brand is supported by five mascot dolls called 'Friendlies' or, since their change of name in October 2006, 'Fuwa' (*fu*/good fortune + *wa*/baby = good and fortunate child). Created specifically to build a merchandizing opportunity, called China, perhaps we mean Brand China, these cute cartoon creatures – Beibei, the fish, Jingjing, the panda, Huanhuan, the Olympic flame, Yingying, the Tibetan antelope and Nini, the swallow – symbolize aspects of China's land, its animals and culture. In fact, the name change came about when 'Friendlies' was seen as woeful branding: not only might the word have been misheard as 'friend*less*', but international visitors might have been reminded of the cloistered 'friendliness' of the state-owned Friendship Store in Beijing, which was intended for foreigners only and, in the days before China embraced capitalism, the only place where foreigners could buy 'export' or luxury items. Predictably, the choice of animals that the Fuwa were to represent was dictated as much by local politics as international branding. The process was driven in part by provincial bids, and Qinghai, a large, cosmopolitan province in the far west with a large Muslim population, was given the antelope.[12] While this may have placated local officials who were hoping that post-Olympics tourism would impact on the entire country, it infuriated Tibetan separatists and campaigners in the 'Free Tibet' movement in the United States. Flagging nationhood moves very quickly from the banal to the hot, and small events can have an impact on that shift. This merchandizing is also part of wider rhetoric for change in the twenty-first century: the 'humanistic' Olympics are under review by Renmin University (the People's University), which is working to give a cultural dimension to the government's directive to build 'a harmonious society' (*hexie shehui*), in the name of which social policy in China is currently being shaped. 'Harmonious society' is a complex political and rhetorical strategy, allowing accelerated change in both the economy and society, while insisting on a post-Confucian version of the stable society or Great Harmony. The insistence on a harmonious society is simultaneously a promise to alleviate the immiseration caused by the Reforms; a continuing determination to build a comfortable environment in which to be assertively prosperous, and a threat that, however diverse the country may be, will remain a single entity in geo-political terms.

---

12 ABC-Radio discussion with Stephanie Hemelryk Donald, *Asia Pacific*, 18 October 2006, archived at http://www.abc.net.au/ra/asiapac/programs/s1768225.htm.

In Hong Kong since 1997 the Beijing method of example and top-down rhetoric has not been popular with the democratic wing of politics:

> Mr Tung Chee-hwa's anticipatory subservience to the real or imagined wishes of China's rulers exposed the congenital flaw in the political architecture of uniting a liberal society with a dictatorship. That flaw infects the heart of the 'one country, two systems' notion: the idea that genuine autonomy can exist in a country whose supreme leaders do not believe in rule by consent (Shaw 2003).

Arguably there are competing forms of patriotism in the contemporary political system, in which the city's branding mechanisms and institutions play a part. Brand-building, patriotism and the love of home have become tense partners in the context of the 1997 transfer of sovereignty and, more recently, in the light of the 2003 and 2004 July demonstrations against Article 23, and the 2004 debate on patriotism in the SAR. The imaginative attention paid to the ideas of home in *McDull* and *1:99*, and the commitment to belonging which inspires political demonstrations, exceed the corporate and state-organized versions of love of country which are promoted by Beijing and departments such as Invest Hong Kong. As we intimated earlier, expressions of love of (home) place are more apparent in the passionate contingencies of cinematic narrative, and in the actions of residents, than in the structures of loyalty managed by government and its agencies. The patriotism debate was certainly in evidence in late 2003 (*Standard*, 5 September 2003, p. B3), but it was not engaged in earnest until 2004, when Beijing and Beijing-oriented politicians called for a Hong Kong where only 'patriots' be permitted to enter the legislature (*SCMP*, Insight, 14 February 2004, p. 1). The debate was an orchestrated policy tool and did not account for the demonstrated love of place, which had been evident – at least to an outside eye – on several occasions during the previous twelve months. Beijing's political unwillingness to accept that love of country (national patriotism) might be complicated, although not necessarily undermined, both by local place-loyalties and by democratic aspirations shows the division between the political imagination of the state and the heterogeneous forms of love which citizens owe both to place and people and also to local histories. Political loyalty to a state-led agenda does not measure the limits of passionate attachment.[13]

In 2004 the online visitor to the Hong Kong tourism campaign website (discoverhongkong.com) was 'welcomed' by Jackie Chan and encouraged to 'share it, hear it, taste it, get it'. Chan's role was to give a recognizable set of characteristics to the city: energy, a 'rags-to-richesness', honesty, bravery, wit and patriotism. Following the initial welcome, the site emphasized shopping, cultural attractions and business opportunities in the post-SARS period (the campaign was entitled Rebound Hong Kong) and in many senses it managed to come quite close to communicating the energy and opportunities for which Hong Kong is famous.

---

13 We are indebted to Professor Meaghan Morris for her suggestion that the intense love of Hong Kongers for home should be seen as a recent *coup de foudre*, a response to the 1997 sovereignty transfer. Her observation points to the need for further deliberation on emotional response to the end of colonialism and the beginning of daily competition with other Chinese cities.

It did not capture the devotion to the city as evidenced by political debates and demonstrations, but whether a tourism website could, or, indeed, should, pay tribute to the debates of its middle classes is itself a debatable point. Nonetheless, the absence of political material or references amounted to the elision of a crucial facet of contemporary Hong Kong, and rendered the brand emotionally incomplete – and it left Jackie Chan's welcome uncharacteristically de-energised. The emotionally eviscerated welcome is echoed in China as the Friendlies become *Fuwa*: pinyin transliterations, neither English nor Chinese. These mascots look and feel like political expediency masked as kitsch. Perhaps it is cruel to describe Jackie Chan in the same category of Olympic branding (one could add that the trio of native Australian animal mascots chosen for the 2000 Sydney Olympics were scarcely more appealing), but the similarity is undeniable. A branding initiative that is itself branded by compromise is a failure. Ironically, it is the ideology that underpins the compromise – a marriage of convenience between the accelerated capitalization and managerial communism of China, or the democratic free enterprise of Hong Kong – which would carry more weight than either the *Fuwa* or Chan's smile.

The current (2006) version of the discoverHongKong.com website dispenses with Jackie Chan (in the generic international portal, at any rate) in favour of a streamlined introduction and navigation model for finding one's way through the SAR's tourist offerings. Shopping is the mainstay, around which country walks, temples, and specially-built attractions are organized. The official Hong Kong brand is nowhere in evidence, suggesting that links between the investment and the tourism portfolios in local government has been severed completely! However, the Hong Kong Tourism Board red junk and the 'Live It! Love It!' logos sit well together in this latest iteration of the site, which now looks focussed, cohesive and familiar, a far cry from the way we saw the campaign earlier. Ironically perhaps, it is the tourism brand campaign that is working out effective brand maintenance after several years when it was difficult to distinguish one brand from the other! The Brand Hong Kong website, with its carefully worked-out quality controls, still exists, but speaks to the business community rather than to tourists. The internal strife, if such it was, has been resolved by a 'one country, two brand systems' model, which mirrors much else that is happening in the city.

Hong Kong's brand-building efforts since 1997 have been focussed on increasing the city's tourism profile, its attractiveness to foreign investors, and on confirming its place in the metropolitan systems of Chinese economic macro-structure (Jessop and Sum 2000). But, despite the timeliness of Hong Kong's recent acknowledgments of its own filmic character, there is a problem at the heart of its international image which undercuts this agenda. It is the second system in China, as agreed in the 1984 'one country, two systems' model that was negotiated by the outgoing British colonial administration and Beijing's central government. It is certainly not regarded as an alternative system, and it is clear that the second system is only in place as long as that is necessary to support Hong Kong's economic contributions to the rest of the PRC. As Barry Naughton has pointed out, these are primarily captured by its role as a financial broker for international investment, given Hong Kong's systemic ability to provide 'property rights arbitrage' for cautious investors in general (1999, pp. 81–

2), and its relationship with Guangdong's industrial development in particular. There are challenges in branding Hong Kong, evidenced by the constant shifts and re-brands from 2000 to 2006, which are essentially political. What is an SAR? Should Hong Kong emphasize its place within China, or should it remember its colonial histories, or position itself as just another Chinese city with significant international expectations and experience, but without the political influence which Shanghai or Beijing can exert.

In October 2003, the *South China Morning Post* quoted brand-guru Henry Steiner's complaint that the Hong Kong brand had not been well developed since 1997, that it had changed too much and too often, but that in none of its several guises had it shown any clear direction or sense of brand maintenance:

> From Harbour Fest to the Disney theme park, to even the new ten-dollar note, Hong Kong's marketeers were failing to send out a coherent message to the world, Mr Steiner said yesterday. The man behind the logos of HSBC, the Hong Kong Jockey Club, and the bank notes issued by Standard Charter Bank, even went so far as to suggest to his Foreign Correspondent's Club audience, that the city could learn a little from Adolf Hitler. Hong Kong had a tendency to go from arrogance to panic with no intervening steps, and this had been particularly true since the onset of the Asian economic crisis. Hong Kong had lurched from being a place where wonders never ceased, to being *The City of Life*, the city had toyed with branding itself the Manhattan of Asia and had more recently morphed into *Asia's World City*, where people were being encouraged to 'Live It, Love It'. In the wake of SARS the city even tried to adopt the famed 'I Love New York' as its own. The problem with these fragmented attempts is very much that they can backfire, Mr Steiner said. The troubled Harbour Fest represented such a flawed attempt.[14]

According to Steiner, then, Hong Kong did/does not respect the branding rules that reportedly support global success. Yet these 'rules' are ubiquitous, and one would suppose that Hong Kong's public servants and marketeers know them very well. It is likely therefore that, if the rules do not work for Hong Kong, it is for specific and contingent reasons, which arise from a sub-national politics and a multiple colonial history. Marketing students will study brands, consumer psychology and corporate globalization, and will discover that the three areas of enquiry are closely linked. They will understand that brands must be strategic, focussed, fast, consistent, and self-knowing in their address to the consumer, and that internationalization of a brand image is especially important for products with a small domestic customer base. In the brand-peak of the commercial world, brand builders are commonly advised to work at the home market for local sustainability, while playing to the global audience as authentic – alive to change, but not a slave to it –, sustained, and bold enough to integrate ideas across company operations and partners in order to look different without looking too new (LePla and Parker 1999). Branding research also suggests that the emotional response of a consumer to a brand is image-dependent, associational and reflective of culture, language, personal experience and social

---

14 This refers to the debacle over the fee demanded by the Rolling Stones for singing at the Festival, which Tung Chee-hwa thought exorbitant, and the too-little-too-late publicity for what was supposed to be a major event for the Hong Kong Recovery.

positioning (Restall and Gordon 1993; Franzen and Bouwman 2001), all of which makes internationalization hard to achieve. In Hong Kong's case the contradiction between a Hong Kong brand of Chinese history, association and experience and the Mainland hopes for Hong Kong's integration into the PRC makes associational branding of the two systems even more difficult to sustain in the long term.

To continue the analogy, a tourism-marketing student will also be expected to glean the basics of sustainability (economic and environmental; not always the same thing), destination profile and product differentiation. Advanced students will be introduced to the various readings of cultural tourism, in which they will discover that, together with cinema, the industry has come to represent modernity itself (MacCannell 1999). International tourists are globally mobile, they consume ideas, images and emotions produced by other people, and their presence re-defines the places that they traverse and the people who provide for them (Graburn 2001, Harrison 2001). International tourists travel to see the authentic, the immutable, the other. Such attractions may be manifested in culture, service and entertainment, and packaged in a process by which these 'authenticities', immutabilities, differences, are created, changed, commodified, in whatever fashion makes them available to classes and groups of people for whom they were never originally intended, and yet for whom they have always only ever been intended (Urry 1990). International tourists come to observe the anthropological present, but they see their own reflections in the temple markets, the keen gradations of price in the hotels, and in the local festivities that have been manufactured as traditions to make their stay more interesting. Domestic tourists, fast becoming the sustaining population for the Chinese and Hong Kong industries, take this concept of the modern tourist much further. The Mainland tourists who arrived in Hong Kong for the (created) tradition of Golden Week in 2003, came to consume the idea of cosmopolitan Hong Kong,[15] to celebrate its return to Chinese sovereignty by a quick photo-opportunity at the Convention Centre (the site of the Handover ceremony in 1997), but, most of all, in obedience to the campaign telling them to shop in upmarket malls at Pacific Place, Festival Walk and Shatin. They came in particularly large numbers in October 2003, as three months earlier Beijing, Shanghai and Tianjin residents had suddenly been relieved of the legal requirement to seek employers' signatures for travel visas. These domestic tourists consumed not only the otherness of Hong Kong, its *unheimlich* relationship to capital, but also its very homely Chineseness; a 'quick fix' of cosmopolitan capitalism with Chinese characteristics for the increasingly sophisticated Mainland businessman, traveller

---

15 According to a survey by the Chinese University's business management department, Mainlanders who visited Hong Kong underlined the fact that the city's international flavour was one of its major attractions. Separately, a heated debate was triggered on a Mainland internet site by an article about one Mainlander's impression of the special administrative region during a three-day individual shopping trip, which highlighted Hong Kong's special role in a country of 1.3 billion people. What impressed him most, he wrote, was the 'feeling of mature capitalism'. 'The feeling of what all youngsters in Hong Kong give you can be summarized in one word: trendy ... I have given up any hope on Guangzhou. Most people in these places do not have a strong desire to absorb the best parts of Western culture. Therefore, they will never attain the special characteristics of a cosmopolitan city.' Chris Yeung, 'One of a Kind', *SCMP*, 8 October 2003.

and relative. (There were worries in casual conversations that the tourists would overflow hotels and sleep rough. In the event, many stayed with family and friends and the city had no problems dealing with the visitors.) For the student of tourism and marketing the problem should be beginning to emerge. How does one brand a city as a self-contained entity representing a peculiar commercial energy and autonomous spirit, when, from one perspective, its main consumers have subsumed its history into the narrative of Mainland Chinese modernity and reform, but still expect the 'taste it' touch of cosmopolitanism, of which political activism and city loyalties are offshoots and progenitors? In the meantime, its domestic loyalty base – the residents themselves[16] – are concerned to preserve a uniquely Hong Kong identity within a Chinese context, and with a political stature that supports cosmopolitan sensibilities, but contradicts the assumption at the sovereign centre of Chinese government, that the second system is only relevant in so far as it supports the macro-economic needs of China PRC.

In 2002–2004, Hong Kong's brand was updated to 'Asia's World City', a self-conscious uptake of the city's role as *entrepôt* during the British colonial administration, but also a challenge to other cities on the West Pacific Rim that might also claim that status, namely Shanghai and Singapore. Hong Kong is the world's busiest container port and a major bullion and stock market. Its current investment literature reminds international companies that the city enjoys a 'high degree of autonomy', that the management of its finances is independent of the Mainland, and that it 'remains a separate customs territory as a full and separate member of the World Trade Organization (WTO) and the Asia-Pacific Economic Co-operation Forum (APEC)' (Invest HK 2003). This, too, is brand, since business and tourist visitors are not differentiated. In this iteration, Hong Kong goes beyond its range of street markets, superb malls and night life, and apparently claims leadership of the region as an 'East meets West' centre of finance, a travel hub and an autonomous partner with China's South, particularly Guangdong, in manufacture and product development. We are obliged to qualify this assertion with 'apparently' as, when it was suggested that Hong Kong was positioning itself as a regional leader, interviewees in one of Hong Kong's government departments (who requested anonymity) were swift to correct the notion. Our informants were certain that Hong Kong was not 'presuming' to offer leadership to the Mainland, simply to complement its existing urban strengths, particularly those of Shanghai and Beijing. This was also the spirit and intention of the 2003 trade and services agreement with Guangdong (CEPA). It represented a cautious understanding of leadership, bred of a new-found political sensibility to Mainland interests.[17] Yet the branding persists, with the conclusions that

---

16 This assertion is based only on the large turnout of between 200,000 and 500,000 people at successive demonstrations, which represents a reasonably significant percentage of the entire population base (6.7 million). According to press releases issued by the Hong Kong Census and Statistics Department (see www.yearbook.gov.hk/2004/en/app.htm), the city's base population in mid-2003 was 6,803,100, of whom 'usual residents' numbered 6,617,800.

17 These sensibilities were forcefully spelled out by Hong Kong CEO, Tung Chee-hwa (see *SCMP*, 7 May 2004). On the same day, the same newspaper carried an article by Jimmy Cheung and Gary Cheung in which David Chu Yu-lin was reported to have said the previous day: 'They include appreciating the impact of Hong Kong's democratic development on the

it inevitably invites with respect to Hong Kong's ambitions and sense of experience in the region. The 'Asia's World City' and 'Live it! Love it!' campaigns echo the East-West intersection that informed Hong Kong's development over the previous century, but they also gesture to a local bravado, suggesting a city that, despite its extraordinary political challenges and local tragedies (most recently the 2003 SARS epidemic), believes itself to be lovable and – very importantly – loves itself.

Recovery

In another *1:99* short, *Who is Miss Hong Kong?* (*shui shi xianggang xiaojie?*, dir. Joe Ma Wai Ho, 2003), a row of beauty queens in a televised pageant line up beside the winner, a small person with a green head shaped like the map of the SAR. Everyone applauds, 'Dream on, the best is yet to come.' The series was remarkable in that it established a precedent in the branding of Hong Kong, an onscreen conversation between the tourism industry and the film industry. Both understood the needs of their combined audience to be based on a local, passionate and even quite sentimental attachment to the place where they reside. The series allowed Hong Kongers to love themselves, laugh at themselves and none of this needed to be couched in a wider nationally-oriented patriotism. This was not Asia's World City, it was Hong Kong, a patriotic sub-national territory – and remarkably attractive in its emotionally cinematic self-confidence.

Image-based media have often been used to support patriotism, particularly on those occasions when that patriotism is allied to a particular regime. However, Hong Kong offers a particular twist to this pattern, as it has a place-based identity which has been cut loose and already survived colonial allegiance. Hong Kong does not respond easily to nationalist patriotism because it imagines the possibility of being patriotic but without surrendering its local affections for itself.

Who is Miss Hong Kong? was partly funded by the Government Tourism Commission, but in partnership with filmmakers, technicians and actors who gave their time and expertise for free. Its sentimental humour is banal but emotionally affective rather than politically effective, and it does not suggest the banal nationalism of a flag fluttering in a primary-school playground or at Ground Zero, nor even the flag of St George draped over the railings of Tavistock Square on the first anniversary of the 7/7 London bombings. Nor does the film use the associative techniques that ally sporting colours with national leaders and the nation itself. But, for all that, the film actually works: like *McDull*, it is a low-key, amusing homage to a place that supports its people and vice versa, the idea of an implausibly small 'island' as an even more implausible beauty queen. It – for that matter, all the *1:99* films – summons a televisual eulogy for a place that can muster love, but for which the hubris of the patriotic appeal is inappropriate. Rather, as the work of film scholar

---

nation's interests and well-being of mainlanders. Understanding the importance of national security and the nation's determination to uphold its territorial integrity was also essential. Be it economic or constitutional development, the mainland plays a pivotal role. We must establish good relations with the mainland, one based on mutual trust and respect. And there is much work that needs to be done.'

Sam Rohdie shows (2001), the image – and, particularly, the cinematic image – can mediate the love-affair between individual and place, and thus be the facilitating third party in a love triangle. The *1:99* films read as love-letters from the residents to Hong Kong, and thus the place serves as a visualized metonym for their own collective memories and aspirations in a very difficult year. As Rohdie writes, 'You meet yourselves, your paths cross, in another universe' (p. 2).

Rohdie's book-length eulogy to cinema itself – which he actually wrote in Hong Kong – is projected as a memorial to a love-affair: 'I projected you into the future of my present, helping you over streams and muddied banks … strolling with you by a Belfast towpath. You accompanied me everywhere' (p. 2). The lover is now absent and Rohdie complains that neither image nor memory (later he remembers that these are one and the same) can tackle the overwhelming strength of absence. He also, once he begins to describe his enduring passion for the cinema, admits that the cinematic image is a necessary condition of modern life (p. 3), and thus intimates the necessity of loss. Image and memory are dependent on absence for their combined value, and, ultimately, for their expressivity in the frame of art. Absence, he argues, affords the image the affective weight that it needs to work as 'cinema'. The value of the image lies in part in the depth of intimacy it allows between the viewer and those memories that the viewer seeks to regain through the capturing eye of film. The value of memories lies in part in the sacramental impulse to memorialize the past, the longed-for present or the fetish. Rohdie is saying something that we have always known about cinema, that it allows nostalgia to become collectivized, in public. The argument here is that absence is another word, not just for romantic love, but also for the love of place that cannot be otherwise expressed in nationalist image culture or national branding.

Rohdie also notes in passing that the earliest cinematic adventure was experienced in a mode of feeling akin to the touristic gaze (see Urry 1990). Rohdie's book is itself a succession of rubber-necking observations; not a series of arguments, rather a sequence of looks, glances and gazes back and forth for the beloved. In these distracted shifts of attention he does, however, contend that the sense-making of cinema was very early on aligned to tourism and to a fascination both with the exotic and the mundane. Thus the thrust of this book's argument that the touristic gaze looks for symbolic traces of the familiar cinematic image in order to visually locate place-character, finds itself citing a looped convergence of fascination and recognition:

> The Dutertre-Kahn film (of Beijing in 1909) was like the films of the Lumières, part tourism, part a fascination with the exotic, part an interest in the mundane and the everyday … Some sequences, shot from the back of moving trains, moving ships and automobiles, as with the earliest films, broke from the immobility and fixity of the camera. These were images in time recording time (Rohdie, p. 7).

That images and the organization of images converge over time and space is not an especially new observation. Lev Manovich (2001) has shown how early cinema restates its conceptual moves in the workings of online narration, and he too argues for the concept of a repository of visual meaning in film. For Manovich, cinema is a 'large cultural tradition' including all 'different elements of cinematic perception, language and reception'. Cinema, the human-computer interface and print are, he argues, the 'main reservoirs of metaphors and strategies for organizing information which feed cultural interfaces' (p. 72). There is a less romantic impulse here than in Rohdie's 'other universe'. Manovich is not looking for an answer to the loss of the beloved, or, here, to the articulation of non-nationalistic love of place, but wants mainly to warn us that we are on a pathway to imprisonment, that the more we adhere to mobility with connections, the further we move away from the magical and sacramental properties of cinema:

> Eventually the VR apparatus may be reduced to a chip implanted in the retina and connected by wireless transmission to the Net. From that moment on, we will carry our prisons with us – not in order to blissfully confuse representations and perceptions (as in cinema), but rather always to 'be in touch', always connected, always plugged in. The retina and the screen will merge (p. 114).

Manovich is nervous that, if we converge ourselves with the screens that we invent and the communicative neuroses that they encourage, we shall lose our grip on the affective value of film as a medium of collective attention. If we move with the screens as part of our bodies we shall lose the perspective on place, both our own and that of the imagined worlds of cinema. Manovich and Rohdie thus describe the sacramental value of affect in modern communications such as cinema, while recognizing that the world, which produces this mass of memories, memorialization and symbolic narrations, is tied to an attentive and disciplined fixation on functional value, productivity and connection. The cinematic image exceeds our expectations, but it also keeps us in place and connected with that place. If we stray into a literal version of place by eliminating the space between ourselves as consumers of the image, the image itself, and the place from where we consume, then we become untethered. In short, we lose access to our structures of attention. So, while he is working in Hong Kong, Rohdie recalls Belfast in the memories of a lover. Meanwhile, Hong Kong memorializes itself in televisual and cinematic products which retain the value of familiar functional forms (advertisements), and which address recognizable generic audiences. The spatial separation allows that the connectivity between the idea of home and the love of the people is retained by the affect of spectatorship of domestic popular cultures in mass-image media, including cinema.

In 2003, the city reacted to the outbreak of SARS urgently and with discipline, and by late-June the epidemic had been contained. The response to crisis had been governmental and pragmatic: the city's streets were cleansed of infection while individuals wore masks to contain sneezes, and small bottles of hand disinfectant were common handbag items. Apparently, SARS was not the 'flu, but it was not unlike the ferocious 'Spanish 'flu' that in 1918 spread with unnerving speed across a world at war (and, therefore, a travelling world of new contingencies). Indeed, when Hong Kong was found to be the site of a bird 'flu in 1997, the scientific network studying animal-to-human virus transmission advised that all chickens in Hong Kong be culled immediately. Hong Kong responded then as it would six years later to the SARS outbreak – efficiently, courageously, but not without an acute understanding of its vulnerability. In other words, there was a local history of response and reaction to crisis, which was self-knowing, consistent and emotionally sustained, all features of an excellent brand. As Anthony Cheung wrote of the 2004 July march:

> Another massive turnout on July 1 this year indicates that there is now a sustainable collective voice for better governance in Hong Kong, which symbolizes the search for a pro-active Hong Kong identity within the new national context. Sceptics might worry that the local population is over-emphasizing its Hongkongness at the expense of national identity. This concern is uncalled for, because striving for the best for Hong Kong should not be seen as adversarial to China's national interest (2004).

On 1 July 2003, the sixth anniversary of the Handover was marked by a march to oppose the implementation of Article 23. The marchers were variously reported as numbering 200,000 (*South China Morning Post*, quoting police sources) and 500,000 (later, unsourced reports), the very same figures as were reported and disputed a year later at the seventh anniversary march. The marches embodied the political anger and expectations of a highly educated middle-class segment of Hong Kong society, which does not regard being Chinese and being a Hong Konger, and choosing a democratic polity, as incompatible. Many of those early marchers were cut from the same cloth as the generation of filmmakers that remembered HKU as their alma mater, and for whom English is still a fluent language of education. But, according to Beijing, these people are apparently not 'patriots', since they so openly contested Tung Chee-hwa's reading of the Basic Law in the July marches.[18] Tung's interpretation is rigidly unhelpful: surely, people who bother to march are clearly in love with their city and are therefore expressing patriotism? They have not called for Hong Kong to be less Chinese, just a bit more intensely Hong Kong. Nor have they indicated that their protests are in any way supportive of the previous, colonial regime, nor that Hong Kong should be independently sovereign – simply that it should be independently beloved.

In 2005, the 1 July turnout was much diminished, to around 20,000 marchers. This was presumably in favourable response to the resignation of Tung Chee-hwa four months earlier and the accession of Donald Tsang to the top (unelected) position in the 'second system' of Beijing rule. In 2006 the number rose again – to 50,000 – with bloggers arguing that the new CEO had used economic improvement to mask general demands for a democratized election process. There was also a backlash against the marchers, with media outlets and bloggers suggesting that the democratic

---

18 In a speech delivered in 2004, Yang Wenchang, Hong Kong Commissioner of the Ministry of Foreign Affairs, said: 'A year has lapsed since I took my current office. During that time, I have witnessed the extraordinary experience of Hong Kong people tiding over difficulties and setbacks, and rebuilding confidence through hard work under the leadership of the special administrative region's government, headed by Chief Executive Tung Chee-hwa. I experienced in person the panic brought on by SARS, the pain in economic restructuring, and the agonising disputes over Hong Kong's political system. As a Chinese poem goes, only the toughest can withstand the wildest storm. In spite of all those difficult moments, the Pearl of the Orient still glitters after the storm, which shows the world that its people are capable not only of building Hong Kong, but also of governing Hong Kong. "One country, two systems" has and will continue to demonstrate its vitality.'

movement had lost its way and should learn more from the … basic principles of branding!

> In a market, the more focused the selling point of a brand is, the greater the effect will be. This is the trick of 'more is little and little is more'. Do you not see that a certain huge sports brand used the slogan 'Just Do It' for many years without fail? Using that as publicity will always be more effective than slogans with dozens of words and any number of variations.

> As said before, the people who participate in the march may have different, even conflicting, views about matters outside of universal suffrage. But they can still articulate their own voices under the banner of universal suffrage and walk side by side. If the organizers insist on selecting certain issues to include under the universal suffrage umbrella, they would be exhibiting preferences and this is divisive and harmful to the overall theme of universal suffrage. Therefore, the biggest threat against the July 1st march is not the penetration by 'Brother Real' and it is not about the oppression by the authorities. Rather, the threat is about having too many brand attributes that will kill the brand. The Civil Human Rights Front does not really need to overthink about the theme – it is a simple 'I want universal suffrage'. The participating citizens can then express themselves freely under this broad umbrella![19]

In the short films of *1:99*, in the media debates on patriotism, and in the honest confusion in branding a city that does not share the character of its political constitution, it is evident that Hong Kong demonstrates the difference between love of country based on nationality and love of place based on belonging and historical memory. In any case, there is an unavoidable incoherence in the 'one country, two systems' policy, where one system is dominant and the other is fragile, and where one territory is ordered by love of home, and the other (which, by dint of sovereignty, history and ethnicity, includes the first) is managed by the reach of a state that defines patriotism strictly according to its own agenda. The contradictions play out in the contrast between the city's address to itself in *1:99* and in the necessary elisions of the city's branding campaigns.

What, then, might be said of the power of love in Hong Kong, a city operating under a regime whose 'one country, two systems' rubric barely manages to disguise its patriotic intentions? The response to SARS offers one answer. The city can defend itself through its systems and its collective determination to continue as an entity in adverse conditions. Secondly, the political work of activists, democrats and marchers offers another suggestion, that the demonstration of a belief in autonomy is dependent on a love of the home, which sustains the possibility of autonomy, and is therefore crucial to continued political participation. Thirdly, the proof of love lies in the cinematic contract between filmmakers and public servants and between cinema and its audience. The generation of *1:99* in a year of demonstration and epidemics was a gentle riposte to the furore of democratic debate and the ravages of disease, but it was none the less passionate for all that.

---

19 Retrieved on August 10 2006, from East-South-West-North blog, citing *Eastweek* (21 June 2006), at <http://www.zonaeuropa.com/20060621_1.htm> (Blogger's translation).

Plate 1   Boy at Circular Quay, Sydney (*Walkabout*, 1971) (reproduced by courtesy of the British Film Institute)

Plate 2   Sydney CBD in the 1970s (*Walkabout*, 1971) (reproduced by courtesy of the British Film Institute)

Plate 3   Hong Kong's Star Ferry (photo: John Gammack)

Plate 4   McDull's Hong Kong (photo: John Gammack)

Plate 5 Sydney sandstone (*Walkabout*, 1971) (reproduced by courtesy of the British Film Institute)

Plate 6 The dome of the Chapel of Hospicios de Cabanas, featuring Jose Clemente Orozco's *The Man of Fire*, Guadalajara, Jalisco, Mexico (reproduced by courtesy of Q.T. Luong, terragalleria.com)

Plate 7　The Oriental Pearl Tower, Shanghai, at night (photo: project team)

Plate 8   The Jinmao Tower, Shanghai (photo: project team)

Chapter 4

Flatlands Revisited

'You Gotta Love This City'

> We have the opportunity of forming our new city world into an imageable landscape: visible, coherent, clear. It will require a new attitude on the part of the city dweller, and a physical reshaping of his domain into forms which entrance the eye, which organise themselves from level to level in time and space, which can stand as symbols for urban life (Lynch 1996 [1960], p. 91).

This chapter discusses the visual contours of Sydney, a global city on the West Pacific Rim, and draws a brief comparison between Australia's 'Emerald City' and a Chinese city with a similar commitment to pleasure, namely Chengdu. Our discussion is written is informed by Kevin Lynch's ideas of a city 'formed' for use and clarity, combined with a sense of the 'making' of a city as a socially realized character (1960). We acknowledge from the outset that Lynch's 'true place' is constrained by his personal ideal of order and legibility. For us, a 'true place' is not an authentic location, any more than a film-shoot creates authenticity, but rather it is never more nor less than the happy coincidence and consensus of people and place in time and representation.

This chapter then refers to our observations of a great city, Sydney, seen through the repertory grids, the maps and the conversations that we have had with its marketers, its residents and its sojourners. As in all our discussions with users and residents of the cities studied in this research, we have tried to emphasize the city as a human construction, comprising urban features that could be metonymically understood in relation to the people who live there, and vice versa. This approach was most clearly endorsed by people in Hong Kong, who were insistent that the idea of *their* city was inextricable from the nature of its people, indeed, that such was the interdependence of people and place that the one was incomprehensible without the other. But Sydney is not Hong Kong; it is a city whose character seems to obliterate that of the people who live there. While Hong Kong's *people* are thrusting, ambitious and hardworking, it is *Sydney herself* who sits like a blowsy, crimson-lipped tart, on the water. Yet, the vigour with which Sydneysiders defend this strumpet suggests that she has a very special relationship with those people who make her a living city every day. The vulgar gendering of cities of such characterizations reflect the discourse that we hear on the streets and in the media, and may seem hard to defend – until we recognize that when a place is so strongly gendered in everyday parlance, it suggests first and foremost that the place in question is accepted by people as possessing the subtlety and complexity of character of an independent human being. This is praise indeed. It may be fair to suggest that the main difference between the Hong Kongers' idea of themselves as the city incarnate and Sydney's distantiation from its own embodiment is simply one of style, or perhaps even of topography? As we suggested in our remarks about the map of Sydney in the British Library – and without wishing to offend those who live there – Sydney was not so much formed as spawned, and it is still watching in fond amazement at its growth and daring. Sydney historian Paul Ashton has written of the Rocks area's 'pleasant, if haphazard process of rustication' (1988, p. 23), noting the romantic irony of applying such description to what was, after all, a no-go area of disease, crime and poverty for most of the nineteenth century. The following discussion suggests that visitors' responses to Sydney recognize these peculiarities of birth and growth, but miss significant aspects of its larger and more haphazard character.

So, Lynch's call for a city formed for use may be practical, but it is also enigmatic, and it needs to be supplemented here with the idea of a city formed by the *attention* it receives, specifically that attention which makes apparent the affective relations imbricated in the city/people relationship. The Whitlams, an Australian rock band, commented in their ballad of the same name: '*You gotta to love this city* ... [he went] into town on Thursday night, ... there was a fireworks display ... the horror, we got the Olympic Games, at least he loves his city. And he screams, my city is a whore ... you gotta love this city, for its body and not its brain.' The song is at once ironic and critical of Sydney, but there is no doubt that the whore is the object of attention, and that without 'this city, this whore', there is nothing to love, however qualified and anguished that love may sometimes be in its lyrical expression. 'You gotta love this city' is not The Whitlams' catch-phrase, although the song has given them a kind of proprietorial right to it. The phrase is commonly used by Sydneysiders, both as a statement of approval and of irony. Standing by the water at Rose Bay, on a perfect day, waiting for the kayaks to turn the corner, 'you gotta love this city'; waiting for a cancelled train at Central Station in the rain, 'you gotta love this city'.

The affective structure of attention, oriented to the transference of human characteristics and types, which the city, any city, invokes, can be recognized in the repetition of landmark phrases which residents use to comment on everyday life, and to articulate recognizable pleasures and gripes. The city's character is thus performed, maintained and (even, perhaps) immortalized in song, on film, and in the casual remarks of strangers in the same place. These path-finding utterances are partners to the topographical and built structures that bring people into connection spatially as they pass alongside Lynch's iconic landmarks of orientation. But, we might ask just how representative of the city as a whole particular utterances are, if we take into account its many different constituencies and the kinds of attention paid by different communities of interest? Sydney is a new city, but also a place (*Eora*) with an ancient history of use by its Indigenous owners (the Garigal people amongst many others). It has different paths for different people and generations, the entirety of which a research team cannot easily access or describe. So, while these remarks concern just one version of the visible city, the principles of attention and affect hold true for other versions and for other cities.

The harbour cities of Hong Kong and Sydney literally look to and from the sea. Their mutual resonances are topographically obvious. Shanghai is a river port, however, and, as we will see, in Lynch's terms, the river city is ordered by a more internalized 'edge'. This prompts us to look further into the hinterland to find cities which resonate with those on the Rim, but which are not necessarily oriented to the sea. In particular, we wanted to find a city that was not strictly comparable in reputation, but had some of the elements of Sydney's character, without its position in the global hierarchy. While travelling recently in the west of China, we discovered the elegance of Chengdu, an ancient river city of ten million people in a fertile basin in Sichuan. Chengdu has always been wealthy and culturally sharp. It has a long political history, but it stands now on the brink of hyper-modernity, though not as exhaustingly so as is the case in Guangzhou or Shanghai. Chengdu has the trappings of the global modern, the confidence of a cosmopolitan – not only is it a centre for minority peoples in China's West, but it also negotiates Sichuan's claims to be quite different from the centres of power on China's eastern seaboard, and yet equivalent to them in culture and history and, particularly, in the sophistication of Sichuan's long political inheritance. As Sydney is to London, so perhaps Chengdu is to Beijing – or to Singapore. The south of the city still boasts fertile farmland, but is developing a creative industries corridor (the fourth largest in China according to the developers), a suite of gated communities to service the new rich, and a number of quietly state-sponsored private schools (a Chinese phenomenon). Chengdu is peripheral in so far as it does not have the immediate competition of Shanghai, although its enormous neighbour, Chongqing, with a population of 32 million, is a challenge to its traditional pre-eminence in the region. Chongqing is an artificially large metropolis, politically merged with other local 'small cities' by Beijing in the late 1990s to challenge Sichuan's provincial power. What Chengdu can boast, however, is a sense of internal style and an orientation to happiness. Its character is intrinsic to its pace and its parochial elegance of spirit. The first phenomenon that returned to the city after the austerity of the late 1960s and early 1970s was not so much money-making: the new rich are here, but more discreetly and in any case the city is used to being wealthy. Rather it was the return of the teahouse. Even in the main downtown shopping areas, the word *cha* (tea) is the most prominent, out-branding Nike, Esprit and McDonalds. Thus, the city accepts the influences of global modernity, but re-sophisticates itself by reference to its own historical status and memory. This is a kind of 'true place'.

Our Chengdu office was in a marble-clad monster of a building in the city centre. Just behind it, we could see a Post Office dating perhaps from the 1930s. Chengdu is still graceful, but its nodes of elegance are derelict or awaiting repair. Temporary hardboard fencing around the Post Office – that has clearly been there for at least a couple of years – bears the weathered, barely legible declaration: 'Let us work on urban infrastructure and make life better for the residents of Chengdu.' Behind the Post Office building looms another, modern, office building, undistinguished but typical of the urban infrastructure that is improving the lives of the residents of Chengdu. It is situated in a downtown area, where most new buildings are quickly built and occupied by general retail, mobile-phone outlets and banks. The area's main road, Zengfu lu, is busy with yellow and blue taxis, green rickshaw-pedal cabs and an increasing number of private cars. The back streets still have a few of the city's famous gingko trees, but newness is characterized mainly by the utter lack of distinguishing or iconic features. It is likely that the old Post Office, once a classic city landmark in Lynch's terms, is now either doomed, or is a vulnerable façade that may not be commandeered by a developer in time to prevent its collapse.

The Post Office building is a microcosm of what Chengdu has been and could become in terms of its visual power, and offers a snapshot of the cinematic city (that has not yet emerged). It is a vivid reminder that Sydney's cinema, although locally reverberant, is internationally mute, and as such is consistent with a historically confident but globally insignificant Western city. Chengdu is much older than Sydney, at least in terms of classic historiography. As the centre of the Kingdom of Shu it was the western capital of the Three Kingdoms (220–265 AD) and still commemorates Liu Pei, the military genius who resisted the Wei at the Battle of the Red Cliff (208 AD). Arguably, Sichuan, gateway to the west, still poses an incipient political challenge to Beijing, and hence the creation of a megalopolis in Chongqing. But for Chengdu, while the weight of history is not in doubt, the legibility of the city – as of so many places in China – is under distinct threat. The Post Office is one example, and the disappearing, multi-tiered covered markets are another. This reminds a Sydneysider of Sydney's own development catastrophes: the ravages of high-rise along the Harbour foreshore, the destruction of the tramways and the problems with the cross-city tunnel are just a few of the past and continuing stories of a city losing its way. Or, as we intimate here, perhaps it is these vagaries that attract attention in the first place. How do we know what to preserve and what to change? What affective glue will hold these cities together, and how will the structures of attention be maintained when so much shifts and crumbles? What is the true place held in common by those who 'gotta love this city', any city, now?

A True Place ...

How are true places found or formed? To organize his image of the city, Kevin Lynch works from the maps people carry in their heads, and which they construct from the visible elements of a city's design. The image is contoured into a 'true place' by means of what Lynch calls its 'paths', 'nodes', 'edges', 'landmarks' and 'districts'. As we maintained earlier, in this context 'true' does not mean 'authentic', but rather it describes the felicitous union of a place's useability, legibility and consistency. By 'consistency' we refer to the quality of 'being immediately familiar to its diverse range of users'. We have already referred to this grammar of the visual city and will briefly summarize Lynch's descriptive concepts, which we believe to be as relevant to seeing the city as a potentially cinematic formation as to making a cognitive map of any urban topography.

Paths need to have both direction and visibility to make a city clearer to those that traverse it. Paths must be usable, although do not need to have been made for use. Thus, a 'path' through Sydney could be the carefully sculpted Wharf walks, or the cut-throughs and double-backs used by drivers avoiding the Parramatta Road on their way between the city centre and the western suburbs, or the magnificent, historically annotated 26-kilometre Circle Walk designed for both residents and visitors.[1] *Edges* must be distinctly marked, by colour, material, planting, or a natural phenomenon such as water, cliffs or mountains. When cities sit on water, as so many do, the water's edge is prime. Hong Kong and Sydney both have their harbours. Sydney also has its rivers, the Georges, the Hawkesbury, the Cooks and the Parramatta. Chengdu's most successful edge is the river, which marks the contours of the city itself. In the valley, it attracts water and mists, both of which contribute to its special attributes as a well-watered, prosperous zone. The edge in Shanghai is also the river, the Huangpu. On the west side of the river there is the Bund, a monument to the quasi-colonial era, and on the east is Pudong (literally east of the river), which houses the rising power of finance in the twenty-first century. *Landmarks* are prominent visual features, which help people orient themselves in a city. The main landmark of Shanghai's status as a media-savvy modern city, the Oriental Pearl Tower, is on the Pudong side. Thus, the city's centre is extremely well oriented both by its edges, its landmarks and the relationship between them. The most compelling stage of its recent development has been this process of equalization between the Bund, the old town on the west, and the brassiness of Pudong. The city is challenging itself across its own edge and on its own terms. Shanghai's topography speaks to Lynch's argument that a truly successful edge is a seam, 'structured to some depth with the regions on either side ... a seam rather than a barrier, a line of exchange along which two areas are sewn together' (p. 100). Sydney is somewhat different. The edge and the landmarks which are clustered on that edge – the Opera House, the Bridge, and every city beach – is also a border, looking outwards to a very wide ocean. How does that effect the formation of the city behind? How much more *on the edge* is a city thus positioned? And why, for instance, does that not translate into an 'edgy' cinematic culture?

Paul Kelly, a Melbourne balladeer, has sung that he would exchange 'all of Sydney Harbour (all that land and all that water) / For that one sweet promenade [in St Kilda, Melbourne]'[2] – but perhaps he was just homesick. Despite the elephant in the corner of Sydney-Melbourne rivalry, Kelly's song captures Sydney just as he is regretting Melbourne. Again, we hear the musical intimation of an affective city – loved, hated, spatially imagined and evocative, despite the refusal of those who sing of it to admit their fascination. Yet, this is a city without a strong cinema. Musically contoured, but filmically flattened, Sydney is still waiting for its great films.[3]

Sydney is not the bloated plutocrat, nor the confident land-owner that Kelly's otherwise powerful line suggests. 'All that land and all that water' is a precarious edge on which people presume to live and build. It never fails to overwhelm. At the

---

1   This walk takes in headland, bush, historical streets and harbour views. Walking Sydney Harbour is a partnership project between community and various authorities who wish 'to improve public access to, and enhance the recreational enjoyment of Sydney harbour and its tributaries for the people of Sydney and visitors to the city'; see Planning.nsw.gov n.d.

2   In a song entitled 'From St Kilda to King's Cross' (White Records, 1997).

3   The trans-national reality behind the film industry woes of Sydney and Australia is told in a number of excellent analyses by Given 2003; Goldsmith and O'Regan 2005 and (tangentially) Scott 2005.

other edge, between city and bush, there are other stories. Eric Rolls (1993) muses, as he drives out of Sydney to Baradine, upon crossing 'the divide between city and country: Pennant Hills, Kurrajong, Lithgow' (p. 12). He notes that, following an outbreak of smallpox in 1913, the government drew an artificial boundary as a circle at a radius of 25 kilometres from the Sydney GPO and ruled that stepping outside that circumference without a medical certificate was punishable.

    Nodes and *districts* are the last two of Lynch's elements for defining legibility, and they need to be considered together. *Nodes* are hubs of activity and mark or facilitate shifts between one part of a city and another. The London tube map is a guide to the nodes by which one moves through London. In Hong Kong, the Tsimshatsui Clock Tower is a landmark, but it is also a nodal point at the edge of the Kowloon district, from where one goes into Kowloon or across the Harbour on the Star Ferry.[4] (By the same token it is also intrinsic to a path.) A node is articulated between and across physical and social areas of a city. *Districts* are the accepted, usually named, districts by which a city is managed. They may be governmental, social, ethnic or use-oriented, but they are most likely to be remembered and referred to by residents if they have a combination of all of these functions. Newtown, an old inner-city suburb of Sydney, is a district used for orientation to other districts in the vicinity that are less well-known. Neighbouring suburbs such as Erskineville, Alexandria, Darlington or Camperdown are regularly said to be located 'near Newtown'. Newtown is both a *district* and a *node*: it has a character, 'bohemian and alternative', that is made visible by its main *path* (King Street), its use value (its vast number of shops, pubs and restaurants), its inhabitants (young, cool, gay, multicultural), and its importance as a route to other places. Newtown is served by buses and trains, while King Street also provides a cut through to the airport in one direction and two major universities in another. Taken out of context, Newtown might not seem particularly special. The main street reflects the suburb's general blend of class and grunge: much of its early-1800s architecture tends to be obscured by under-regulated lights and signage. Newtown's non-conformist, radical character has been retained by resisting over-commercialization: an unwelcome McDonald's franchise closed within a year. A 'true place', Newtown's strong community feel means that, despite some gentrification and a younger demographic, its particular character endures. An annual festival, established nearly 30 years ago, and a strengthening theatre culture give the suburb a certain kind of inclusivity, that more than offsets the 'outside invasion' that gentrification necessarily implies (Petty 2005). Its power lies in part in its contradictions: while an eating strip is a desirable feature in many cities, this is at odds with Newtown's main path also serving as an arterial road for cars. 'Anyone mad enough to think of having a coffee on the pavement in King St Newtown or

---

    4   The Star Ferry route from Central to Kowloon closed in November 2006, shortly after this research was completed, in order to accommodate the new Harbour regeneration plans. The loss of affect is likely to be substantial both in terms of international cinematic memory – just remember the opening sequence of *The World of Suzie Wong* (dir. Richard Quine, 1960) – and in terms of local memories of romance, in which the ferry represented an amorous crossing where lovers met, or positioned their love in the wider context of Hong Kong on the Harbour.

Military Rd Neutral Bay', wrote Peter Spearritt, 'soon retreats to shore up their life expectancy' (2002). But, retorts a Sydneysider, whoever thought of having coffee on the street in King Street? Everyone knows that you should perch on the ledge between the café and the footpath?

Similarly, Kings Cross, with which Paul Kelly has such an ambivalent relationship, is an absolutely crucial *district* for Sydney's path-making, a *node* between the wealthy Eastern Suburbs, the central business district (CBD) and the rough *edges* of Woolloomooloo, and one which is well used in a number of ways. Kings Cross is the iconic drugs and red-light capital of Australia, a district that is both part of, and antithetical to, a number of fashionable residential areas. It has the best small restaurants for late-night meals and early breakfasts, the easiest access to the city centre, and a great position in the transport system. It is also the location for a rather exclusive Christian girls' school. Kings Cross – or, to locals, simply 'The Cross' – is a 'true place', and one of the reasons why Sydney gets the attention a city needs. But its brothels and strip joints are also why the city is so readily and properly referred to as a strumpet, a whore or a bawd. The mix of antithesis, affect and unfulfilled promise which Sydney encapsulates is a textbook study of a difficult branding exercise and a city whose cultural producers have not yet grasped or been offered the opportunity that the city's perversity seems to offer. Yet, it also makes the point that this city's character is less an expression of its perfection than of its contradictions. Who cares if King Street is too narrow, or the Foreshore too exquisite, or the children at Luna Park, the fun palace at harbour-side Miller's Point, too loud for its wealthy neighbours? Surely, these are the bizarre combinations that make a city a 'true place'?

In his own work, Lynch looks for 'true places' among those cities of the world that he himself traverses. He cites Florence as a city that is visible, coherent and that gives a certain sensation of pleasure to anyone simply walking its streets and sighting its contours:

> [T]here are fundamental functions of which the city forms may be expressive: circulation, major land-uses, key focal points. The common hopes and pleasures, the sense of community may be made flesh. Above all, if the environment is visibly organised and sharply identified, then the citizen can inform it with his own meanings and connections. Then it will become a *true place*, remarkable and unmistakeable (pp. 91–2).

A 'true place' combines design, natural elements, presence and the facility of inducing expectation. To be in a true place, one has only to arrive in order to know where one is and what it feels like to be there. The Globalization and World Cities (GaWC) index (Beaverstock, Smith and Taylor 1999), which we have mentioned already and to which we shall return, is not interested in such qualitative judgements on place. It is concerned with measurable qualities such as the levels of networking, the effectiveness of transport systems and the amount of finance and investment flowing through a city's virtual portals. Virtual edges, nodes and paths of world cities are a conceptual advance on the thinking of Lynch, whose work preceded by several years the outbreak of the IT revolution. They do not obviate judgements on the aesthetic and planning decisions, which create place value. These are also vital to the creation of a world city as a true place. And so is everything else. To be both of itself and of its people, a true place, a true city must be have powerful local signifiers. Kings Cross and Newtown should have the power to summon up a broader picture of Sydney as a whole city, as if the suburbs to which they directly refer could not exist outside of Sydney the 'true place'. But also, a true place should also elude, exceed and confuse those who think they know what to expect. Its stories must be both explicit and mysteriously fragile. 'To create a true place, a "there" there, requires more than solid architecture and snappy graphic elements. It takes an understanding of urban design, a sensitivity to the history, context and scale of the community … [C]ustomers want to be surprised, to find themselves in the story of a place' (RTKL.com 2006b).

Flatlands

Edward Tufte, a professor of statistics and graphic design, exhorts us to 'escape flatland', to get out of the two-dimensional information space and to find strategies 'for extending the dimensional and informational reach of display flatlands' (1990, p. 15). Tufte's main concern is to allow statistics to speak clearly and effectively to those who must understand them. In practice, this requires a *visualization* of well-chosen statistical, evidential or topographical material. A major case study of Tufte's concerned the cholera epidemic in London in 1854 and the 'classic of medical detective work' (1997, p. 5) conducted by Dr John Snow, who, in order to determine the epicentre and possible cause of the disease, made a dot map showing both where deaths from the disease occurred and the location of eleven water pumps in the area. He isolated a water pump in Broad Street, W1. Tufte uses this case to illustrate, first, that Snow had a good idea and so collected the right kind of evidence and, second, that Snow had been unfailingly logical in pursuing a conclusion that could only be reached visually. The Broad Street pump was the closest to the death clusters, and Snow persuaded the parish council to remove its handle, so putting an end to the epidemic. He also accounted for deaths that did not occur in the immediate vicinity of the Broad Street pump: the local brewery and the workhouse had relatively few deaths, the brewery, Snow determined, because workers drank 'small' beers instead of water and the workhouse because it had a singular water source. It was Snow's map visualization, not the time-series graph of the data, which told the story, just as Euclid's 3-D pop-out had illustrated his geometry book.

As we have seen, Lynch had introduced the idea of place legibility into thinking about urban design and cityscapes in 1960, thirty years before Tufte. Indeed, Lynch validated the very idea of 'thinking about a city' by means of visual schemas, in so far as he allowed its useability to be entertained as a category of thought by those who designed and planned urban space for everyday life. His experimental work on urban navigation by icon, landmark and features of the streetscape combined with an index of imageability, which took into close account the experience and visual memories of residents and visitors. Lynch visualized the responses of his subjects as cognitive maps, which were coded to describe not a flatland, but a thick description of what it felt like to move around in a particular space. It is from Kevin Lynch that we learn that it is the navigational ease of the city, its *paths*, which are in large measure responsible for its success or failure.

But other lines can be drawn: the cultural critic McKenzie Wark describes how as a child he would trace the outlines of countries and colour their natural terrains: 'The geography of place. All craggy and squiggly and never the same twice.' Then he would mark big black dots and join them with straight, ruled lines: '[C]ities and highways. The geography of space ... of second nature.' Then, on a third map he would remember distant car trips when radio reception was lost and television channels changed: '[T]he geography of telesthesia ... connecting and coordinating the movements of people' (1997, p. 32). Wark develops his argument in describing the inner-city suburb of Ultimo. Once an important shipping and manufacturing centre, latterly a tourist location and the home radio and TV stations, Ultimo has a large Chinese population. Drawing a line from Castle Hill to the airport divides those in Sydney's (rich, educated) eastern suburbs from those (obese, unemployed) in the west, identifying new spaces of flows and patterns of proximity such that those in the east are more likely to fly overseas than to visit a western suburb (pp. 34–5).

The popular image of Western Sydney as a badlands of crime and neglect is specifically considered in an article by Lesley Johnson, entitled 'Feral Suburbia?' (1997), in which she seeks to denaturalize this totalizing and media-reinforced way of seeing the city and the assumption that this structure of perception is objective. Apart from being factually unfair, the homogenized image is largely constructed by media that find it convenient and, by contrast, regard Sydney's North Shore, northern beaches, and Harbour-side suburbs as a kind of Arcadia. An interviewee from Tourism NSW commented directly on this, noting that many Sydney marketers lived 'in the nice bits' and easily forgot that Sydney was not all 'nice'. On the other hand, it was incumbent upon him as a state marketer to ensure that the propositions of other tourism precincts were represented. Many of these do give local depth of experience and genuine cultural exchange, but some are undeniably mediocre and of little interest to visitors. Even getting to some other parts of the city, he thought, involved long trips by car or rail 'through some pretty bloody awful stuff'. (Presumably, he was thinking of a Saturday afternoon on a heavily-congested Parramatta Road, once referred to as a 'varicose vein'.) The brand, he noted, was not yet 'embraced by all stakeholders' with planning issues interacting with tourism requirements, and tension between 'pushing the best product that you have to offer rather than good product mix in with [the] sort of stuff that is okay but still has a fair way to go in terms of being a right-up-there sort of world-standard in terms of tourism precincts'.

In our own research we were particularly concerned to test these truisms and find more about how the true place is articulated by outsiders, young sojourners who offer fresh, and critical, perceptions of the city's appeal and drawbacks. We also wanted to both utilize Tufte's flatlands thesis as part of our methodology and as a descriptive analogy for thinking about how certain places are understood by strangers. Focussing on paths, icons and way-making, we used elicitation techniques to prompt respondents to think visually. Unlike Wark, none of the map-makers involved in this exercise were brought up in Sydney: indeed, many of them had only been in the city for a few months. So, using a methodology derived from Lynch's premise of mapping and plotting spatial meaningfulness, we sought out the paths of Sydney from maps drawn by international students and other short-term residents of the city. The method moved us away from the flatlands and into a realm where Sydney's spatial character was only feebly manifest. Sydney has many paths, but very few of these are known to the visitor. Those that *are* there are strong and predictable, street-equivalents of the Central, Victoria and Piccadilly lines on the London Underground. They run across the city from the airport in the east to the northern beaches. In the maps we collected, there is only one mention of the western suburbs and no hint of the inner west, or the south, or the shires, and only the odd flourish of colour to indicate the Blue Mountains. All paths converge in the CBD, where there is a seemingly inescapable set of visual landmarks and where the built environment takes meaning from its proximity to what we might call 'key signs of place', or 'indicators of image-ability'. The pattern is striking.

If, as John Snow expected and filmmakers assume, urban paths are indicative of narrative contours, they must be matched with a particular city's visual field. Dr Snow came to understand his city, London, by exhuming an 'imageability' from the numbers of cholera deaths and the very particular landmarks associated with them. Lynch understood that the city could never be known in any lasting way without such landmarks, points of reference and distinctions. In the images that we have collected, and which are reproduced below, we see the city's paths enunciated in simple accounts of iconographic landmarks and their relative positioning. We learn from these responses that Sydney's landmarks are well-known to the new arrivals, but that, in the way that they draw it, there is very little evidence of an imagined hinterland to the city. It is unconnected to a larger world, or to an inner world of identity. It is a city of desirable destinations without journeys, and of functional arrivals without any imaginative possibilities beyond the limits of safe space. There is often emptiness between locations, and restricted human activity. In only a narrow sense is the city successful: it can be clearly articulated on paper. Yet, as the maps remove us from the flatlands of representation of space, they deliver us back into a flatland of experience.

Sojourners in the Flatlands

The maps fall into three descriptive categories. Sydney is a university city, a beach city, and a tourist city. The first (Figure 4.1) is organized by campus and affords little sense of the city as a human or natural environment. The logic of the relationship between the campuses orders the path, and that in turn curtails the possibility of an urban character emerging through the visualization. The second (Figure 4.2) is a little more promising. There are people on this map, and they are all on the beach, or perhaps they are at Circular Quay? Geographical exactitude is not in much evidence, and while that is not quite the point of the exercise, it is fair to say that in these visual accounts Sydney is undersold. The people stay at the water's edge, and something that might be George Street meanders from nowhere to the Opera House. The third map (Figure 4.3) provides much more detailed information than the first two, but is more sterile than the second, and less demographically specific than the first. Here, there is an itinerary to fill three days of central Sydney tourism, including a trip to the markets in Balmain and Glebe, and to the Zoo. There is, however, precious little character or context, or any sense of Sydney extending beyond the path detailed by tourism activity. In these visualizations – and they were typical of this particular group of respondents – a Sydney emerges that is predictable, water-hugging and tightly drawn around the CBD. It has one path, which starts at the airport or in a dead end (or a dead beginning).

The respondents to the cognitive mapping exercise were mainly young and international, and many were students. So, the city that they drew reflects their demographic predilections. They go to university and they go to the beach. And they go to the Opera House: they at least have to say that they've seen it! However, the data is also supported by a much larger sample of 300 responses to questionnaires about the 'character of the city'. Summarized, these comments separate out 'Sydney' from 'the west', and even in the centre of the city only certain aspects are classified as 'of Sydney'. These aspects are clustered around the path identified in the maps. On Sydney:

> A harbour city with vibrant nightlife – geographically beautiful, architecturally confused.

> Vivid light and starkness of colour – mostly a blue city with water and sky dominating.

> Parts of the inner city resemble cities everywhere – the downtown of Central and environs are grey, dirty and noisy.

And on 'the west':

> A huge, expansive, amorphous tangle of human wasteland.

Figure 4.1 was drawn by a new arrival, an ESL student from Italy, and shows a path that runs from the Airport past the University of New South Wales (UNSW), the University of Technology, Sydney (UTS), the University of Sydney (USYD) and Macquarie (MQ). There are recreational paths, beaches in the east and south, and four landmarks clustered in the CBD. The Zoo is mentioned, but beyond the path weaving from campus to campus, and Central station in the middle, the orientation east to north follows the logic of student aspirations and needs.

This figure is drawn by a visitor, resident in Sydney for one year, and shows the city's liminal spaces. Here the city is more familiar. There is less naming of landmarks as though they are likely not to require, or deserve, labels. The Opera House and the Ocean are still named, as the Sydney 'fixers'. There is activity in this image. There are people, all on the beach. Although the map is crudely drawn and highly inaccurate in its orientation, it effectively suggests that the path through the city runs past nothing worth naming but leads to the major tourist icon, and that all human interest is focussed exclusively on the sea shore.

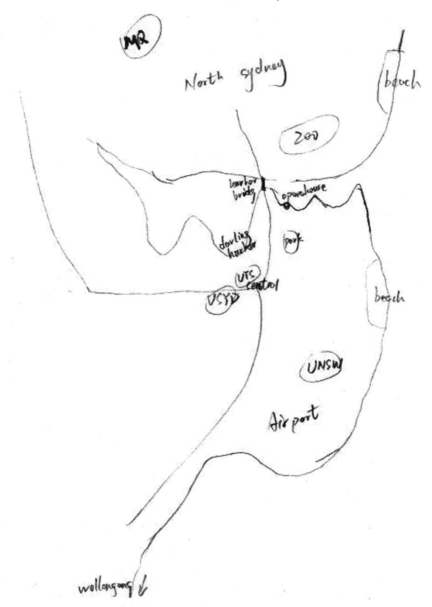

Figure 4.1   Drawing Sydney – new arrival, 2004 (ESL student from Italy)

Figure 4.2   Drawing Sydney – one-year visitor-resident: liminal spaces

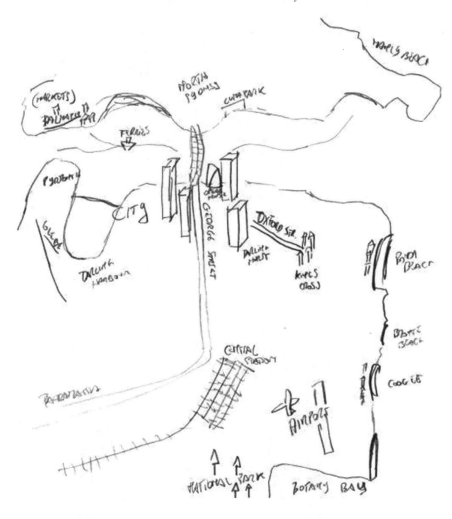

Figure 4.3   Drawing Sydney – six-month student visitor: orientation to the CBD

Figure 4.3, drawn by a student visiting for 6 months, illustrates an orientation towards the CBD. It is a developed image of Sydney, again focussed on the main tourism centre, but with some sense of central suburbs (Glebe, Kings Cross and Balmain). Naming is used to manage the spatial accuracy of the 'map' (the three big tourist beaches are in correct geographical sequence) and transport is highlighted: the Bridge, the Airport and Central railway station indicate possibilities of arrival (and departure). Again, the city path is singular, the George Street / Parramatta Road indicates the main route, and its environs cluster round it as the defining stretch of the city's spatial identity.

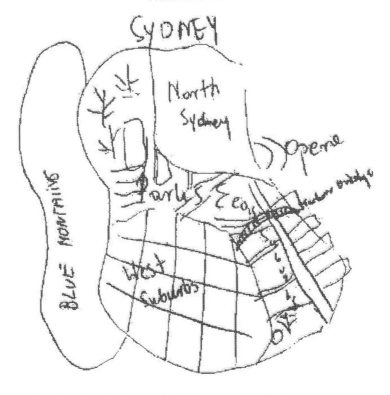

Figure 4.4   Drawing Sydney – the Unimaginable West!

Here Sydney is a cluster of conceptual areas: the parks, the Blue Mountains, the north, the east and the west, again, 'fixed' by the Harbour Bridge and the Opera House. There is no path in any area apart from the familiar route from an unidentified place (the Airport?) to the Bridge. Each named area is divided from the others. The woman who drew this map told us that she had visited the western suburbs, or the West, as some would have it, and found the experience very 'despairing'. We read her response as having been conditioned in part by a European view of the outer suburbs, usually depressed, marginalized and under-represented in the élite imaginations of European urban culture. Is she correct in believing that Sydney is moving in the same direction? Or does she fall into the trap of thinking that liminality and marginality are necessarily the same thing? Incidentally, despite the real problems of some famously problematic suburbs such as Macquarie Fields, the west is by no means a human wasteland. It is a more or less comfortable set of suburbs, with small-strip shopping centres, satellite 'city' centres, developments and quarter-acre blocks. By contrast to most British metro-sprawl, Sydney's West would look reasonably extensive, not too clogged with traffic and enjoying good weather for much of the year. On some routes through the West it is possible to glimpse views of water and to slip down easily towards the sea via the Hume Highway. What the West is *not*, of course, is in any sense the close neighbour of a magnificent harbour and an Opera House.

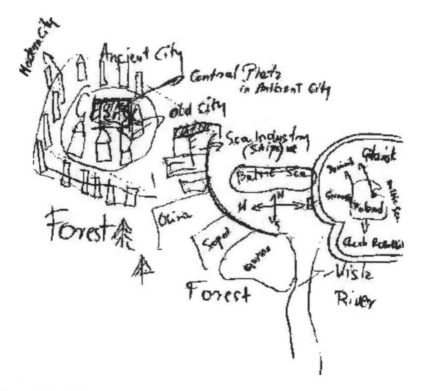

Figure 4.5   Gdansk (Home)

Drawn from memory by the respondent who drew Figure 4.4, this map of Gdansk emphasizes industry, the Wisła (Vistula) River, national boundaries and balance of ancient and modern in the central tourist area. It differs from Figure 4.4 in one important respect: the European understanding of Sydney is limited because Australia is not seen to share borders with other nation states. Poland's national borders have changed in response to invasion and occupation across its all too porous inland frontiers. Australia does have those inland borders, of course: the states are a modern example and the rivers, which divided up Indigenous tribal areas and still divide up cultural groups along their banks, are another. But Sydney does not advertise its rivers as central to its identity politics. Yet Sydney's rivers are the focus of many cultural groups and, of course, while Australia's borders and Sydney's edges are sea-bound, the rivers are by no means unimportant.

These four cognitive maps of Sydney fall somewhere between wayfaring diagrams and pictures of what Sydney means to the respondents who drew them after a short period of residency. They cannot pretend to offer more than a snapshot of a visitor's experience. Our point in reproducing them, however, is to suggest that Sydney would appear to present itself in a peculiarly simple and uncomplicated manner: our evidence places a noticeable emphasis on the city's principal iconic features, and hardly any sense of movement through the city, except for one main street – which is drawn as a feature of orientation in relation to the landmarks, rather than as an indication of human traffic. If we return to Edward Tufte's premise, the flatlands of these conceptual pictures do seem very flat indeed. Where are the flashes of narrative energy ? Where are the mysteries, the private places, and the 'best bits' of a city for young and presumably adventurous visitors? Why are they strangely submissive to just one path, which leads them from nowhere (other than the Airport) to a bridge and a featureless north? Where, again, is the cinematic depth and narrative sense of adventure?

Arriving in New York, the imagination is already prying into stories, the resonance of which gives narrative substance to buildings and streets that might otherwise be impenetrable. This may be in part because of a long-term financial commitment on behalf of the city of New York to sponsoring filmmakers and locations. It may also be because New York has a contour that draws on both known actual and also imagined paths. The city is full of a specific bravura based on stories that travel across time, and of landmarks which refer to them in their various iterations. Whether it is the original King Kong, or the Marshmallow Man from *Ghostbusters*, the Empire State Building is as much reliant on these fictional creatures for its fame as they are dependent on its symbolic vulnerability for their cinematic impact. The sharing of cinema and place is evident in the iconic yellow of New York taxi cabs and the (yellow) gridlock that always indicates incipient disaster as the streets grind to a halt in the face of flood, global freezing or monster marshmallow men! If Sydney has such stories, and the cinematic tropes to sustain them, they have yet to be told to the rest of the world. Nor can Sydney boast the literary depths of London or Paris. When we asked in a Woollahra bookshop for 'the defining' Sydney novel, we drew a blank. Someone suggested Ruth Park's *Playing Beatie Bow*, the children's time-travel novel, set in the Rocks area in the nineteenth century, and a friend found the memoirs of a Jewish childhood spent in Kings Cross. These were exquisite fragments, but they hardly constituted a shared story, and were certainly not sufficiently well-known to amount to the layering of place and image that might let us escape the flatlands of the international imagination. Sydney is a true place, but who knows that, and what do they think they mean? How much of the truth of Sydney is missing from the image the rest of the world has of it?

One approach might be to take the notion of flatlands literally. Is Sydney too flat to develop the contours of cinematic affect? Can Sydney evoke a structure of attention that moves beyond the everyday pleasures of sun, sea and easy living? Can the sojourner even see the undulations of history and landscape that exist but which can apparently go unnoticed? A marketing official we interviewed described the winding lanes and surprising vistas of Sydney, whose older paths and roads were often shaped by the curves and lines of creeks, noting how this contrasted with the city-block regularity of other cities. The way in which the natural environment shapes Sydney's topographical edges is truly stunning, but do they attract the attention of the sojourner? Apart from its natural undulations, the visual layering of Sydney's *built* environment barely adds a vertical dimension, except for the towering sky-scrapers of its CBD. From the water the skyline features appear conservatively spaced, and beyond the concentration of buildings in the central area if the city the horizon is essentially flat. Although the

Centrepoint Tower (aka Sydney Tower) is locally prominent, and is the second tallest free-standing structure in Australia, no Sydney building figures in any list of the world's 100 tallest structures. On the other hand, both Hong Kong and Shanghai are represented in the top 10. Is this a cause for pride, or does it simply betray timidity on the part of planners and developers? The modernist notion that progressive cities need skyscrapers is expressed by George Bailey in Frank Capra's *It's a Wonderful Life* (1946). When his wife Mary asks him 'What d'you wish, George', he answers: 'A whole hatful, Mary … I'm gonna build skyscrapers a hundred stories high.'

But this ideal is contested in a celebrated article entitled 'The End of Tall Buildings', written only days after 9/11. The authors, James Howard Kunstler and Nikos A. Salingaros, consider skyscrapers to be a failed building typology and predict that in time the only ones left standing will be in those third-world countries that uncritically imported the idea of the megatower from the USA. While conceding that a city will need some high buildings, they advocate increased attention to certain ideas of people in the New Urbanism and New Architecture movement, particularly those of Christopher Alexander (1977), who urges the inappropriateness of tall buildings for human habitation. Paris refuses skyscrapers in the city centre and its great Eiffel Tower is visible from miles away. Despite the high-profile criticism it attracted, London's Canary Wharf Tower, the tallest in Britain, was designed as a 'beacon' to attract investment to East London, its height a symbolic necessity to reassure prospective city-based investors to move east (Open University 2006). To create an 'exciting and dynamic' CBD in 2006, the city of Brisbane – which is shaded by Q1, the world's tallest residential tower, on the nearby Gold Coast – is considering removing height restrictions on building development other than around certain heritage and other specially designated areas (ABC 2006). By contrast, Melbourne, Sydney's traditional competitor, has taller and architecturally often more adventurous skyscrapers. Although the larger Sydney has more tall buildings, overshadowing traditional landmarks (Spearritt 2000) and visually reflecting its prominence as a regional financial node, its city-block and tall-building developments are never going to be purely iconic. One marketing manager made this point unambiguously:

> A city block cannot be an icon as it is not unique ... [An icon] has to be something that stands out on its own. You might argue that the Sydney Tower is a reference point. It's not an icon of the strength of the Opera House and Harbour Bridge. But the Sydney Tower is a visual cue as to which city you are in, if you are reasonably familiar with the city ... but is not otherwise well-known).

There are subtle compensations for size, however. Norman Foster's Deutsche Bank Place at 126 Phillip St emphasizes functional efficacy rather than external spectacle, natural light and fluid connections rather than sheer height. Perhaps the brashness of which Sydney is so readily accused is not entirely deserved. Although some financial investors may be reassured by the height of buildings, brand competition based on tall buildings is unlikely for Sydney, which effortlessly differentiates it from that of other cities in the South.

Future residents are rather more likely to find themselves living up in the air than flat on the ground. Like other Australian cities, Sydney has always been surrounded by sufficient land to avoid any need for vertical development. Indeed, prior to 1959 no building taller than 45m (150ft) was permitted. Nevertheless, the trend towards higher-density development in the inner suburbs and elsewhere continues. As apartments are expected to comprise two-thirds of Sydney's new housing over the next 25 years, there is a trade-off (between environmental targets and perceived affordability) that will not only impact on Sydney's future residents, but also risk compromising the environmental component that strengthens Sydney's brand. By comparison to other housing forms, the residential high-rise apartment blocks that currently exist emit more greenhouse gases and, furthermore, the building industry claims that installing energy-saving measures in new flats would make them too expensive to buy (Nixon 2006). An exemplary 'new model for living in Sydney' was established during the 'Green Games' Olympic period, when the reduction in greenhouse gases and water consumption achieved by the Olympic Village was matched by the sale of all its permanent accommodation at above-forecast prices (Leece 2001). Although there are signs of increased awareness of the business value of green building – for example, Deutsche Bank Place has been recognized for its environmental sustainability (Green Building Council Australia 2006)[5] – local debate continues as to whether environmental standards should be relaxed so as to boost affordability: the issue epitomizes Sydney's ambivalence about its natural environment values on the one hand and its real-estate values on the other.

Architectural confusion is a feature of many cities, an outcome of attempts to balance heritage and developmental agendas, fashion and necessity. In Francesca Morrison's view (1997), Sydney's architecture is characterized by a pragmatic concern with particular local problems, rather than with globally engaging or leading theoretical design, preferring to affirm its regional identity around the Harbour's edge rather than at the traditional centre. Union-led 'green bans' of the early 1970s preserved bushland and heritage areas from speculative development, particularly the Rocks area, Woolloomooloo and the Botanic Gardens, which was destined to become a car park for the Opera House (Burgmann 1993). Morrison also notes the various strategies and results of attempts to reconcile the historic with the progressive, where authentic patches of maintained identity and the imaginative response to climate and landscape are juxtaposed with anachronistic or clichéd trappings, imitation styles and façades poorly integrated into their context. Sydney's European and, more recently, Americanized style is visually dominant, but, as Greg Cowan (n.d.) observes, the Western concept of architecture differs radically from the 'nomadic dwelling traditions of ancient Australia' and that the rhizomatic structure of 'opportunism, ephemerality and collapsibility' epitomized by the 1972 Canberra Tent Embassy, by suggesting different concepts of environmental responsibility and sustainable permanence, propose new ways to help theorize the future of Australian culture.

Sydney's disengagement from its past is another aspect of a shallow flatland. Sydney city's colonial and convict origin is not an attractive theme for commemoration, and is essentially denied, with the Indigenous and older ancestral understandings of the place removed from mainstream presentation. Christine Gates (2004) describes how, 'as a member of a group of white Australians, newcomers to a land of ancient traditions', she endeavoured 'to find a place ... and

---

5   For a contrasting perspective, see Vivian (2006).

achieve an understanding of the spirit of place', that incorporates something called 'European heritage' but 'enriched by the culture we have invaded' (Introduction, n.p.). The prevailing emphasis on economic rationalism has now necessitated 'a new way to interact with environment' (Gates, p. 27), but it ignores deeper sources of understanding. Gates describes how, for Indigenous Australians (in Sydney as elsewhere, the land is documented in song-maps, equating topographic and mythic features in guiding human paths in life. Without any embracing cosmology such as is found in Indigenous understanding, these deeper sources are unattainable by modern Sydneysiders.

Sydney's Aboriginal history, of course, is not a thing of the past, nor do we presume to offer any detailed discussion of it here, except to say that there is a clear disconnect between 60,000 years of belonging to the place and 200 years of real-estate development. Sydney the city attempts little in the way of serious engagement with its past, and such efforts as it does make come across more like a class-room 'show and tell' than an integral and informing experience involving the two-way exchange of cultural insights. An Aboriginal troupe performing at Circular Quay, an art gallery exhibiting Aboriginal artefacts, or a lesson about Aboriginal history posted on a government website seem little more than token gestures and, at this point, inadequate to the needs of the (usually very) ill-informed visitor – or the local non-Indigenous person either, for that matter – who may be anxious for more than a shallow tourist engagement with Indigenous experience. Despite having expressed a significant interest in Aboriginal tourism, however, very many international visitors in 2000 left Australia without taking part in any Aboriginal tourism experience, whether it be 'rock-art tours, politically-themed art exhibitions, live theatre [or] stories from the Dreamtime told around a campfire'. According to the *Survey of Indigenous Tourism 2000*, this was due in part to an 'inability to find appropriate information' (Robertson-Friend 2004). The distinction made by Aboriginal Tourism Australia between 'authenticity' and 'authenticated products' is also important in establishing appropriate ways in which stories and other cultural material may be shared. Although the heterogenous uses of authenticity as a category in tourism and the extent to which it is really sought are currently subject to question (Reisinger and Steiner 2006), having an authentic experience is an important aspect of tourist expectations (Belhassen and Caton 2006). Authentic and appropriate use of musical heritage can promote re-signification and a deeper contemporary identification (Mason 2004). But with a presentation that, at least by comparison with the historical depth of Chinese and European tourism propositions, is shallowly rooted. Sydney remains historically undersold and juvenile in its political approach to its deeper history, a failing – shared by Melbourne and Brisbane – which shows up in its visual prospect.

One highly-placed respondent, who preferred to remain anonymous, bitterly lamented Australia's (Sydney's) failure in this regard after the extraordinary triumph of the Olympics. The unprecedented goodwill, positive international attention, characteristic Sydneysider optimism along with Cathy Freeman's emblematic triumph in the 400 metres – all perfectly timed to coincide with the dawning of a new millennium – were not translated into any political effort of reconciliation: the opportunity was missed, and missed badly.

There are several branches of the Eora nation. Sydney historian Denis Foley is from the northern area and is a Gai-mariegal man, but his relatives include Guringah. Other coastal clans include Bidgingal, Gadigal and Wangal (Foley 2001).[6] Indeed, the City of Sydney's official website, entitled 'Barani' (meaning 'yesterday') lists no fewer than 34 Aboriginal language groups in the Greater Sydney area. Much of the content of this website was compiled and written by an Indigenous author, and it was designed by a (now defunct) Indigenous multimedia company. However, at the time of writing (November 2006), the site seems not to have been updated for four years, which suggests that little in the way of a continuing or integrative relationship or commitment has been maintained.

The City of Sydney's coat of arms was re-designed in 1996; in its revised form a shield bearing stylized maritime imagery is supported by a coiled rope and a representation of the Rainbow Serpent with markings similar to those used by the Eora people. The intertwining of the rope and the serpent represents cultural harmony. The impression one receives is not of the intertwining rope and serpent, of cultural harmony, but of parallel, and rather superficially understood, layers. Given the intensity of history and experience, which Indigenous owners could bring to the place of contemporary Sydney, it is a shame that here –as, indeed, in the case of all other capital cities in Australia – there is so much yet to be imagined and done.

'Superficiality' is a term often used in descriptions of Sydney: it was mentioned by several of our respondents and it was highlighted in a recent *Sydney Morning Herald* opinion piece. The Sydney people currently celebrated, wrote author Steve Cannane, are 'chefs, models, celebrity real-estate agents and wine snobs … [T]he interesting people simply have left town'. In other words, Sydney has lost the very real and creative characters a great city needs and '[w]ithout them, [it] has become more like one of those silly B-grade celebrities we see in the media constantly. They might look beautiful, but, when you peel back the makeover, there's not much going on there' (Cannane 2004). A resonant opinion and one that is echoed in critical discussion of Sydney's imaging, where attention is drawn again to the city's 'glittering tart' typology, a place of 'overwhelming natural beauty', but with 'a narrative underbelly of crime, drugs and hedonism' (Simpson and Lambert 2005).

When hedonism, the shallowest of ethics, is the underbelly, we have a city that is, as Andy Warhol said of himself, 'deeply superficial'. It is perhaps appropriate, then, that the 'face of Sydney', the representative visual identity of the broader City of Sydney community, is a digitally layered composite photograph of 1400 Sydneysiders exquisitely superimposed to produce the collective male and the female faces of Sydney. Each night during Sydney's 2006 Art and About event, the composite faces and some individual component portraits were projected onto a tall building. The symbolism highlights similarities and differences in the 'City of Villages' – the local action-plans strategy that protects the characteristics of the various areas of greater Sydney (City of Sydney 2006). Reflecting media

---

6   Material in this section is partly based on a personal conversation which Donald's younger daughter, Ellen, held in 2005 with Mr Foley at the University of Sydney, to both of whom we are most grateful.

artist Nick Ritar's philosophy of 'audiovisual architecture for better living', and following in a tradition of art in public places that includes immersive video animations on architectural surfaces, these portrait-projections seek to 're-enliven and celebrate public space' and find micro-narratives that might lie behind those surfaces (Cicada 2006).

Living in the present sometimes means being superficial. It is as though to turn ones back on the past, that which is substantial and has depth, necessarily means embracing that which is, by definition, insubstantial and shallow. But perhaps it is rather a matter of being economically realistic. As one respondent, a Sydney marketing manager, put it, 'Sydney is not big on nostalgia.' And tourist attractions based on nostalgic themes have not been successful. This may change as Sydney, still a young city, matures. Aboriginal galleries and web exhibitions of old Sydney and its underworld can be found in growing numbers, and are becoming more integrated in mainstream tourism promotions. An increased appreciation of heritage is also becoming evident – at a local-, if not a state-government level. In June 2006 the New South Wales Government's plan to replace with new high-rise buildings the historic brewery buildings located in a unique precinct of laneways and public spaces that are important to the character of Chippendale met with vociferous opposition. Recalling the green bans that saved the Rocks from similar development in the 1970s, Lord Mayor Clover Moore said, 'As a sophisticated global city, we should have moved beyond urban vandalism' (Sydney Media 2006). She subsequently moved to have all buildings over 50 years old heritage-listed. This places an onus on many residents to make an official case for home renovations, weighing aspirational values against nostalgic values, and halting the urban vandalism that has blighted Bradford and threatens to blight Shanghai. Another reading of Sydney's presentism is that it is less conservatively attached to the nineteenth and early twentieth century than some other cities in Australia: it recognizes *from its past* the vertiginous challenges of a city on the edge of the ocean and at the cusp of Australian international relationships.

However one reads the city's obsession with the present, it seems that a maturing Sydney is beginning to appreciate its 'heritage'. Nonetheless, as with any wilful and bloody-minded adolescent, growing up will take time and involve much drama. A *Sydney Morning Herald* editorial considered the decision to rename part of Hickson Road as 'The Hungry Mile', in order to reflect the Sydney waterside workers' struggle for work during the Great Depression (29 September 2006). The Maritime Union of Australia (MUA) had campaigned for the new name to apply to the whole East Darling Harbour district: National Secretary Paddy Crumlin commented: 'Place names in great cities add value and colour if they seek to touch in a real way all of the elements of its history' (quoted in Davies 2006). The State Government, however, feared that the connotations of the new name might discourage investors. Critical of Government proposals to add historical stevedoring exhibits and 'sentimental propaganda installations', the *SMH* editorial suggested that renaming the district would suffice to preserve its heritage, and that developers would quickly see the asset value of a central waterfront location with a 'vivid, memorable and intriguing' name. To call Hickson Road 'The Hungry Mile' would be quite apposite in local terms, as the street is shared between the working Harbour-side, the Sydney Theatre Company, the Sydney Dance Company and élite apartments on the redeveloped

Figure 4.6   Man by ship (*The Hungry Mile*, 1953) (reproduced by courtesy of the Maritime Union of Australia)

wharves. The name 'Hungry Mile' belongs to an older set of shared catch phrases and mythologies, which structure the city's attention. For the Sydney waterside- and shipworkers (wharfies) the Hungry Mile was the equivalent of a daily Jarrow March for work, and the tramp of hunger was the subject of *The Hungry Miles*, a documentary made by the MUA film unit in 1953 (see Figure 4.6). Strongly influenced by Soviet cinematography, montage and didacticism, the film explains a 1950s dispute – workers were contesting 24-hour shifts, ticketed labour and a lack of protective regulations over conditions – with reference to the sufferings of Sydney wharfies during the Depression. The MUA – arguably Australia's best-known and feared workers' union – fought its most recent, and most contentious, battle in 1998, when the Patrick Corporation (a stevedoring and transportation company) and the Federal Government sought to improve efficiency on the nation's wharves by reducing workers' entitlements and the power of the MUA. The Union's website (www.mua.org.au/home/), a supremely sophisticated political noticeboard, has films and audio material relating to the 1998 waterfront dispute. The past is archived here, along with clues to the class warfare, post-globalization conflicts and mediated strategies of resistance, which have now attached place branding to the portfolio.

Is Sydney a city that peaked with 'the best Olympics ever', and had no development vision beyond 2000? Or is this an unfair, synchronic judgement? After all, Sydney's advertised proposition is in many ways a timeless one: a tolerant city offering consistent opportunity and lifestyle to anyone, a 'fair-go, level playing field'. Its 'flatness' is a promise of predictability and stability, which is arguably only a problem if unfavourably compared to the energy of the emerging megacities of China? The changes that Sydney *is* going through remain perceptually dominated by the classic icons that everyone knows, with only a gradual awareness of emerging alternatives. By Australian standards, Sydney is fast, brash and 'the big city': elsewhere people don't think or act as fast. (Similarly, an Expo official said Shanghainese in China are 'just like New Yorkers in the US. We walk faster. We work more efficiently. We dress better.' (Zhou 2003, p. 58) Our Sydney marketing director compared Sydney to other Australian cities as follows: 'It takes Melbourne people [a couple of drinks] to be the same as us ... sober ... and ... you really got to give Queensland people ... a line of coke until ...you know ... they are with us.' This is all very well, but it says little about Sydney's 'world-city' speed in comparison to that of contemporary Shanghai, New York or Hong Kong.

Domestic tourists may be expected to have more awareness of Sydney, but, even within New South Wales, the same challenge applies. One city marketer summarized the domestic perception for us as: 'Yeah, yeah, no, Darling Harbour ... We went there with the kids five years ago ...' and added that her marketing challenge was to say, 'Well, are you aware that Darling Harbour has changed completely?', or to help domestic tourists to understand that 'Newtown has an eat street' and that 'Surry Hills has antiques shops' and 'what was a dump ten years ago has changed.' The same inner suburb, Surry Hills, is examined by Fiona Adams (1997) through two 1948 texts: Ruth Park's narrative of its slum dwellers, *Fishing in the Styx*, and the Council's plan for a 'better city' such as Le Corbusier might have designed. Park's stories of characters and experiences are partly validated in her autobiographical writings about a factory's 'acrid chemical' smell and its 'pink-lit smoke ... poisonous and enigmatic, like so many things in Surry Hills' (Park 1993, p. 138). Adams says that the 'real place' and the 'unreal space' of a utopia envisioned by planners do not tally: the slum dwellers' views were not evidently solicited, and high rises in parklands would house them efficiently, sweeping away social class-structures and eyesore slums. For Adams, the real voices, the 'real' images of the city, did not intersect with the town-planners' vision, nor did the dreams intersect with the acceptance of real life. She suggests therefore that 'we have to find sources (images, descriptions, narratives) that *are* good for this essential task' (p. 94).

For another respondent, a tourism officer, the key proposition differentiating Sydney from other Asian cities was the interplay between the strong elements of the natural world and the bustling cosmopolitanism of the built environment, with imagery in which the harbour-side dominates. For the domestic market, however, he focussed on the range and variety of the forty-odd precincts (suburban areas), and the possibility of building a richer marketing proposition around their different visual signatures: the taller buildings and iconic parts of the CBD, the historical look of Parramatta and Windsor, the bohemian Newtown, the nestling harbour-side areas, the beach zones and the more rural suburbs on the approaches to rivers and mountains, natural edges defining places within Sydney. Just how varied the suburbs are becomes the more obvious as one travels unhurriedly between them, 'self-contained and village-like' due to their varied landforms (Hall 1988, p. 14), but in danger of being reshaped by planning around the tyrannical private car and higher-density living. The same tourism official expressed the view of many Australians:

[T]here is a lot of fear and loathing and safety and other concerns about coming to Sydney, because it is sort of a world city. ... [W]hat is exciting about the city is that it is an edgy, bustling, exciting place ...[W]hat is dangerous about Sydney ... well, it is dangerous. You could get robbed and da da da. You know, they are all both sides of the same coin.

In her description of Sydney's suburbs, Dina Zavrski-Makaric (n.d.) acknowledges that people do get mugged in Sydney and, although she cautions against using its lanes at night, recommends Kings Cross strongly: 'Every city that wants to call itself worldly has [its red-light district].' Yet local government has tried to sanitize the area, prohibiting new sex-industry businesses from opening and, notwithstanding its art-deco buildings and restaurants, putting its established character at risk. As Jeremy Johnson writes, the Cross is a 'national icon for sex and erotic behaviour ... [I]t will be a shame to see it fade away completely. The promiscuity in all of us will feel the nostalgia at the "Kings" extinction' (n.d., p. 63).

Sydney real estate may now have become virtually unaffordable. Nevertheless, there is no sense with Sydney, as there is with, say, Prague, that it's already too late to buy, or, with Shanghai, that it very soon will be. Indeed, the 2006 slump in property values revealed the extent of household debt and financial precariousness in which many Sydneysiders live. Yet, going to Sydney, whether it was in 1986 or in 2006, means finding a party pretty quickly, meeting fun people, drinking good coffee, seeing lovely places and experiencing terrific weather. There is work and opportunity, and, as the chances are that no-one will be rushing to take that opportunity it will still be there tomorrow. Sydney is 'laid-back' and is more than happy to be seen as such: if it started rushing around like Shanghai it wouldn't be Sydney. It may be superficial and beautiful, but the city understands this facet of its edginess. What is more, it celebrates it in its marketing communications. Comments made to us by those responsible for the marketing of Sydney were very clear about what messages they were choosing to send and what was on offer. Furthermore, analysis of the logos and other branding materials using visual art categories supported the view that Sydney was irreverent, free-spirited, fluid, beach-, sun- and water-themed, fun, bold and vibrant. While some critics remain snobbish about Ken Done's art, it *does* epitomize a design sensibility that is very Sydney – hedonistic, vibrant, outdoors, non-elitist, colourful and bold.

Despite disappointments that only hindsight can bring to light, the 2000 Olympics marked a highpoint for the perception of Sydney (and Australia) in its key tourist markets. In 2001, with a view towards future brand development and identifying the perceptual drivers of visitation, the Australian Tourism Commission (ATC 2001) commissioned a brand stock-take, hypothesizing that TV coverage would have moved perceptions (of Australia) beyond images of nature and landscape in the direction of something more contemporary. Overall this was achieved: as well as an increased awareness and reinforcement of the familiar brand attributes (i.e. clean, beautiful, friendly and laid-back), as far consumer groups across Europe, Asia and North American were concerned, the brand was given a broader dimensionality. For example, the Olympic coverage demonstrated more noticeably than before that modern, urban and professional cities co-existed with the Australian landscape, which was now seen to comprise forests, mountains and snow in addition to sea, beach and desert: 'What the world knows about Australia today it would not have known about for another ten years, if Australia hadn't had the Games' (Morse 2001). The Olympics also helped increase knowledge and awareness of the possibilities for participating in an attractive lifestyle with 'interesting Indigenous culture', a multicultural diversity of cuisine and an 'open, inclusive and welcoming' Australian people, all of which was likely to prove a powerful attraction for visitors in the future.

From a tourism viewpoint, however, the anticipated post-Olympics boom never eventuated. That the city 'felt flat' immediately afterwards is well-documented – after the high of the Olympics came the downer: twelve months later, on 11 September, any chance of leveraging the international recognition and positive image to Australia's advantage was destroyed with the Twin Towers. Although tourism and marketing chiefs we spoke to knew that the immediate post-Olympic period was the time to take advantage of the successful showcasing of Sydney. But, by 2003, the impetus had gone: as one Sydney marketing director put it, 'Too many boys worry about what corporate box they are going to sit in rather than getting off their arse and leveraging on the event.' The moment had been lost. Although all the world 'loved Australia' during the Olympic glow, it 'loved us less' after 9/11: so reviled was Australia's new image in Vietnam that one highly-placed Australian brand manager who was visiting there pretended to be from New Zealand. Good work was undone, and visitation numbers continue to remain essentially flat. For example, the Japanese interest in visiting Australia, which had doubled over the Olympic period – 63 per cent of those surveyed agreed, or strongly agreed, that they could see themselves visiting – has since declined. Market share has been lost, despite a recovering economy, and in March 2007 Japan Airlines' suspended its under-performing Brisbane-Sydney-Osaka route. Japan's dominant perception of Australia as 'a place to see nature' does not fit this market's preference to 'wander small alleys, …visit art and craft galleries and experience exotic cultures', and Chinese destinations, including Hong Kong, are benefiting accordingly (Cameron 2006).

A perceived lack of depth is an issue for Australia generally, and for Sydney in particular. Simon Anholt's view that the national brand is now 'stagnant' results from the lack of cultural depth and consumer education, particularly with regard to Aboriginal heritage. Speaking in 2003, a Sydney marketing director recognized the challenge: 'Australia has not bothered to promote culture … [Visitors to Sydney] don't have two months to go to the Northern territory … so we have to develop product.' Indigenous culture offers 'a commercial opportunity' and, after a brief comment in which he mentioned artwork, the same director talked more about 'new Australian culture … food and wine big-time … great chefs … bright young things, music, fashion, art, everything from the visual arts to performing arts, dances, poets, comedians … whatever … to try to give the city more layers.' But, as we write this, we can only suggest that the layers of potential in the oldest land with the oldest peoples among the newest cities and the newest technologies are yet to emerge.

… the Image of the City

Kevin Lynch's image of the city derives from an investment in spatial dynamics, based on the notation and formation of an ideal of mobility in which landmarks, iconographic features and paths are the routes and signposts by which urban social and cultural life is made good. As a result, Lynch values people as wayfarers and way-makers in urban space. If a path makes sense to a *resident,* whatever its status on the map, it is indeed a path. If people cluster, traverse or make rendezvous in particular places over time, then that place is a node. The process is greatly assisted or countermanded by planning decisions, but it gives value to people as the city's source of energy and motion. His ideas are borne out by our research, which found that residents either declared themselves to be metonyms of the city's character or else spoke with such personalized fervour of the city in question that they demonstrated an affective relationship both in their criticism and their praise.

Sydney is a city where locals are passionate about their glamorous, sexy, smug and beautiful home, and where the easy slurs cast by outsiders on the city as superficial are just as easily rebutted. Following a presentation of these findings to a large group of academics, the discussion was heated, with one born and bred Sydneysider recalling that 'its depth lies in its edges' – and that the edges of the city centre, as opposed to the more thickly populated Parramatta, used to be marked by hotels (public houses), and that everyone could make their way to the 'depths' by these landmarks of sociality. This memorial to a set of paths which are no longer as well understood or effective, points to an issue at the heart of Sydney's brand. While the central icons and landmarks are effective, at the same time they limit any affective depth which they may or may not afford to sojourners and tourists. This is underscored by the absence of any filmic identity, something which may, we suggest, be a clue to the flatlands of experience which newcomers report. Sydney's cinematic status is as an occasional offshore production centre, the home of *Superman* (dir. Richard Donner) in 2005 and *The Matrix* series before that (see Donald 2007; Goldsmith and O'Regan 2005). These are not films that get into the many hearts of a city with complexity both in its topography and population. Films that do exploit the Sydney experience are unlikely to prove financial successes on the international circuits. *Lantana* (dir. Ray Lawrence, 2001) is a Sydney film, but does not read as one to people from elsewhere. The same is true of *Little Fish* (dir. Rowan Woods, 2005).

Perhaps it is *Looking for Alibrandi* that most perfectly captures, for a teen audience, that mixture of local pride, Harbour views, ambition and ethnic rivalries and misunderstandings that make the city at once profoundly interesting and yet perversely able to ignore the challenges of difference by focussing on a multicultural 'survival' rationale. In other words, the city survives not by an agonistic embrace of the rough and tumble of ethnic rivalry, but by means of the 'food, clothes and lifestyle' form of multiculturalism which promotes mutual ignorance. This 'tectonic' technique, which has also been ascribed to parts of London (Butler and Robson 2003, p. 92), means that we like the idea of multiculturalism and we have some shared grounds of mutual interest, but that is as far as it goes in terms of real cross-cultural knowledge. But *Alibrandi*, while a very entertaining and locally exact case in point, is not an international film of any standing. Likewise, despite international status, (and having opening and closing sequences that are all about Sydney, with stills of the other side of a Sydney in which Hungry Mile men of the 1950s men waited for work (see Figure 4.7), Nicolas Roeg's *Walkabout* remains a classic film of the interior, and not of Sydney itself. Furthermore, how many tourists and visitors are sufficiently aware of these Sydney images to expect and anticipate them on arrival? Who actually knows to expect The Hungry Mile in the same way that they look forward, well

Figure 4.7   Men at wharf (*The Hungry Mile*, 1953) (reproduced by courtesy of the Maritime Union of Australia)

before arriving, to their first sight of the Opera House? (see Plate 1). An internationally known, cinematic Hungry Mile could be actively sought out – and missed if it were not easily recognizable, just as Hong Kong's Star Ferry crossing will begin to be missed since the 2006 closure of its most famous Central to Kowloon route, to make way for building on reclaimed land. But the affect of loss can only occur if the stories are told in the right places and for a global market. Thus the idea of Sydney is riven with contradiction. It is on the scale of the global world-city index, and yet comparable to the space and pace of Chengdu, an older capital in the far west of China with no film industry. It has a history that spans Indigenous occupation, invasion, settlement, Depression and the multi-ethnic populations whose arrivals over two hundred years have initiated new 'Australian' histories, which take shape in the new land, but which stem from global events. Alfred Hitchcock saw the point in *Under Capricorn* (1949), tying together issues of class and ethnic hatred between the English and the Irish, while at the same time making a passable attempt at capturing an idea of Sydney. The film was not shot on location and so does not really give a sense of what Sydney in the 1830s meant for those who lived there at the time. But, given the enormous numbers of inter-generational, regional and global tensions and passions that might be explored, even a studio set from 1949 is welcome. In sum, Sydney has a strong visual image, which emphasizes the edges and nodes of the waterfront, but it has not developed the deeper cinematic image which would give every stone and every building the promise of more stories and more adventures outside of George Street, that central thoroughfare from Central to Circular Quay, which for our sojourner-respondents comprised Sydney's single path from the Airport to the northern beaches!

Chapter 5

Chromatic Contours

Grey. The air, the buildings, the clothing, the faces, the mood. ... The States, France, Italy all felt modern. ... England by contrast was dowdy, rigid and, above all, unrelentingly *grey*, grey to its core (Levy 2002, pp. 3–4).

In the previous chapters we have noted that the consistency of a city's image may be described in terms of its cinematic ambition, its experiential approximation of a true place, even the solidarity of its citizenry. This chapter looks closely at the concept of chromatic place identity, with particular emphasis on the characteristics conferred through incarnation in the natural and cultural environment. As Michel Pastoureau (2000) has noted in reference to the ways in which it is culturally perceived, colour is understood by its mood, its tone and its literal 'consistency'. It is, he writes, 'of fundamental importance to know whether a colour is dry or damp, smooth or rough, mute or sonorous, joyful or sad' (p. 175). Pastoureau demands, therefore, that we take up colour as a phenomenologically profound aspect of our relation to the world. And, as others have noted in respect to the architecture, public art and geological tones of urban place, the depth and sensuous spectrum of colour perception is at the heart of its role as a recognized marker of spatial affect (Lenclos and Lenclos 2004).

Colour's impact is immediate and preverbal: up to 90 per cent of an initial assessment of a person or a product is based on colours (Singh 2006), and in semiosis it plays a role of the first importance (Kristeva 1980). Embracing both physical and psychological aspects, colour is a critical category in art, architecture and film. In numerous everyday contexts colour has been shown to draw attention to, associate with and evoke particular emotions affecting behaviour (Valdez and Mehrabian 1994): one's perceived appetite in restaurants may vary with décor, and email response-rates have been shown to differ according to variations in background colour (Zviran et al. 2006).

To those working to create cultural and commercial images of the city the colour spectrum is of obvious importance, not the least vital aspect of which is the capacity of colour to define the perceived nature of *space* and the cultural and emotional characteristics of *place*. The role of light, public art and display, urban colour schemes and the symbolic value of colours is clearly related to logos, civic and heraldic emblems, as well as to other designed representations of city identity. Similarly, film narration is dependent on colour to give stylistic form and emotional intensity to a specific narrative act in a specific location. As urban locations draw repeatedly on a particular colour or spectrum of colours, so the structure of attention for that city is itself coloured by that repetitive visual, perhaps cinematic, experience. Indeed, having viewed a number of 'old British films' a four-year-old relative once asked what it was like to live in the days when towns were black and white. He was not far off the mark. The greyness of London, described by Shawn Levy in his book about the swinging sixties when London invented 'cool' is arguably indelible for anyone who has seen London films in monochrome. And, much more recent and powerful London films, *The Long Good Friday* (dir. John Mackenzie, 1980), *London* (dir. Patrick Keiller, 1994); *Lock, Stock and Two Smoking Barrels* (dir. Guy Ritchie, 1998), while intensely coloured, remain wedded to a monochromatic view of London as a shady city – where blue skies, when they occur, are uncanny, even frankly misleading. The climactic scene in John Mackenzie's *The Long Good Friday*, a summer boat-trip on the Thames under blue skies, leads directly to a scene in which IRA gangsters capture and probably murder the protagonist and his wife. Meanwhile, for those who saw the Sydney film about the handsome charm of Italian migrants and the strange homeliness of Australian summers, Michael Powell's *They're a Weird Mob* (1966) could never imagine Sydney as anything other than shining and piercingly blue. The consistency of the colour's tone within a place-specific visual tradition is vital to understanding its spatial and emotional impact. Whereas blue is now often perceived in Europe as cold and clean – it is a favourite bathroom colour in England – it was thought of at one time, by Goethe in his *Theory of Colours* (*Zur Farbenlehre*), as 'beautiful and dynamic', and yellow as 'weak', 'cold and passive' (quoted by Pastoureau, p. 133). In *Weird Mob*, the affect of Sydney blue is the youthful and energetically optimistic reading that Goethe attached to it in 1810 and, with its implied critique of affluent snobbisms, that the French found in it as a Revolutionary colour in 1789.

So, colour operates as a dynamic and emplaced mode of distinction in imaging the city as a lived environment, as a site of historical memory, as a repository of emotional identity for the population and, arguably, as a key component in the identification of a sustainable brand. In these operations, colour is both manageable and magical, giving form to feelings, and accurately visualizing the cultural norms and topographical possibilities of people and place. It is magical in the sense that *how* colour works is still little understood, but the fact that it *does* work in certain ways in particular places, cultures and contexts is beyond doubt. First, then, this chapter relates basic concepts in the psychology and symbology of colour, noting, although without assuming any causal connections within a psychology model, its properties under different media renderings and its role in logo and brand designs.

Secondly, the chapter discusses colour as affect in the experience of urban residence, belonging and political articulation. As its opening point of reference, the discussion takes those colours nominated by visitors and residents as most representative of a particular city. The data we use for this discussion was collected in administered and online questionnaires, available in English and Chinese. Respondents were given a spectrum of colours and a shortlist of ten world cities, and were asked to make matches where they felt such were possible or sufficiently meaningful to them. The results were echoed in the long-form interviews with professional branding experts and filmmakers, where the colours of the West Pacific Rim were seen overwhelmingly to be red, yellow, blue and grey. For contextual explanations of these preferences we therefore look to the histories of these colours in both regional and imported semiotic systems, from the palettes of academy and social-realist works in Shanghai, to temple decorations in Hong Kong and hybrid Settler-Indigenous understandings of colour and form in Australian visual expression. The chapter makes a gesture towards the composite rendering of the form of the city through the chromatic scales of film, painting and architecture. We enlist both our own analyses of colour perception and such as have been observed and noted in different cultural traditions over many years.

The visual form of a city is complemented by its signature colour spectrum, which is at least partly understood as the perceived hues of the natural and built environment under particular lighting and atmospheric conditions. The cinematic equivalent of this is at one further remove, as filmmakers negotiate light, form and space to tell stories which are generically apposite to the city and which can be told with available technologies of cinematography. In an interview with us, the Hong Kong filmmaker, Derek Yee, noted that Hong Kong lends itself to night shoots because the daylight there is too bright for successful daylight work. Films from the Mandarin period in the 1960s are, however, more often that not shot in daylight and involve romantic sequences on the Peak, in Central and around the water's edge. *The Wild Wild Rose* (*Ye mei gui zhi lian*: dir. Tianlin Wang, 1960), a re-telling of the Carmen tragedy, is the best-known nightclub *film noir* of the period and it is shot almost entirely in dark interiors. Yet, one sequence does feature the light of an open window, offering the prospect of a summer's day and a view over the sea. This moment of daylight accompanies a promise of domestic happiness and passion fulfilled, as the heroine (played by Ge Lan) waits for the release of her lover. Even the classic Hollywood movie of Hong Kong, Richard Quine's *The World of Suzie Wong*, which dwells for the most part on the darkened fleshpots of Wanchai, opens on a perfect day on the old Star Ferry route between Central and Kowloon (see Plate 3). Perhaps what Derek Yee was actually explaining to us is that some contemporary indigenous Hong Kong stories are not especially comfortable in the quality of light which the city affords, that their forays into darkness, as in Johnny To's *PTU* (2003) or the hyperactive night-light as in the work of Wong Kar-wai and Chris Doyle, are necessary to express Hong Kong's complex, claustrophobic level of human occupation, industry and activity (including the criminal and the emotional). Sydney's cinema does not have a sufficiently nuanced repertoire of genres and types to compete with Hong Kong on film. Nonetheless, while the brightness of the sky in the innocent *Weird Mob* and in modern tourist advertisement lends the city its aura of perpetual summer, in *Lantana* and *Muriel's Wedding* (dir. P.J. Hogan, 1994), for example, the quality of the light is such that the tragedy inherent in both narratives almost evades us. From the perspective of branding, one might say that, while these films work hard to give a close reading of human life in suburban Sydney, they do so in despite of its signature colours and the formations of feeling and attention which that spectrum naturally evokes. The intelligence behind both films is therefore geared provocatively to a cinematic narrative that defies optimism: by means of delicately performed relationships and the exploration of exceptional textures and colours, both achieve in emotional and visual close-up to counteract the insistent optimism of the blue sky in the background. Muriel's ghastly but powerful leopard-print dress is a good example, or the lantana plant in which the body is found, or the multiple layers of relationship across class, in *Lantana*.

The literal categories of form (edge, line, position, scale, path and juncture) may be considered analogous to drawing in black and white: they are aesthetically complemented by the colours, tones and modal qualities that compose a fuller pictorial experience of the city and its affective and sensory qualities. Not only the environment, but also the skin colours and climate- or life-style-related fashion preferences of the people, confer local qualities that can visually characterize a place and suggest underlying determinants of brand. It may be a generalization to say so, but regional colour preferences vary, some cities being considered more stylish, and some markets more conservative, than others, as fashion industry forecasters and buyers know very well.[1] In Australia, it is a given, verifiable by a quick trip to the various capital cities, that (a) more white is worn in Sydney than in any other city, (b) Melburnians wear a great deal of black – but a smart black tending either towards designer chic or to the office, rather than a studiedly relaxed street-style orientation, as in London, and (c) young people in Brisbane tend to show a lot of flesh, while women often wear large floral prints. The weather in each city has something to do with these variations, but so does the political age of the states in which these cities are situated, and the ways in which wealth and social or cultural capital is measured and esteemed in very different milieux.

It is presumed, therefore, that associations go beyond the arbitrary or personal colour preferences of a product designer or individual consumer to a symbolic cultural referent, and engage larger frames of meaning. For example, in China colours are traditionally associated with compass-points, natural elements and other modes of classification (Eberhard 1986). South, fire and red, for example, are meaningfully associated in a cosmology underlying public interpretations, at conscious or unconscious levels. Colours have socially entrenched symbolic associations, and also imply meanings with affective value, such as 'happy, bright, angry, calm…'. But meanings and wider associations can vary between cultures. Named colour-distinctions are also both culture- and language-specific, whereas physical properties can be measured and defined to ensure a consistent understanding, as, for example, is the case with house paints or international fashion palettes. Familiar colour *names* describe a perceptually nuanced range of hues, and a colour's perceptual quality will be influenced by saturation, brightness and effects from an ambient context. So, colour, disembodied as a descriptive category, remains elusive. Nonetheless, colours can be formally described and located in a colour system, for example, the Natural Colour System (Hård 1969), or the Web-safe colour palette (Priester 2006), which, by avoiding the range of interpretations and nuances an ambiguous linguistic term such as 'red' can imply, allows a particular specification for trading purposes. This is also important in comparative research, and when colours are rendered using computer media, since different display properties may produce unintended effects. There is also an international language of film colour, which begins famously with

---

1   The International Colour Authority publishes colour forecasts biannually to inform industry buying. See www.internationalcolourauthority.com/index.html (Williams 1996, quoted by Crozier 1999).

Technicolour, and is exemplified by Douglas Sirk's signature palette of highly-charged, Mannerist paintings on film. Or, indeed, by the *shock and awe* that Abel Gance (amongst other early adventurers) achieved through the earlier craft of hand-colouring his epic film, *Napoléon*, in red, white and blue in 1927. That which filmmakers know by training and instinct may be learnt by visual communicators as they work to capture and give impact to place.

Charles Riley (1995) describes the difficulties of establishing any fixed code for colour, but shows that colour has qualities which suggest that it springs essentially from thought and is not simply a secondary decoration. Examining colour in philosophy, psychology, architecture, literature and art, he considers ways in which it has been used metaphorically, in specific discourses, to pursue an ideal, while its literal coding remains elusive and polyvalent. In his discussion of Jung's 1932 article on Picasso – not only did Jung paint, but both he and Picasso studied alchemy – he considers the artist's transition from his Blue to his Rose Period via a phase of Harlequinesque motley, a transition the artist refers to as an Orphean 'descent into the unconscious … With the change of colour, we enter the underworld' (quoted by Riley, p. 305). Blue is consistently primordial, elemental, pure, male and linked to the philosophers' stone and Krishna the Virgin. Pink, shocking or otherwise, is modernist, youthful, glamorous, avant-garde and stereotypically female or gay. Although transgressions may be identified, this links colours to a mythic ordering, embodying temporal and progressional qualities. Seductive as it may be, we would not support the circular causality built into such Jungian analyses of colour, psychology and art. Taken to extremes, such a position would leap to attest that such and such a colour proves such and such psychological conditions and pre-notates all art in already existing structures of attention approved by that schema. It presumes a necessary narrative of chromatic meaning within a hierarchy of consciousness. However, if analyses of this kind are taken as just one example of the way in which people attempt to interpret colour, and common and repetitive, symbolic and psychological associations with colour and fields of affective meaning have been put to the test, then we can claim that there are sociological grounds for stating that colour can have predictive effects. They will be bound up with a number of competing and converging conditions: culture, history, political allegiance, weather, topography and age, to name just a few. However, to the extent that not one of these factors is absolute, they will always be unreliable.

A considerable body of work has also been done on the universality of colour perceptions and the extent to which their specific associations inform their instrumental use in visual culture and design. Many qualities and associations hold across cultures in terms of majority preferences and symbology: historically studies have generally shown blue to be the most liked colour (Crozier 1999)[2] and

---

2   Ray Crozier considers various explanations for the consistent preference for blue in the general ordering of blue, red, green, violet, orange, yellow. These include, among other things, the relative neutrality of blue against extremes of judgement, its largely positive associations and its evolutionary significance. Using such preferences simplistically for public designs is problematic, as the critical response to Vitaly Komar and Alex Melamid's (1997) project to produce 'America's most wanted painting' suggests.

in a study of logo colours (Madden, Hewett and Roth 2000) similar meanings of 'peaceful', 'gentle' and 'calming' were found across several countries for green, blue and white clusters, consistently distinct from 'active',' hot' and' vibrant' for red. Although susceptible to multiple interpretations, as are other systems of signs, social and ethno-specific colour choices shape perception and interaction, but can also connote specific nostalgias, such as the colours of 1950s kitchen plastics or cars. Le Corbusier, for example, asserted the common belief that the effect of red on the body is stimulative, whereas blue is calmative and he related this to the specific appreciations of designed space (Davey 1998). It is possible, therefore, to maintain discourse on the qualified basis that (universally) an exemplary 'blue' is not an exemplary 'red', and for general purposes the distinction is sensible.[3]

Colours, Culture and Branding

Enhancing experience of spaces and suggesting both moods and modes of appreciation, colour satisfies narrative requirements involving both an emotional and a rational logic. As discussed in Chapter 2, branding, advertising and tourism promises have shifted ground, from the merely functional toward concepts of emotional resonance and personal engagement, entirely consistent with neuroscience affirming that emotion is the primary driver of decision-making to which reason must accommodate (Damasio 1994). Together with formal qualities, colour affects the visual equity of a brand, and may or may not be congruent with other meanings and understandings (Bottomley and Doyle 2006).

Colour is a primary associate of brand image, whether in a logo or generally as a visual property of a product, and can be enough on its own to signify a brand. This has encouraged efforts to trademark specific colours: Kodak yellow, Coca-Cola red, Cadbury purple, and other signature colours give a distinct 'sensory strike' (Elliott 2005) and their message remains, even if the product is 'smashed into pieces'.[4] Colour associations increasingly become part of a brand's meaning as hedonistic/ indulgent or deeper emotional choices are made, until they actively express a brand's meaning (Reay 1990). For example, the red and black of Alfa Romeo deliberately express the cars' values of passion and technology. Reverse associations can also occur: ever since the packaging was introduced in the 1960s, packets of Benson and Hedges cigarettes have carried connotations of gold and conversely, particular colours will bring to mind certain products through familiar association.

Particular colours are consistently used or strategically avoided in product marketing to connote culturally understood associations and values, both affective and symbolic. While colour is a salient feature of a brand's packaging, colour choice

---

3   We are aware of the ongoing debates about the universality or otherwise of colour naming, of culture-specific distinctions, particularly in the blue-green spectrum and of the controversy following the Sapir-Whorf hypothesis regarding the relationship between language and thought (see Berlin and Kay 1969; Saunders and Van Braekel 1997; Alford 2002). Our general concern here is to consider colour as a critical, rather than an empirical, category.

4   The concept of 'smashability' is Martin Lindstrom's (2005).

is also vitally important feature of its logo design. The logo is a visual mnemonic representing the essence of the brand, a recognized identifier that triggers associations in a wide range of contexts, media and applications. As Mark Rowden puts it, the intention of a logo is 'to stir emotion … [T]he best [immediately] gain recognition, promote a particular set of values and act as endorsement for the bearer' (2000, p. 143). Nowhere is this more strongly reinforced by colour use than in primary markets, where it is consciously used in design to communicate instantly and clearly, attracting the eye and partitioning information and space. While only part of a brand identity, logos summarize the central message to which others are tied and in doing so suggest an honest promise of a brand's underlying values to the pre-conscious mind. For example, the vitality of bright colours suggests 'youth and optimism', while darker tones indicate a historically oriented maturity (Rowden 2000).

Any projected image or symbol, however, is effectively non-existent until it is meaningfully recognized, consciously or subconsciously by its target recipient. Achieving the intended perception by the market (i.e. consumers and general public) is the mark of the success, or failure, of the logo design or a wider campaign. Despite this, Pamela Henderson and Joseph Cote note that there is 'no systematic research on the effect of design on consumer evaluation of logo' and logo selection is often only subjectively informed (1998, p. 14). Their paper, 'Guidelines for selecting or modifying logos', demonstrates that there is a transfer of evaluations from logo to the host brand and notes a need for further research into both the effectiveness of linkages between a logo and recognition of its host's identity and the influence of the choice of colour on this.

Although scholars are beginning to show an interest, it is principally in the work of practitioners that guidelines and understandings are described. Steven Skaggs (1994) discusses the requirements for effective logos, distinguishing between recognition and connotation aspects. Chief among the recognition requirements are memorability, visibility (i.e. ability to attract attention) and versatility (of usage). And the main requirements of connotation are that there is an effective identification association with the host; that the intended interpretation frame is evoked and that the logo is appropriately expressive of the desired feeling for the brand. This last aspect is crucial to the creative design of the logo and typically is realized by means of appropriate graphic design features such as typefaces, colours and shapes. Although colour is the most memorable visual component, different elements work together (Sandin and Äkäslompolo 2004). There needs to be consonance between colour, text and shape, together with a lively interaction with other aspects of context, all of which requires a more complex design effort than is implied in a series of prescriptive guidelines and the designer's own aesthetic. When the way in which brands are attempting to position themselves (primarily as functional or as sensory-social products) is properly understood, fairer judgements can be made regarding the appropriateness of colours and their congruity with intended image.

Colours, either represented or coded in images and words, have been theorized as important in forming memory networks,[5] and particular story contexts help form

---

5   There is a considerable body of theory and empirical work around the role of colours in signification and cognition. Julia Kristeva (1980) finds it both more profound and

associations with specific emotions at both cultural and individual levels (Rusinek 2004). Research conducted by Nader Tavassoli and Jin Han (2000) has found that, since reading logographs places greater reliance on visual processing, the capacity of Chinese readers to remember the colours of logographs is better than that of American readers to remember alphabetic words. It has been suggested that connotative colour meanings could well be more important in communicating a desired brand image in Eastern cultures.[6] Follow-up work found that visual identifiers integrated more memorably with Chinese brand names, whereas auditory identifiers integrated better for names in English (Tavassoli and Han 2002). This finding resonates with the noted relationship between the written word and the drawn picture in a range of contexts: visual narrative in Chinese political art, specifically posters of the 1960s-1980s (Evans and Donald 1999); modern advertising that is redolent of older forms of visual address; and the deeply saturated filmic worlds of Zhang Yimou and Wong Kar-wai. The work of DoP Chris Doyle, who has collaborated with both of these directors, is especially relevant here. Doyle has discussed his strategic use of colour on several occasions, perhaps most illuminatingly for our present purpose in an interview published online, in which he links culture, place, narrative and technological possibility in a fluid movement of aesthetic decision-making:

> [U]p to *In the Mood for Love* [2000], there's no red in Wong Kar-wai's films. For Chinese, red has a very special significance … it's a very auspicious color. In *Hero*, we [Doyle and Zhang Yimou] wanted …cultural associations … [W]e were choosing colors depending on the locations … [In one location] green was the choice … Fuji has an interesting green (Rodriguez-Ortega 2004).

In our own interview with Doyle in Hong Kong in March 2003, he was in more of a party mood and rather less reflective. However, the night-time tour around the clubs and streets of Hong Kong Central to which we (Donald and our research assistant Jeanie Wong) were treated was, as Doyle doubtless intended, an education in the logic of the colour of some of his films with Wong Kar-wai. At night the city is drenched in energy, libido and danger, but it is not necessarily best captured by the 'auspicious' red. At one point we were turfed out of a fashionable film-set bar, as whispers of a triad fight threatened. The colours that shape Donald's memory of that night are dark blue (for the outside) and green (for the interiors), both of them especially opaque. So, when reading brand theorists on their use of colour, it is worth remembering the hyper-affect of colour in 'real life'. To what extent does brand colour edge anywhere close to lived excess? What are the determining or limiting factors of its reach and impact?

Now, culture is known to influence consumer acceptance of designs, and branding researchers have considered the issue of globalization of package design

---

essential than the structures of dominant semiotic systems, motivating an understanding in psychoanalytic categories and relating to instinct, while representation codes for (learned) memory, emotional and colour associations have been explored in cognitive psychology by, e.g., Patricia Valdez and Albert Mehrabian (1994).

6   Tavassoli and Han's Chinese-American study is quoted, and discussed with further analysis, in Bottomley and Doyle (2006).

in relation to culture. Lianne van den Berg-Weitzel and Gaston van de Laar (2001) ask whether one single design communication is preferable to several different versions, each targeting a different market. Effects of product type and colour preference) were found to differ from culture to culture. For example, contrasting or brighter colours might be preferred in one market, but not in another. The authors duly conclude, therefore, that, if global designs are chosen, elements should be kept as neutral as possible so as to minimize disparities of cultural effect. This is the very opposite of what a filmmaker like Doyle would choose to do: in his work it is exactly the heady impact of culturally resonant and place-specific colour signatures that makes his cinematography powerful. *In the Mood for Love* (*fa yeung nin wa* (Mandarin: *huaying nianhua*), 2000) is an evocative love story about the visual eloquence of desire and moral restraint (Teo 2001), but it is also the most extraordinary advertisement for Hong Kong. The love story, shaped by the parochialisms of a small boarding house, but articulated in the exquisite contours and colours of the cosmopolitan dresses (*qipao*) of Maggie Cheung, is not cultural by virtue of its moral restraint – as is the case with David Lean, whose *Brief Encounter* (1945) reflects the austerity and morality of post-war England – but in the chromatic tones of its expression.

It is quite a leap, and possibly a reduction, to think of Cheung's numerous *qipao* in the film as a cinematic logo, although they certainly constitute a trope. Furthermore, they are obedient to Pastoureau's dictum that colour should have tone and texture, mood and emotional capacity: Cheung's *qipao* are either silky, or embroidered, or cotton-brisk. Pamela Henderson and her colleagues (2003) argued that Asian companies should use visual strategies to develop strong brands and recommended elaborate, natural and harmonious logo designs for creating positive affect and a perception of quality. Some years earlier, studying the psycho-semantics of icon perception, Robert Rieber's research team enquired into the ways in which cultural differences in perception might be applied to international communication and understanding. They found 'icons tapped deeper areas of emotional resonance [than] most verbal stimuli... [They are] the sort of thing dreams and myths are made of' (1989, p. 189). It goes without saying that Maggie Cheung in *In the Mood for Love* is very much the 'stuff that dreams are made of'.

With the globalization of tourism and other consumer markets and the need for tourist destinations to have a (regularly updated) international web presence, the construction and positioning of iconic images that are understood across cultures have become increasingly pressing issues. Whether the constant influx of international talent into the US and Hollywood has been responsible, or whether the narratives of the American Dream have proved especially seductive, is hard to say, but, thanks to film, America has succeeded in this task for over a century. The intensity of Technicolor used to reflect more realistically the complexities of the human condition, as opposed to the overbright colour filmstock used in the revolutionary realism of Chinese and Soviet films, seemed to touch chords the world over. From the hard ironies of director Douglas Sirk (born Hans Detlef Sierck) to the exuberance of the musicals of Stanley Donen, colour invested the America of the 1950s with a sense of real possibility. As the three sailors bound off the boat singing 'New York, New York' at the opening of Donen's film version of *On the Town* (1949), the blue morning light on the Hudson River is transformed into a set for homely recognition of the ordinary American-boy-meets-girl romance, but also a literal tour round the sights and lights of the city.

Whatever the nexus of reasons for the success of American cinema, the current imperative to communicate to a world-wide audience as successfully as possible is especially critical for global cities, whose perceived image, and credibility, depend on wide exposure. Any great city will serve various markets, and must service traditionally differentiated segments. Yet a logo must portray a consistent image that implies certain commitments, qualities and an underlying authentic substance. Conversely, it must be able to adapt and function effectively in multiple contexts, and to illustrate a variety of readings. In relation to global branding, Mubeen Aslam (2006) asks whether colour choices should be pan-cultural or culture-specific, and argues that, in light of the numerous cross-cultural associations of colour, a cross-cultural perspective on colour is indispensable to the development of global marketing strategies. This will become increasingly important as native businesses who understand their local environments become more competitive. Aslam relates colour associations, not only to atmospherics (a means of attracting customers into shops), but also – and in this her work relates to Tavassoli's – to synaesthesia, where affinities between colours and sounds, whether natural or induced, can be used powerfully in marketing.

For websites, a culture-specific strategy may be indicated: the Hong Kong Tourism Board's front page (www.hktb.com/login.html) differentiates the attractions it offers by key markets: some may be attracted to the food, others to culture and heritage, and the website access responds to this. Although this website family is substantially similar, analysis of one tourism site for Dalian, a trading and financial centre in north-eastern China, revealed major differences between the Chinese and the English versions. In Chinese Dalian presented as 'dynamic, open and interesting, [whereas in English it was] static and dull' (Holt 2002). Furthermore, on the Chinese website, bright and colourful title-graphics for 'Dalian' and the specific colour choices and typeface effects used in the supporting graphics and image-content, conspired to project the city as 'forward-looking [and] on the move', and this message was consistent with its external touristic promotions. The extra visual complexity was still evident in our informal analysis of this website in its updated 2006 form. Holt's discussion of ethnocentrism and communicative intent for the touristic imaging of Chinese cities is also relevant to the future of China's inbound tourism. Websites can provide an introduction, an initial sense of a place, and, as they become increasingly sophisticated, virtual tours can be a surrogate for a physical visit, encouraging greater physical engagement but causing the visitors to risk dissatisfaction if their expectations are not actually met. This suggests design approaches closely related to the particular market expectations to be served, domestic, global, tourist, investor and residents.

In Japan, extensive research (Kobayashi 1990) has identified the associations between colour combinations and key image words typically used in branding, such as 'romantic' or 'authoritative': work that has informed product design and manufacturing choices. These colour combinations are made to be consistent with brand values and may be used to project a brand proposition (romantic, natural), and to imply and underlying identity and its social-symbolic value. The semantics of colour were nowhere better illustrated than in Hong Kong in 1997, when all its post-boxes were repainted green and purple, thus symbolically shaking off the imagery of British pillar-box red.

Brand makeovers are required to dissociate from inappropriate, unrecognized or negative imagery. They might also be required if a competitor takes up their visual or emotional space thus altering a hitherto special relationship between the product and the market. More abstract logo designs prevent excessively narrow and local associations, and can also withstand the mergers, acquisitions and divestitures that large global concerns can face. Ideally, a makeover should give the impression of having evolved from an earlier design, often by the use of design elements which have already established the identity of the product in question. This was the case with two of Hong Kong's iconic brands: the Hong Kong and Shanghai Banking Corporation (HSBC) and the Bank of China (Huppatz 2005). Although global from its birth in 1865, the top half of the HSBC's original company seal featured the British Royal coat of arms, and, although a Chinese junk is visible in the bottom half, the image as a whole strongly connoted British colonialism. In 1983, Henry Steiner designed a new corporate image, the now-familiar hexagon of red and white triangles, so as to provide a more appropriate identity for an increasingly international audience. HSBC was established by Scottish businessmen, and Steiner's design consciously drew upon the Corporation's original flag, based on the Scottish cross of St Andrew.[7] The new design evolved from an established brand identity and, in an interview we conducted with him in 2004, Steiner described how he had approached similar rebrandings at the time of the 1997 Handover. In particular, banknote designs with colonial connotations were given fresh imagery with a distinctly local identity. The fact that this had passed virtually unnoticed was seen as a tribute to the success of the design's makeover.[8] The Bank of China's corporate image was reworked in 1992 by Chinese designer Kan Tai-Keung: beside the simple logo of a red square enclosed within a red circle (designed by Kan in 1981) he added the words *Zhongguo Yinhang* (Bank of China) in traditional characters and the English words in capitals below. In so doing, writes Huppatz, Kan functions in the manner of a *comprador*, 'a [nineteenth-century] Chinese merchant whose knowledge of both Chinese and Western commercial practices and culture made him an invaluable figure in the country's economy,

> aestheticizing the Chinese bank in an appropriate language for the global marketplace. The China evoked in Kan's logo is not the Communist China of the 1970s or early 1980s, but one constructed from an existing Western code of representation in which calligraphy and Chinese coins already have an iconic status (pp. 359–60).

---

7   Huppatz offers an alternative reading, in which the logo is seen as a folded out Chinese purse (p. 359). In view of contemporaneous developments, this is quite plausible, even though the designer may have had no such intention.

8   He could not say the same for Hong Kong's own image marketing, as we described in Chapter 3.

In an acute semiological analysis, Huppatz reads both bank logos as images that encode compressed historical narratives but which downplay local identity in favour of a globally referenced positioning.

Colours and Places

There are few more succinct ways of expressing the broad spectrum of associations that might exist between colour and place than in the phrase 'Lincoln green', which derives from the manufacture of cloth of this colour in the English city of Lincoln in the Middle Ages. In addition to geographical, we might describe the associations in this instance as historical and commercial. If we think, as we invariably will, of this as the colour worn by Robin Hood (a figure with links to Robin Goodfellow, the pagan god of the forest), we could add 'folk-mythological' to our list. Victoria Finlay (2002) traveled across the face of the earth, and beneath it, in search of the origins of colour, tracing the use of ochre, the first colour used in art, to central Australia and the 'ultramarine blue' paint used by Michaelangelo exclusively to lapis mines in Afghanistan. Okkes Gençay and his fellow researchers (2005) have explored the historical and cultural interaction between the people of Turkey and the colours worn by over 200 soccer clubs in various regions of the country. Specific football club colours were found to derive from the cultural symbolism of wars and other significant historical events, as well as from the signature colours of local onyx, forests and flora. In our own work we discovered a strong link between Brisbane (Queensland) and maroon, largely attributable to an informal tradition that held maroon to be the colour of Brisbane's major sports teams. In late 2003, however, it was officially proclaimed the official state colour (Queensland Government 2006). While the natural environmental colours of Brisbane – green, blue and yellow – also featured frequently in our study, the choice of maroon prioritizes a manufactured, cultural basis for association, and one that differentiates Brisbane from other Australian cities, where characteristic colours tend to be dictated by the natural world. Beijing – never as colourful as Shanghai – has declared its official colour to be grey, the tone of traditional Beijing architecture, of the Great Wall and the courtyards (*siheyuan*) in the city's lanes (*hutongs*). Grey also carries connotations of winter, of seniority and authority, is consistent with the city's generally conservative *jingpai* style.[9]

Tom Porter (1997) suggests that the colour of a city is a significant feature of its history and, while he does not advocate that a particular palette remain frozen, argues that, once identified, a colour map facilitates appropriate chromatic evolution. Environmental colour mapping is an urban-planning process pioneered in the early 1980s by Jean-Philippe Lenclos that aims to profile the chromatic identity of a place. In documenting this indicator of local identity, historically informed preservation, restoration and development, as well as colour pollution and built-environment cohesion, can be managed. Zena O'Connor (2006) develops this argument in a

---

9   This is associated with the Olympic Games 'Image and look' and is described in an official article entitled 'Introduction of the Colours: The Great Wall Grey'; see Olympic Games (2005).

case study in which she applies digital technology to the colour mapping of a small apartment building on Berry's Bay in Sydney.

There is also a diverse body of research in place-identity and characterisation that identifies the colours that *belong* to places by means of their natural, emergent or characteristic properties. The Indigenous Australian artist and cultural theorist Janelle Cugley (2000) has described how local 'pattern and colour [tell] a visual story, celebrating a local vernacular particular to site', and suggests that cognizance of this palette can feed back into built-environment and interior design in such a way as to reinforce a sense of home and belonging. Her work has inspired further thought by Western Australian artist Natalija Brunovs regarding the development of what in the title of her blog article she calls a 'palette for Perth'. Here in Perth, she writes,

> soulless developments don't provide a "sense of place" ... They'll just keep on tearing down our history, maybe a tokenistic plaque here or there, but no substance will remain. Soon there will be no earthly materials, just plastic surgery hollowness making up our landscape, our home. Perth will truly gain a dead heart, because these cold shapes won't reverberate our creativity (Brunovs 2006).

This comment could apply to many cities, which have not designed around their local chromatics or other characteristics. Alongside the Sydney sojourners' focus groups, to which we referred in Chapter 4, we also spoke with residents' associations. In these sessions, tellingly, most people tried – and failed - to express on paper the colour of Sydney sandstone. As Plate 5 shows, it is neither yellow nor brown nor beige, but offers an absorptive light and sandy tone which complements and soaks up blue.

Different physical qualities, natural and designed interplay (local stone, heritage paint colour palettes, quality of light, distinctive flora or natural earthtones ...) together with other atmospherics, such as smells, sounds, buzz or calm can evoke palpable moods and emotionally resonant experiences. Essentially grounded, as it were, in locality, these counteract homogenizing forces of globalization and imply distinctive brand propositions. These are instantly distinguishable by colour. It is very similar to the concept of terroir in wine-grape cultivation. Lois Swirnoff's work (2000) on the colour of cities illustrates one approach in this tradition. She photographed various cities and analyzed their light quality in order to produce a typology of *brightness* that distinguished cities as light (Santa Fe), shadow (Stockholm), or median. The angle of the sun and the clarity of the air affect the natural visuality. In a thoroughgoing study (2004), Jean-Philippe and Dominique Lenclos developed a method of analyzing the geography of colour, and used it to demonstrate the 'chromatic personalities' of regions and cities across the world. Combinations of light, geology, climate, local traditions and vernacular techniques all express distinction and 'contribute to the affirmation of a national, regional or local identity' (p. 15). Other work of this type looks at the traditional colours used in the built environment, often stemming from pigments that are available locally, or that may be acquired relatively cheaply. Zsuzsa Karman (2000), for example, has looked at the traditional colouring of Hungarian houses, and, mindful that this heritage is fast disappearing, urges that many of the facades of these houses be preserved, as their colourings, dating from the mid-nineteenth century and earlier, represent rich vernacular art that is of national value.

Bente Lange describes how cities may be characterized in the public mind by the dominance of certain colours. Her analysis of the colours of Rome (1995) and Copenhagen (1997) show historical patterns of favoured colours and how disharmony can emerge as a result of insensitive colour choices, as when twinned buildings, for example, are painted in clashing colours. Clare Gunn (1988) lists various US cities that have enacted ordinances instituting specified colour policies to ensure, on the one hand, that the visual appearance of heritage areas is preserved and, on the other, to designate other city areas that are specifically permitted loud signage and bright lights for the excitement of visitor and residents. In Sydney, conscious of the international significance of 'inappropriate developments overshadowing the Opera House', former Australian Prime Minister Paul Keating took an active interest in the development of the immediately adjacent area.

> The other thing I said to them was I wanted the materials to be in the colour of Sydney, which is Sydney sandstone, the same as the MSB Building [now the Museum of Contemporary Art] on the other side [of Circular Quay] and the Customs House. Now, I was diddled on that part of the deal. They went for a more greyish sort of stone. Architects are in love with grey. I don't know why it is, but they are. Grey and white are their favourite colours (ABC 2000).

Many historic European cities have also understood this issue and the threat to their image that uncontrolled colour decoration implies. Among several case studies undertaken in collaboration with the Sikkens Foundation in the Netherlands are those of Maastricht, whose current building policy extends its signature colour palette and use of natural materials beyond the historic centre to new suburban developments; and of Barcelona, where the colours of the entire urban fabric, as well as the historically appropriate restoration of the Rambla, are co-ordinated to retain their character (Sikkens, n.d.).[10] City councils have also commissioned colour plans from eminent colour consultants such as Werner Spillmann to give both visual variety and continuity to proposed developments. Spillmann's colour plan for the development of Kirchsteigfeld, a suburb 5 kilometres from the city centre of Potsdam, is discussed by Verena Schindler (2004a). The desire to preserve the artistic, cultural and nostalgic value of historic areas that are being demolished to make way for 'urban renewal', has provoked the town council of Yerevan, in Armenia, to undertake an extraordinary project: nineteen significant, traditionally-painted buildings in 'Old Yerevan', buildings that best represent nineteenth- and early-twentieth-century architecture and ornamentation, are all being rebuilt and relocated on one street. The project is looking to recreate in one area an environment with archways, backyards, old style taverns and the like 'to show the routine lifestyle and traditions of previous times', attractive both to international visitors and to the domestic market in ways that 'skyscrapers would never be' (Abrahamyan 2005).

---

10 The Sikkens Foundation website (www.sikkens.com/en/About/Foundation) carries descriptions of case studies conducted in a wide range of European cities.

Writing about the contemporary role of colour in the light of shifting ideas on gender stereotypes, Paul Overy (2005) writes that in modern architecture '[c]olour has often been considered the "feminine" element, which changes according to fashion. ... Form and structure ... have traditionally been perceived as "masculine" and enduring' (p. 122). Effectively downplayed in the architecture of much of the last century, ideas on integrating colour are now re-emerging in architecture and urban design globally (Davey 1998). Conscious decisions are being made about its communicative and expressive potential in city projects, and examples abound of colour policy being considered at early urban-planning stages (see Schindler 2004b). Anna Maria Fontana and Nora Matias claim that '[c]olor in the urban space fulfils an essential function for the identification of place' (2004, p. 29), motivating a localized study searching for chromatic identity in its architecture. Similarly, Emilia Rabuini (2004) describes how an old area of Buenos Aires, La Boca, the city's first port, recovered and strengthened its traditional identity through the palette of Benito Quinquela Martín, an important local artist. Quinquela's Palette was subsequently included in a law, enabling colour to be used to enhance the identity and value of other cities. Walking around the Mexican city of Guadalajara, one can see its historical memories are expressed and made emotionally present in the murals of Orozco, which retain a sense of poverty, oppression and the trauma of revolution within a contemporary, pleasant and well heeled city in Jalisco, one of Mexico's more conservative provinces (see Plate 6). Orozco's man of fire in his swirling reds and black sits in the centre of calm grey-blue, which is also the blue of suffering and immiseration.

Delegates at a 2004 symposium on China's Color Industry agreed that, as modern development continued apace, in most cities colour science was seriously lacking in city planning. Accordingly, the traditional beauty and architectural grace of Chinese cities was becoming obliterated by the colour pollution of advertisements, garish lighting, a kind of general 'visual spam'. Faced with similar problems during its rapid of development in the 1970s, Japan passed legislation to control colour usage (Zhang 2004). Similar regulations are already in place in many cities and regions, with moves afoot to preserve heritage colours and styles in others. But policy must be sensitive to the nature of the place, not just particular stakeholders. As French architect Michel Cler told a recent symposium:

> [D]ecorations on facades designed by foreign groups living in the city may lead to an insidious loss of cultural memory ... [T]he adoption of a [*sic*] historicism which consists of preserving or reconstructing a 'fake' ... appearance, can hinder new colour developments. Equally ... [m]ore and more cities are changing their colour mood and colour identity to fulfil the international visitor's exotic expectations. Thereby, the chromaticscape is expressly conceived and maintained not for citizens, but for visitors (Cler 2004).

In India, the symbolic and mood-affecting qualities of colour have been used, the authorities hope, to positive effect in Aurangabad, a city in the badlands of Bihar. In order to lift residents' morale and deter crime during a prolonged insurgency – the city is a hotbed of Maoist rebel activity – in late 2006 all municipal and private buildings were painted bright pink, a colour said to 'symbolise good mood ... and

foster communal amity and harmony' (Tewary 2006). The long-term effects of
this initiative have yet to be measured. A similar face-lift was given to Fremantle
in Western Australia in the 1980s. In celebration of an Australian victory in the
America's Cup yacht race in 1983, which brought to an end America's 132-year
winning run, the once-dowdy heritage port city was dressed up in pink and pastel
green, and made to look like some Mediterranean city by the Indian Ocean.
Fremantle is now a successful tourist destination with a distinctive identity and
feel.

Colours in the built environment can signal unifications, harmonies or
diversities, and can symbolically identify a brand, an identity or a value. Dutch
architect Rem Koolhaas (2001) considers colour to be a formal medium in
architecture, exploring many definitional possibilities of colour as an architectural
element that lie between crude application as a decorative treatment and a simple
property of material. He traces the trajectory of colour from paint's ability to
transform and get rid of history, through the multicoloured firework displays of the
late 1960s to the 'good taste' of the 1980s, at which point the subtle colours of real
materials such as granite dominated and 'entire cities changed their colour palette
overnight' (Koolhaas, Foster and Mendini p. 11). Describing various cultural
differences in the use of colour in structuring urban spaces, Giordano Beretta
and Yoko Nonaka (1999) contrast the signature architectural colours of Lugano
(Switzerland) with those appropriate to Kyoto (Japan). They discuss the ways in
which these colours interact with each other and with light, and go on to indicate
methods for achieving appropriate colour schemes with dynamic equilibrium.
They reference architect Kuma Kengo (1999), who describes the way Japanese
architects use colour 'to intensify the natural effect of light', and in neutralizing
structural form, make shape secondary to colour. This is in line with the Japanese
tendency to use colour 'to make things fade towards nothingness', as opposed to
the Western tendency to use it 'to bring extra life to things'. Colour, which can
of course either reinforce or subvert shape, thus increasing a feeling of distance
or presence, was brought back into architectural thinking by Le Corbusier, who
tried to find a system with a basis in a historical and natural standard (Davey
1998). Le Corbusier's work on colour keyboards, though relatively unknown,
provides colour associations with an order analogous to musical structures,
characterized both by 'a strong relation to Nature', and as an element to provide
space, 'introducing a new kind of fluidity between the inside and the outside'
(Schindler 2004b).

Lighting, both natural and artificial, is critical to highlight the colouring and
general appearance of a place, and is of course intrinsic to cinematography. Natural
lighting is required in the building codes of many countries – and the installation
of the solar collector in the HSBC in Hong Kong and the extensive use made of
natural light in the Shanghai Pudong Development's Bank are by no means the only
examples of architects' strenuous efforts to comply. The natural light of Shanghai,
it should be remembered, however, is filtered through pollution, and often presents
as pink or orange, producing a very attractive effect that visitors often comment
on. Indeed, it featured in the 2003 tourism promotion CD 'Seven Wonders of the
World' and related marketing, and documented by photographers anxious to record

for posterity a disappearing Shanghai.[11] A reviewer of Greg Girard's photographic work on Shanghai describes the pink sky as 'shockingly artificial, like the street scenes in Hitchcock's *Marnie*. Actually, the entire street looks like a film set. A large concrete building extends beyond the frame. In the middle of its wall, ten wire steps are embedded in the cement, leading nowhere and coming from nowhere' (Burnham 2006).

In discussing 'light branding' as a means of enriching sensory branding, Carrie Liu (2002) draws an analogy with the cinematographic techniques of, particularly, *films noirs*, that employ light and lighting effects as elements of the narrative. Having analyzed the role of lighting in the narrative of *The Natural* (dir. Barry Levinson, 1984), she comments on how architects create similar effects in order to make walking amongst the glass towers of contemporary New York a very different experience from walking amongst the stone buildings of a medieval town (p. 32). Light has also started to become a feature in the presentation of the physical city, and of its imaging. While architectural lighting has always allowed aesthetic display of the city nightscape, highlighting certain features and shading others, much more ambitious displays are now becoming common. Hong Kong's *A Symphony of Lights* is a nightly show of coloured laser beams projected onto buildings on both sides of the Harbour, synchronized to music and narration. Designed by Laservision,[12] a Sydney company, it unifies the architecture, but uses film to inform about culture and history. Laservision creatives indicated to us in an interview in 2004 that designing this was a major technical as well as artistic achievement. Previously, light beams on major buildings had been inefficient, uncoordinated and had caused considerable light pollution. Yet it was unlikely that coordination of lighting would be possible between competing companies owning skyscrapers, such as banks, since, for security reasons as much as anything else, their electrical systems would not be designed to interface with each other. Around twenty skyscrapers were involved, and it was necessary for the owners of iconic buildings as well as government representatives and other stakeholders not only to agree to work together and invest in the project, but also to allow the lighting of their buildings to be managed centrally. In addition to exterior lighting, interior staircases and corridors that were visible from outside needed 'aesthetic' lighting to be specially designed. The lighting was also customized to provide different displays during the day or when the show was not occurring. Colours and designs were able to be changed to reflect corporate policies: for example, the red and white triangles of the HSBC logo could be represented or connoted by strategic lighting on the HSBC building. Significantly, and surprisingly, the superior design,

---

11 The promotional video for the Shanghai World Financial Centre (www.youtube.com/watch?v=cPqCe9QnQM) also shows the building against a pink sky – with an airship flying through the hole at the top of the building! The bygone pink-lit smoke of Surry Hills in Sydney described so vividly by Ruth Park also comes to mind.

12 The founder of Laservision comes from a lighting background in television. In conjunction with the HKTB, Laservision has made several films, including *The Colours of Hong Kong*, which drew on the mythical five colours. They were also involved in the Sydney Olympics and Paralympics spectaculars as well as in recent projects in Shanghai.

with its innovative technologies for centrally and securely managing the lighting effects, actually reduced the electricity bills.

This kind of activity is a challenge to cinematic phenomenology. The light show is both a body in itself and a mediation of the body of the city. Shows seen from the Harbour in Hong Kong include a vision of the Harbour and, through secondary aesthetic engagement with the city's form, create structural participation in place branding, invoking natural colours of the day and the light-scape of the city at night. Where does contemporary city cinema achieve this 'wow' factor? Arguably in Christopher Doyle's works with Wong Kar-wai, and in Johnny To's dark and febrile meditations on Kowloon. But perhaps we should not leave this simply as an open question, but as a suggested category of critical appreciation and one that is necessary in order that film may play its part in capturing and moulding the structures of attention through which its cities will be viewed.

By comparison with *A Symphony of Lights*, outdoor lighting in Shanghai is relatively uncluttered: major tall buildings and stadia are lit in particular colours at night, with dark and lower-rise areas visually separating them. The roofs of residential high-rises are modestly outlined in neon trim, considerations of power (i.e. costs) as much as aesthetics being at the forefront of municipal thinking. Interior lighting also is an important aspect of the design of one of Shanghai's new luxury hotels: the JW Marriott in Puxi's Tomorrow Square illustrates how physical spaces can be signalled through light and colour to provide emotional effects. The lobby of this 60-storey hotel is on the 38th floor, so it was necessary 'to create a welcoming environment … for guests as soon as they enter the building and maintain a special environment for them between the ground floor and the [lobby]' (Lutron.com 2006). At each lift entrance, ready to offer an elegant smoothness to the guests' journey upstairs, stand the young, evidently Shanghaiese, hotel staff, females tall and dressed in embroidered orange body-hugging *qipaos* and men in smart military-looking Sun Yat-sen suits. The embodiment of style and city identity is both literal in their persons, but also implicit in the hotel itself and in the discreetly elegant luxury that it evinces. In its other spaces, lighting control allows different ambient atmospherics, such as a blue-tinted entrance to the pool complex on the sixth floor. The executive floor, of course, gives privileged access (via a hidden bookcase-doorway) to the roof and the lights of the city's newest skyscrapers on the Pudong. Shanghai's Westin Hotel also features an unusual staircase, this one a three-tiered cantilevered glass affair that changes colour, sometimes in time to musical accompaniment (Color Kinetics 2006).

Elsewhere in Hong Kong, intelligent lighting is shaping the experience of some shopping malls, with different zones displaying projected images, ranging from sports logos to Monet's garden at Giverny. A 'kidsworld' zone has images of ducks and lions, each accompanied by the appropriate animal sound (Martin.com 2001). Animation is also now part of the urban environment in Guangzhou: an underground business precinct, Cartoon and Animation City is 'equipped with the first national "interactive sensor and projection system" which makes visitors feel as if they are in a science fiction world'. Animation is a big local industry and this design proved commercially very popular: it was the first theme precinct to be given underground property rights and all the tenancies were rapidly let (*Guangzhou Daily*, 22 August 2006). Such developments increase the sensory nature of the everyday experience of the city, and in the case of Guangzhou they do so with specific fidelity to the city's local qualities. This is in line with recent ideas in urban design that suggest a sense of the city gained through involving sensory modes other than the visual.[13]

In engendering intense and resonant experiences, the visual form and other sensory qualities of a place brand become strengthened, and differentiated as an identity. Associations between sounds and colours can, however, be experienced as assonant or dissonant. Synesthesia is a neurological condition in which two or more bodily senses are coupled (as, for example, when involuntarily one hears colours, or tastes shapes). Although the condition is more common in younger people, creative artists often retain it into adulthood, taking aesthetic advantage of it to inform their designs, whether textual, visual or auditory. Synesthetic experience is related to memorability and to a certain sort of satisfaction of knowing a true experience. Although particular synesthesias are often unique to individuals, there have been many attempts in both science and art, supported by underlying mathematical and neurological explanations, to establish generally harmonious associations between, in particular, colours and sounds (Gammack 2002).

Shaping the interface between space (real or imagined) and surface colour can dissolve or accentuate boundaries, can change moods and perceptions, can act as a material, or present itself through interplays of light and materials such as glass. Priya Metcalfe (2001) has described how colour can gender space, relating it to Bourdieu's concept of *habitus* – in which an expected way of being in a place is suggested by physical and design qualities. The visual city, whether as immediate tourist spectacle or presented on film, displays powerful chromatic qualities that access feelings and resonances to reinforce (or diminish) its brand equity. The idea of a true place is echoed here in the presentation of a truly sens*ed* place, recalling Carolyn Cartier's 'touris*ted* spaces'.

Colour and City Branding

Colour is also a central feature of formal or representative identity: a commitment made in corporate or civic marks or heraldic identity, and represented in logos, livery and publicity. Blue is a dominant colour in the logos of many large corporates, and has also been found to be the most popular in the civic logos of Canadian cities (Mills 2005). As signs, these may function more or less strongly as representative of their referents, be more or less mutable, and more or less understood or accepted. In addition, particular feelings and qualities such as vibrancy, trust, contemporaneity, excitement or calm, may be conveyed by design. Such symbolic meanings 'increasingly form a basis for brands' positioning and differentiation' (Siguaw, Mattila and Austin 1999).

---

13 In Canada, Mirko Zardini curated an exhibition, 'Sense of the City', that ran from September 2005 to October 2006. It proposed 'a sensorial urbanism [challenging] practices that privilege vision over the other senses, thus editing out a whole spectrum of experiences and limiting both the designer's and citizen's holistic sense of the city' (Carroll 2006, p. 286). The book Zardini edited, *Sense of the City: An Alternate Approach to Urbanism*, was published in 2005.

Within the city too suburbs have distinctive colour profiles that contribute to their sense of place. Writer and filmmaker Kathryn Millard (1994) describes her Adelaide childhood street of ordered cream- and red-brick houses which, around the corner, turned into another street, peopled by Bulgarian market gardeners and defined in pink and black. She describes how the springtime jacaranda blossoms in Sydney's Penrith evoked specific memories and associations for its residents; how the extensive green in the suburban gardens of Vietnamese migrants is 'reminiscent of cities in Vietnam', but also how the restricted palette of 'heritage colours' valorizes an Anglo tradition to memorially eradicate the visual history of later migrants' colour preferences. Noting colour's role in evoking lost and imagined homelands, and defining a sense of place, Millard suggests that 'colour can and should reflect the distinctive histories of particular suburbs' (p. 186)

In our own work on branding the city, an understanding of the colour associations and their propositional rationale complements the formal drawings of the previous chapter to provide access to the emotional and sensory experiences applicable to understanding a city and its particular qualities, such as those located there, residents, visitors or other stakeholders, perceive them to be. Following the use of colour as a 'quest for essence' (see Riley 1995), we aimed to use colour categories as 'markers' for the city's brand. If colour can bring to the surface some essential qualities of a place, ideally complementing any verbal rationalizations of salient aspects of a city's identity, then distinctive colours allow distinctive branding. If the colour is 'right', then memorable portrayals of character and designed artworks may follow. While city branding goes beyond its role as destination imaging for the tourist market, colour-infused city imagery is likely to be commonly agreed and to reflect the most visited landmarks of the place in question.

When eliciting affective responses, or associations that may be non-conscious or implicit, an indirect approach is preferable (LePla and Parker 1999). Projective methods, which contrive to ask questions of interest in ways that elicit values and thoughts unattainable through direct questioning, have long been used practically in forming design briefs for corporate identity. Projective methods use metaphors as a mean of accessing an issue – asking, for example, 'If this company was a chair, what would it be like?' – and organize discussion around chosen examples intended to elicit values that are, say, 'comfortable' or 'old-fashioned', which it may not be socially acceptable to confront directly and which therefore might not otherwise be disclosed. Such methods have the advantage of avoiding preconceived wordings or other biases on the part of the questioner leading the response, while at the same time avoiding the need for the respondent to be particularly articulate on matters of which they have limited, or an emotionally coded, understanding. They also use the fact that, while people may find it hard initially to articulate a preference or its rationale, they can recognize it when they see it. We thus approached the topic of colour and city branding by way of a series of indirect explorations.

Martina Gallarza, Irene Saura and Haydée Garcia (2002) provide a review and taxonomy of methods used in the literature on destination image. We took a mixed-methods approach, using qualitative methods (interviews and free elicitation) as the first stage. This is in line with the typical rationale for destination image research (O'Leary and Deegan 2002), and ensures that the attributes elicited are genuinely identified by the stakeholders and participants themselves and in no way intimated to them by the researcher. Our aim was to identify key and current attributes that could potentially be used in subsequent quantitative, experimental studies or in a convergent interviewing approach by researchers into city brand. We were looking for a way into the structures of attention that allowed people to see, hear, smell and move in the city space.

Cinematographers and tourism-marketing professionals were interviewed on the general themes of city icons, colours, nostalgia, everyday life and aspiration. A separate group, of international and domestic tourists, completed a questionnaire addressing their favourite cities and the colours they associated with Sydney and other Australian cities. Pilot studies involved small convenience samples of international travellers, internationals resident in Sydney and native Australians, all of whom completed their questionnaires in Sydney during early 2003. Made up of more less equal numbers of males and females, and aged from 18 to 27, they had all travelled internationally. For the sake of the particular focus of our research, versions of the same questionnaire were also trialled in Hong Kong and Shanghai, rather than only in Australian cities. These sources were analyzed for significant content directly related to the conceptual themes identified, and descriptive statistics were used for the most prevalent words and thematic concepts that occurred in the responses. They also served to ensure that the questions were understood meaningfully and to elicit some of the recurring attributes of the sort market researchers might use. Although we were not attempting quantitative brand research, which might have involved grouping our respondents into categories based on demographic variables, we were interested in identifying a sense of the salient perceptions across a broad range of stakeholders since city branding requires such breadth.

Many respondents considered Sydney among their favourite cities and, when asked, 'If Sydney was a colour, what would it be?', most of them, thinking of the sea and sky, said blue, although individuals mentioned several other colours along with an associated rationale. Adjectives most frequently used to describe Sydney were 'vibrant', 'beautiful', 'busy', 'friendly' and 'multicultural'. The colour blue and the descriptive words were less frequently used to describe other Australian cities, for which a common adjective was 'boring'. These categories were also compared with the interview transcripts from senior Sydney tourism marketers, who were asked other specific questions in relation to narrative constructs, colour and logo. One marketing manager said, 'We have … a colour palette … [T]here are certain colours you can look at and you know that is not really Sydney, [but] you can write the word Sydney in any font, any colour and any type size …' Another said, 'The colour of Sydney is blue and gold … the blue water and the blue sky … But the yellow is the sand and the sunshine.' Another (New South Wales) marketer emphasized the slogan 'Feel free', connoting friendly welcome and tolerance, and the blue and the green in the logo's colour palette. The tourism logos feature stylized designs of the Harbour Bridge and Opera House, the accepted and recognized icons, and emphasize those colours. The words 'beautiful', 'vibrant', 'multicultural' and 'friendly' also appeared frequently throughout the interview transcripts of other individual respondents. In response to the question on colours, one interviewee, an architect of the national brand, immediately described Sydney as blue before pausing, then suggesting green and another colour that was harder to name but might be cerise (for vibrancy). His first descriptor for Sydney, however, was 'male',[14] though 'flashy', 'showy', 'superficial', 'welcoming', 'vibrant' and 'optimistic' were also mentioned – perhaps sub-characteristics of the Sydney male? His staff had been directed to watch *Billy Connolly's World Tour of Australia*, as that TV programme by the Scottish comedian, he said, 'really got it'.

The extent of the similarities in our responses suggests a consistency of perception across a range of stakeholders. Moreover, attributes identified in Sydney's own previous market research and used promotionally also appear to be stable. These also include themes of youth, fun, vibrancy, contemporaneity and friendliness, all of which frequently occurred in spontaneous responses, and suggest that these brand elements are both substantiated and successfully conveyed. Beauty, nature, sunshine and beaches, as well as human-made icons, were also recognized and appreciated. Both the anthropomorphized traits and the physical attributes are identified with the people in Sydney and help define the city's personality and attraction. Although ten respondents nominating 'blue' may have had ten different shades of blue in mind, our later studies – which we shall report presently – required choice within a specified palette of representative colours. Even then, any such palette could only be a sample of the possible colour space, and will always be subject to such things as the effects of uncontrolled ambient light, for example. But, for present purposes, establishing that Sydney is predominantly blue rather than red provides a general basis for an understanding of this marker of its brand essence. Parallel studies with Chinese respondents in Shanghai and in Hong Kong clearly established red as the dominant colour marker for Hong Kong, attributed to its vibrancy and energy, although red is also signalled in the symbolism of *feng shui*. The colour of Shanghai emerged less conclusively, but in pilot studies it evoked pinks, oranges and browns, colours at the red end of the spectrum, though there were occasional mentions of green and blue.

Having established that our questions made sense across key demographics and elicited largely consistent perceptions, we proceeded to use an online survey in order to examine the perception of cities and their underlying attributes across a wide section of society. Again respondents were asked the colours they would choose to characterize specific cities. To avoid any problems arising from interpretations of the *name* of any colour, respondents were given a reference palette (Gerritsen 1975). This palette, used widely in art theory, has twenty colour swatches covering a spectrum of hues, including white, grey and black.[15] Follow-up questions then

---

14 Readers will recall Charles Riley's observation that '[b]lue is consistently primordial, elemental, pure, male and linked to the philosopher's stone' (1995). Although colour can gender places, we did not emphasize this in our analysis. Shanghai, on the other hand, is a 'female city', suggesting that particular emergent identities can summarize a constellation of identifying attributes.

15 Hue is what is commonly understood as colour, i.e. the quality of redness, blueness etc. Although some formal colour systems distinguish achromatic values (e.g. white, black) from hue, using greyness as a dimension nuancing the hue, identifying distinctive basic colours was seen as the relevant characteristic here and thus white, grey and black were included as elementary colours like any other.

sought reasons for the respondents' choices and probed them regarding the city's visual qualities generally.

The online survey was conducted between November 2004 and January 2005, and attracted responses from all over the world. However, only those respondents based in Australia are reported here, since numbers in other demographics were too statistically small to permit of any meaningful comparison. No significant differences between Sydneysiders and other Australians were found, so these were aggregated and 127 usable responses were analyzed. This affirmed that Sydney was considered blue, with the top three choices corresponding to the three blues offered in the Frans Gerritsen palette. Yellow came a distant second, and the number of times red was mentioned was negligible. Conversely, Hong Kong was clearly seen as red; orange was mentioned reasonably often, but blue very rarely.

Although there is inevitably some blurring of nuance, for the sake of analysis the colours can be put into broad groupings, including linguistic groupings, so as to enable general comparisons to be drawn. Thus, for example, the familiar rainbow spectrum, or the eleven basic colour terms of Berlin and Kay (1969) can be mapped onto Gerritsen's palette in such as way that all the blue responses regarding Sydney, for example, are treated as one. This would mean that Sydney was blue for 90 of the 127 respondents, the overwhelming majority. The results for Hong Kong were less clear-cut, but over half the responses were in the relatively narrow orange-to-red section of the spectrum, corroborating the results of our previous studies with a larger sample. Once collapsed into these broader categories, chi-square analysis showed that the patterns observed for Sydney, and also for Hong Kong, had frequency distributions that were highly unlikely to be due to chance. For both cities the difference highlighted by chi-square analysis is highly significant suggesting that Sydney is meaningfully associated with the colour blue, and Hong Kong with red (Donald and Gammack 2005). As with the pre-tests in both the English and Chinese versions, Shanghai had a similar profile to that of Hong Kong, again with a range of responses based on what was significant to respondents, and most responses were clustered towards the red end of the spectrum (Gammack and Donald 2006).

In determining the reasons for these choices, the open questions in the survey and those in the relevant pre-tests were analyzed for content. Positive assessments, adjectives such as 'clear', 'clean', 'vibrant' and 'beautiful', appeared in respondents' descriptions of the visual qualities of Sydney, together with frequent references to the Harbour, the sky, and natural environment. Many respondents also commented upon the quality of light, and some noted that, despite the busyness of a city, there was a relaxed, laidback quality about being in Sydney. These descriptors relate to the water, as much as the built city. Sydney is 'a water city', even for those who do not look upon it: 'What remains constant is the water' rather than the city, with waterfront suburbs held intimately together by the Harbour, each with its own character shaped by its landform and organic history, charming but with irregular roads tracing the paths of old creeks causing 'impossible traffic conditions' (Hall 1988).

When asked for a rationale for a particular choice of colour, respondents were far more ambivalent in their descriptions of Shanghai than in their stories about Sydney and Hong Kong. Sydney's blue was consistently associated with the water, and the sky's natural light. For our Chinese respondents, red typically symbolized 'vibrancy', 'life', 'warmth', 'passion', 'China', 'prosperity', 'sunrise' and 'keeping busy', and was clearly associated with Hong Kong. For Shanghai, however, it was a rather different story. Certainly, red continued to imply prosperity and 'increasing strength', but Shanghai's 'deep and mysterious' features also suggested blue. A few noted that the reality of pollution and local bureaucracy combined to make Shanghai 'brown'. One female Chinese respondent currently living in Shanghai proposed an 'ever-changing rainbow colour', because no single colour was adequate to describe Shanghai. Although Sydney was occasionally described as 'a rainbow', due to its presumed multicultural quality, by comparison to Shanghai both Sydney and Hong Kong were chromatically consistent, Sydney essentially because of its natural environment and Hong Kong its buzz.

A logo analysis confirmed the values generally identified in our other studies, and that the national tourism brand architecture in which Sydney plays a role is consistent. Much of what is said of Sydney (that it is 'blue' and 'laid-back') can also be said of other places in Australia, and the colours blue and gold, reflected in the Sydney's tourism marketing and logos, are often used in Australia generally to reflect the dominant physical characteristics of the country's coastal destinations. Slogans such as *feel free* represent Australia's (here New South Wales) expansive skies, water and coastlines and also connote the laidback, tolerant and friendly attitudes for which Australia is recognized. This sense is reflected in the appreciation of those charged with marketing the city, and reflects in the colours identified with the city, as our logo analysis showed. The fonts used are generally fluid, sans serif and unfussy, as if handwritten or drawn in sand. The dominant colours in the logos of the marketing bodies for both Sydney and New South Wales reflect the water, beach, forest parks and red inland, and make visual references to the shape of the state, the Opera House, the Harbour Bridge and the water. Again blue is dominant in many logos, suggesting that Sydney has a coherent sense of its attractiveness and the values that underline its brand.

Some of these logos, marketing images and colour choices were consciously aligned with the 2000 Olympic Games, developed for the Paralympics. They were the outcomes of deep reflection by many people on the relationships between colour, brand and presenting the city. Deliberate colour choices were made by the Sydney Organizing Committee for the Olympic Games (SOCOG) design team and by professional colour forecasters whose job it was to predict, three or four years in advance, the colours that would be relevant in 2000.[16] The program manager in charge of the Games' image describes a palette using the three colours of the logo, a vivid, deep, Sydney blue, red, and a rich, golden yellow, together with 'hot colours like rubine red, lime green ... deep purple and vivid orange. White and silver were used, but gold was deliberately excluded from the identity, being seen as not a new millennium metallic colour'. Pastel shades were also eschewed entirely in favour of bold, partly because of Sydney's quality of natural light, but also to capture the feeling expressed in a migrant's comment that 'she'd left the pastel colours behind her and

---

16 See Van de Ven and Cox (2000), an edited transcript of an interview with Jonathan Nolan, Program Manager, Image, SOCOG, on the look and image of the 2000 Games, conducted by Anne Maria Van de Ven and Peter Cox, Curators, Powerhouse Museum.

[had come to] the world of shocking hues'. These remarks express a common feeling for many first time-visitors to Australia. The silver and white were seen in relation to architectural resonances, silver having the feel of nautical architecture and white making visual reference to the extensive work of the Philip Cox group, such as the Sydney Football Stadium (among other sporting venues) and the Maritime Museum and Exhibition Centre at Darling Harbour. Also, from a practical perspective, blue is considered the best backdrop for filming movement for TV audiences. In the event, four blues were used, selected in conjunction with the Sydney Olympic Broadcasting Organization, but all vivid (Van de Ven and Cox 2000). These considerations show an awareness of the natural light quality, the media requirements and the perceived psychological qualities of colour in presenting a city.

In a parallel strand of the same research, we tested the chromatic metonyms for global cities as well as Australian state capitals. Several cities had some chromatic characteristics – Hobart, for example, was a deep green, Perth a yellow – but were not without some consistent variations and contradictions. Sydney was somewhat unusual: it was invariably seen as simply, utterly, blue. Some respondents questioned whether the palette that we provided gave them the right set of blues to choose from, but the vast majority chose from that spectrum nonetheless. These results have given us pause for thought. Blue holds connotations of cold clarity, of fear, of endless horizons. How does blue work with the path through Sydney's suburbs? How could it warm an audience to the perfect autumns, or the dense wet heat of summer? How could it distinguish the energy and loneliness of cultural difference, or the settled parochialism of suburban loyalties? How might the chromatic character contribute to the complex narrative of arrival, striving, and stasis which characterize Sydney's urban character? The blueness of the city has been on display in recent cinema and television – an eclectic list of recent films might include *Looking for Alibrandi*, *Finding Nemo* (dir. Andrew Stanton and Lee Unkrich, 2003) and the ABC-TV film *Hell has Harbour Views* (dir. Peter Duncan, 2005), although it is not evident in dramas such as *Lantana*. Nonetheless, the relationship between the perception of city residents and visitors on the one hand, and professional knowledge in a particular industry on the other, is not always one of perfect consonance. We wonder, for instance, whether some tourists visiting Sydney in search of a particular life-style, clarity of colour and iconic simplicity are disappointed when they arrive and encounter them? We may speculate that blue characterizes a quality of light and spirit that is not often described in the narrative films of mainstream Anglo-American story-telling, but which may be reflected in other worldviews, particularly those of Indigenous story-tellers. Indigenous philosophy, art and sense of space all locate Sydney in a much broader context, a more complex vision of land and occupation, with a more developed, and less modern, spatial-temporal expression of the meaning of human experience (Muecke 2004a).

It may well be that such stories and the chromatics of those stories are waiting to be told anew. The blue skies and waters of *They're a Weird Mob* announced both the corruptibility of affluence, but also, and this seems to have been the popular view, the possibility of happiness within a prototype of contemporary European notions of multiculturalism. The critique is starker five years later in *Walkabout*, the film that captured a sense of Australia for many Britons in the 1970s and which still accuses

Australia of its deepest failure. The glimpses of Sydney blue in the sky, the Harbour views and the swimming pool do not speak of optimism. In the closing sequence – as the audience is left with the depressing memory of David Gulpilil's on-screen death and Jenny Agutter's adult slump into aspirational domesticity – the blueness of Sydney is shockingly intense. But this blue says little about Sydney per se: it is a harsh shade of blue that recalls the blue of the walkabout skies. It turns the city into an urban metonym for the imagined hinterlands, at the same time implying its inability to match the emotional scope of the bush.

The colour of film is dictated by a number of factors and derives from a number of sources: the perceived colour-scape of the locations used, the emotional palette of the filmmaker, the film-stock and styles of filmmaking current at the time of the film's making. These are just some of the reasons why a film looks the way it does. Cinematographers and production designers are also hugely influential on the relationship between colour, space and narrative. Cao Jiuping, who worked as production designer with Zhang Yimou on several films – including the red-saturated *Shanghai Triad* (1995) – famously used the dye mill in *Ju Dou* (1990) as an emotional space in which colours are used to literally paint the emotions of the characters on screen. So, colour on film is not a realistic translation of the colours seen with the naked eye, but rather the result of stylistic, affective and aesthetic negotiations between the eye of the filmmaker-as-artist, the narrative in hand and the emotional weight that a place and the atmosphere the filmmaker is seeking to create might bring to bear on the imagination of the audience. Thus, our discussion of city colours is an acknowledgment of the genius of the cinematic city in prefiguring the marketed city and in taking up the power of topography, urban character and human affect.

Chapter 6

Shanghai: World City?

[Y]ou can't get too sentimental about Shanghai, a place built, like Bombay, on the back of the opium trade (Mishra 2006, p. 3).

The structure of attention required of visitors to contemporary Shanghai is, as Panjak Mishra recently noted, not sentimental. The city was the major port for the English opium traders in the nineteenth century, the site of the Shanghai strikes and massacre in 1926, and the victim of Japanese invasion in 1937 and occupation in 1942–1945 (Wakeman 1996). Sentimentalism is out of place in this most historically experienced of cities. Nonetheless, the structure of attention that prevails in making sense of Shanghai entails a complicated relationship with its various pasts and its future, which borders on something that might be misread as sentimentalism, but which we term 'pragmatic nostalgia'. In this chapter we shall discuss the way in which the image and narratives of Shanghai as a city combine to produce a complex place-brand which, despite the obvious success of Shanghai as a global city of the world's imagination, has a number of inconsistencies. We shall also suggest that, while these inconsistencies may be irritating to purists in the tourism industry, they are the grist to Shanghai's enduring fascination.

The favoured past of Shanghai is that of the 'modern girl' in a *qipao*, the feminine city of exquisite Russian refugees, decadent European expatriates, Chinese gangsters and Marlene Dietrich in *Shanghai Express* (dir. Joseph von Sternberg, 1932). These are clichéd character sketches of the city, but they resonate powerfully with the international imagination. Dietrich, in the person of Shanghai Lil, continues to produce affect in cinema-goers worldwide as a persona for Shanghai. One *baidu* blogger, writing on the popular Chinese blog site in 2006, even went so far as to suggest that Zhang Yimou and Gong Li, director and star respectively of *Shanghai Triad* (1995), are the new Sternberg and Dietrich! (Post. baidu.com n.d.) This is a compliment to the Europeans as much as to Zhang and Li. Meanwhile, the new modern girls of Shanghai pick up in their fashion, their assurance and their ambition, the elegance –all with just a hint of desperation –of all these pasts. Theirs is a work of pragmatic nostalgia, using the fetish of past glamour to create a currency for an aspirational present. Shanghai has its physical landmarks: it has Pudong and the Bund, but it also has the walking icons of its women. If cinema has done nothing else for Shanghai, it has convinced the world and the city itself that they are, simply and utterly, superior to any others. Shanghai woman is the epitome of modern China, and the image of 1930s is the enduring foundation of the magnetism of Shanghai's identity.

A number of internationally successful films in the 1990s (some better than others) have reiterated the point. Notably, it is the non-Mainland directors who film the feminine aspect of the city's historical image with most subtlety. Chen Kaige's *Temptress Moon (Feng Yue*, 1996) and *Shanghai Triad* are possibly less interesting, perhaps because they assume that Shanghai's louche status will be adequately personified in the contemporary star, Gong Li. If she has indeed assumed the Dietrich mantle, then they may be correct. However, the films lack the immediate and slightly dangerous glamour of the 1930s film, which was responding to an idea of Shanghai that was current and febrile. In the 1990s, there is no specifically 'Shanghai' currency in Gong Li's exquisite aplomb, although as ever the actress deploys her generalist Chinese *femme fatale* and White Queen of Chinese film to elegant effect. But Mainland films offer scarce visual or narrative questioning of Shanghai's moral identity, or, in the case of *Temptress Moon*, of its effect on the code of morality to which its playboys subscribe. The city is presented as a museum of depravity and a convenient backdrop to a period pastiche. We would argue, therefore, that these films deploy Shanghai much as *Mission Impossible II* (dir. John Woo, 2000) used Sydney, as a brand without an emotional core. The Taiwanese Hou Hsiao-hsien's *Flowers of Shanghai (Hai shang hua*, 1998) and Stanley Kwan's *Centre Stage (Yuen ling yuk / Yuan ling wang*, 1992) work harder to seduce us. Perhaps, as outsiders, the directors themselves feel the need to get to know the city on its own terms, rather than rely on the stereotypical positioning of Shanghai as 'depraved' within Mainland popular discourse. These films acknowledge the idea that Shanghai becomes the richer in cinematic vitality and energy, if the city is made an active player in the small tragedies that unfold on screen. In *Flowers*, the women are not all played by Chinese actresses, just one sign that their power as women is not assumed as a national certainty in the way that Gong Li's screen persona demands. Hou's characters are urban creatures in the emotional tradition of Dietrich and Ruan Ling-yu's modern girls, their survival dependent on their location in the brothel, and on the interest taken in them by fickle clients, also played by an array of trans-national stars, led by Tony Leung. The city is not used on-screen as a painted backdrop in these latter films, but is rather a palpable off-screen presence to the extent that characters are fleshed out by our understanding of the period, and the place, in which their lives take shape. *Flowers* and *Centre Stage* draw complexity from the audience's knowledge of the city's future and the likely fates of its protagonists, and in the process make the city itself seem more vulnerable to its own history.

Apart from these these subtle intimations of future loss, Shanghai's post-Liberation (1949) revolutionary inheritance is largely elided in its presentation in popular film[1] and in tourism guides, except where that story may be meshed together with glamorous architecture or intrigue dating back to the 1920s. Thus, Madame Song Qingling's house on Xiangshan Road, a comfortable European-style residence with French gardens, encapsulates the symbolic leadership of her husband Sun Yatsen. Likewise, another beautiful house, the site of the founding of the Chinese Communist Party in Xintiandi district, is now a rather expensive restaurant.

---

1   We mean the 'mainstream melody films' made for domestic consumption, which deal with Shanghai as a heroic zone (Wu Jing 2006).

Shanghai's role as a highly political city is assumed and known by those who live there, rather than emphasized to its sojourners and guests. As David Goodman (1981, p. 146 ff) argued – while that history was still unfolding – Shanghai has been home to powerful factions (not least the Gang of Four), and in the 1970s was a centre for the education (p. 136) and 'sending down' of politically active young people to foment radicalism in other less engaged provinces. It has also been the city most prone to industrial strikes (Perry 1994), and the place where the Nationalists had to subdue the workers as a key strategy in undermining the growing strength of the CCP in 1926 and 1927. An awareness of these violent political histories is crucial to understanding the city's current entrepreneurial energy, aspirational vigour and pragmatism. One cannot get too sentimental about Shanghai, but you do need to get a little bit intimate with her if you want to spend time with her. In 1949, in a speech to the Second Plenary Session in which he outlined the Party's intention to set up government in Beijing, Mao made a strong attack on 'the interests of the bourgeoisie in Shanghai' (Mao 1949, p. 9). He then introduced his famous remark about 'sugar-coated bullets', clearly linking Shanghai (a potential rival to his seat of power in Beijing) with decadence and potential class treachery, and setting up a justification for Party purges in the following decade: 'However, the flattery of the bourgeoisie may conquer the weak-willed in our ranks. There may be some Communists, who were not conquered by enemies with guns and were worthy of the name of heroes for standing up to these enemies, but who cannot withstand sugar-coated bullets; they will be defeated by sugar-coated bullets' (p. 11).

These remarks were taken up in subsequent years to strengthen an image of Shanghai as potentially dangerous, essentially corrupt, and needing to be managed with force where necessary (Lü 2000, pp. 32–5; Lewis 1965, p. 133). Mao's aggressive characterization of Shanghai was prompted by the same ambivalence towards the city as that shown by nationalists in the 1920s strikes. Nevertheless, despite this continuous history of radicalism and confrontation, often provoked by those outside the city itself, a sense of 'history beyond pragmatic nostalgia' does not structure the attention, which the city evokes in its cultural address to the present. Indeed, the idea of the *present* in Shanghai seems almost unnecessary, given the pace and scale of development and change. The future has always already arrived, and more of it is always expected. Others have noted Shanghai's nostalgia for the 1930s (Wu Jing 2006), but that is not sufficient. Nostalgia is not simply an attachment to the past; it is a necessary anchor for the future. It is *because* Shanghai develops so quickly that it must be as nostalgic as it is aspirational. This pragmatic nostalgia answers the need for a fulcrum of urban identity, bound over to hold the centre while all else moves on.

If Shanghai's image depends for its coherence on a preferred version of its past, so its scale of chromatic identity is similarly oriented towards the feminine and the nostalgic. Despite its credentials as an ultra-red political hub, its redness is subdued. Shanghai is a city with pink skies, a forgotten brown aspect – 'an old brown riverside city', Paul Theroux called it (1989, p. 105) – and a cinematic inheritance firmly ensconced in black and white. A city of extremes and extreme contrasts, Shanghai has nurtured both radical leftist filmmakers (Du 1988; Fu 2003; Li 2005; Pang 2002) and romantic film stars, whose personal beauty and dramatic love-lives rivalled the extravagant elegance of Hollywood in the 1920s (Harris 1997; Meyer 2005; Zhang 2007). Indeed, the triumph of allure over ideology rather undermined the political radicalism in some of the best leftist films of the 1930s (Berry 1988).

> If you are lucky enough to fly into Shanghai in the late afternoon, up along the coast from Hong Kong, you will be treated to a remarkable sight. As the sun fades to twilight, the pink and then purple light reflects back up at you, first off the East China Sea, then off the Huangpu River, and finally off the 1,000 dappled mirrors of Shanghai's exploding commercial district (Ramo 1998, p. 64, quoted by Wu 2006, pp. 296–7).

In colour, the pink skies of Shanghai look beautiful and support a new iteration of the feminine. They are eloquent in Wilson Yip's *Leaving Me, Loving You* (*Dai sing siu si*, 2004). Yip's film, a 'break up and make up' romantic comedy, is not only not very comic, neither is it a great Shanghai movie. A slow narrative dims the star qualities of Faye Wong (who plays a party organizer) and Leon Lai (a doctor). Where there are tensions in the film's plot, they are undermined by the absence of sexual buzz between the main protagonists. However, the film is extremely successful as a paean of praise to Shanghai the international city. This is achieved by shameless exploitation of the city's landmarks, fashionable paths and river edges. Several sequences include a panorama of either the Bund or Pudong, while characters hang out in the Huaihai shopping strip, occupy residential blocks in the French quarter, pop up on mega-screens and eat in funky restaurants. Faye Wong's character lives in a series of brightly coloured apartments which remind one of Amélie's flat in *Le fabuleux destin d'Amélie Poulain* (dir. J.-P. Jeunet, 2001). These not only reflect the hyper-modernity of Wong's personal style, but also make a textual gesture towards Shanghai's claim to be the Paris of the East.

Yip traces the passing of time in fast fades of the skies at night and morning, the lights of the city seen across the river, and the blinking of progressively fewer lights as the day dawns. This is *the view*, Shanghai's projection of itself as a world city in full colour. The view from élite restaurants in the higher buildings on the Bund and the executive suites in the best hotels all rely on this electric lightshow for their credibility. It is this which legitimates Shanghai's visual status as Paris of the East and as the world city with the liveliest future on the West Pacific Rim. But, we should also note that sometimes the view can be appropriated by a more overt articulation of the political ethos which underpins the city's development. Fifth-generation filmmaker Peng Xiaolian's mini-epic *Once Upon a Time in Shanghai* (*Shanghai jishi*, 1998) narrates the trials and heroics of a reporter trying to inform the US authorities of Chiang Kai Shek's corruption at the end of the 1940s and witnessing the arrival of the Communist troops at Liberation. The film opens with a panorama of modern Shanghai, as the hero, now much older, returns to the city and recalls his own leap in time from the late-forties to the present.[2] While this aerial shot of 'the view' reiterates everything in Yip's film at one level, it seeks temporal resolution, not so much in nostalgia, as in a reminder of the city's contemporary formations. The

---

2	The film's historical sequences were shot, not on location, but in the replica of 'old Shanghai' at the Shanghai Film Studios.

film was made in 1999 to celebrate the fiftieth anniversary of Liberation, and here at least the last shot of the Pudong skyline shows the cityscape against a deep red sky.

'Small Potatoes'

In *Leaving Me, Loving You*, the postman and the traffic warden are two secondary characters, who operate like avatars in a virtual tour. They pop up in street-scene after street-scene to encounter the leading characters of the doctor (Leon Lai) and his girlfriend (Faye Wong), who break up, and then make up, with the postman's help. In Kevin Lynch's schema these characters would be the 'walkers' on the city pathways, the people who use landmarks to guide them from one everyday activity to another. Wong is more of a *flâneuse*, a little self-aware in her journeys around the cool spots. She is a busy party-organizer but, despite her work schedule, she is herself a mobile icon, the modern woman of the world city. The traffic warden, on the other hand, is good-looking and well-dressed and as such is also an embodiment of Shanghai's brand attributes, but she and the (rather less glamorous) postman operate more at the level of a sub-brand. Or else they are the little people, the ones that make the city work, the 'ordinary heroes' and 'small potatoes' that McDull represents in Hong Kong. They are, if you like, the parochial reality beneath 'the view', and a gentle reminder of Shanghai's non-international population. There are, of course, other films that deal with ordinary people in Shanghai. *Suzhou River* (*Suzhou he*, dir. Lou Ye, 2000)[3] manages to portray an everydayness in its otherwise extraordinary main characters (a video-maker, a drifter and a girl who might also be a mermaid) that conveys the ambivalence of city folk in a truly world city. They are ordinary small potatoes but, as they walk the city and occupy its dirtiest corners, they embody its other aspects too: modern, tough and good-looking survivors.

The emergence of Shanghai's urban identity in the early part of last century is traced by Lu Hanchao (1999), who is not interested in 'exotic Shanghai' as much as in its alleyways and side streets and the people who lived there, away from the main streets. These are Shanghai's 'little urbanites', the peasants who formed most of its population, and whose everyday lives still provide the economic base for the internationalized superstructure. Lu argues that place and kinship did not immediately produce a sense of belonging to the city. Despite their families having resided for several generations in shanties and communal *lilong* or *longtang* (alleyway structures comparable to Beijing's *hutong*) (Fu, M. 2006), people did not produce a Shanghai-ness or even sub-urban communities. 'The city' was, for many, just the few blocks of urban village around their home, a city-equivalent of the provincial villages from which workers had migrated. Bryna Goodman's (1995) study of Shanghai between 1853 and 1937 describes the countervailing influence of incomers from other provinces, whose retention of their own native-place identities, cuisines and practices shaped social life, and hindered the development of a unified urban identity. It is Lu's contention that, while native-place ties helped establish trade, the people of

---

3   A good plot summary and analysis of the film's strengths is given online by Clode (2002).

Shanghai were 'not always ready (to identify with) the city' (p. 50), but rather made their way in it, tracing, one imagines, the same paths that constitute its cinematic edges today. If we are seeking out brand descriptors from Shanghai's world-city image, we might choose 'style', 'elegance' and 'international'. If we were to look to the small potatoes, we should discover another, rather different, level of description. Adaptability, resilience, mercantility and enterprise are common characteristics in migrants and survivors, so might also serve as appropriate descriptors for Shanghai, given its history of migrancy from within and without China. Yet, Lu and Goodman's observations suggest that, while these may be more general starting-points for the emergence of the city's character, they are still not satisfactory markers of its elusive identity.

Lu goes on to make the very useful point that the very idea of a city differs in crucial aspects between Europe and China. The European idea of cities as superior centres of culture is markedly dissimilar to the Chinese tradition that blurs urban and rural boundaries, and formerly even devalued the city. Furthermore, he notes that categories such as 'citizen' (*shimin*) and 'corporate civic identity' were largely alien to the city's administrative character in the years of the Treaty Port system, although Shanghai had begun to challenge this by the early twentieth century. Lu's caveats are themselves to some degree generalizations. Beijing *was* a superior centre of *wenhua* (Chinese culture) with regard to China's opinion of barbarian challenges from beyond the borders of empire, and the southern cities of Kaifeng and Suzhou have been characterized in art and poetry as places of cultural significance and beauty as well as operating centres for imperial administration and trade. So Lu evidently regards Shanghai as a very particular case: 'The Chinese have seen Shanghai in many different ways, but in the final analysis there are only two views that count: the city is a symbol of economic opportunity to be seized, or it is a trap of moral degeneration ... to be shunned or condemned' (p. 11). Lu is not the first to have observed this *ambivalence*, but he may be unusual in believing that these two rather different views of the city may be held simultaneously. As we point out later in this chapter, Shanghai's moral degeracy is in part a Communist Party fiction, itself indicative of the uncertain relationship between Shanghai and 'China' as represented in the dominant power systems emanating from Beijing. Shanghai's otherness is extremely important in understanding how even Chinese residents may both belong to and be distanced from its urban personality. It is not very helpful to a brand designer to be asked to slip in 'ambivalence' as an attribute, but an ambivalent approach to the city's feel and style is perhaps what has been responsible for some films working better than others in the recent Shanghai canon.

The small potatoes in Shanghai's story have been witnesses to its rapid contemporary transformations and, as we have suggested, are guides to both its past topography and the shape it may assume in the future. They are also ambivalent carriers of both 'industry' and 'moral depravity', adaptive innovation and nostalgia. They are provincial migrants who may not speak Shanghainese, but who in the days of silent cinema would flock to the cinema, brought together by films that put their chosen city before them on the screen. They are embodiments of the political energy of the recent past and 'brittle fashionistas' of the brand new present tense. Likewise, Shanghai's rapid physical transformation does not lend itself to a 'static analysis'. Describing its urban infrastructure development, the architectural writer Darryl Chen sees the city's architecture as 'the physical corollary of the paradoxes and conflicts in current political dogma, a turbulent modern history and an inherently flexible and resourceful people'. In Chen's view, Shanghai offers relatively few opportunities for *flâneurs* and, indeed, it is the committed walkers, the small potatoes, who must make their tortuous pathways through a rambling modern city that has not quite taken control of the shape of its undoubted destiny. Legibility, Chen argues, is not yet apparent in the financial districts and 'engineering-led planning [leaves] little opportunity for an urbane pedestrian environment' (2003, pp. 31–2).

Brand and World Expo

> Hong Kong …was a small entrepot port when Shanghai was a world city (Alley 1973, p. 274).

Shanghai's brand, even more so than Hong Kong's, is in a state of visual transition. If it is not exactly illegible, it has an ambivalence that is partly attributable to the character of its past/s and partly to the headlong top-down planning for its present rate of change. In the years between Liberation and the present era of Reform, Shanghai appeared rather nondescript, the city essentially serving as an industrial centre with a penchant for political factionalism. The time when it was best known for opium, foreign intervention and vice was long past and in any case this former identity caused it to be stigmatized as a capitalist degenerate (Wong 1996). Even witty essays on the cruelty and contrasts of Shanghai were few and far between, and it is worth noting that it was in 1949, in the immediate aftermath of Liberation rather than in the Communist era itself, that the Kunlun Film Studios first brought the cartoon tales of children's hero Sanmao to the screen in *The Travels of Sanmao* (*San mao liuliang ji*, dir. Zhao Ming and Yan Gong). As Yomi Braester has argued (2005, p. 418ff), the film complied with the CCP's use of cinema to conquer Shanghai, then portray it as a liberated city, its public spaces claimed by parades and celebrations of the new regime. The film's performative energy and humour, however, sets it apart from other propaganda efforts – which Braester discusses in detail (p. 420ff) – and also from later remakes such as *Sanmao Joins the Army* (*San mao cun jun ji*, dir. Zhang Jianya, 1993), in which the boy's face is spliced into documentary sequences showing parades and quoting propaganda films of the 1949 Liberation Movement. Despite the transitive role of Sanmao in creating a benign, Communist version of Shanghai,[4] the character survives into the present as a charming example of the ambivalence of which the city is capable, but also of its ability to shift gears and regenerate. In 1927, Shanghai gained a huge clock on the Bund, a pinnacle of urban confidence demonstrating the city's commitment to scale and self-promotion

---

4   Braester's main argument, however, is that, in the 1950s especially, Shanghai was vilified in film images, as the CCP sought to manage the city's wayward autonomy from Beijing.

(Wasserstrom 2006).[5] In 1985, Shanghai had only one skyscraper (Harvey n.d.), but over the past twenty years has energetically used architectural statements and scale in order to again position itself as a major international city. The iconic Oriental Pearl Tower (see Plate 7), completed in the mid-1990s and thousands of skyscrapers and other construction developments have altered Shanghai's physical image quite dramatically, while the commercial nature and sponsorship for these developments have reinforced its national and international role image as China's trading hub. In his own evaluation of Shanghai's architectural capital, Wang Tianyun, then Vice-President of the Shanghai Film Group, contests Chen's analysis:

> The development planning for Shanghai has moved from disorder to order, from basic to advanced, from singular to plural, from backward to vanguard. It has made a flying leap in terms of quality and quantity. The Bund now has over 3000 buildings, which gives a wonderful base for cinematography. It is excellent for film. But is also has relics from previous periods. Genuine *shikumen* buildings in Chedun were used in the recent epic *Deng Xiaoping 1928*. A director, Chen Kexin, recently came to us in Shanghai to shoot some historic architecture. He used Shenzhen for the modern parts and Beijing to capture a sense of ancient culture.

Shanghai has also consciously addressed its brand proposition, particularly in its successful bid to host the World Expo in 2010. A World Expo can be considered something of a coming-of-age event, a debut on the world stage, and like the Olympics, it provides the opportunity to showcase a city's maturity. The Shanghai Expo is expected to attract 72 million visitors, more than half of which number will probably come from China itself (World Expo 2003, p. 58). The bid required consideration of the style that would successfully present the dominant idea of the city. The success of the bid presentation has prompted the acceleration of city development in order to substantiate that proposition. This effort coincided with the emergence of a consciousness of city branding in China and elsewhere. In the case of Shanghai's case, the question of how a city could be a brand required immediate and pragmatic address.

Professor Zhou Hanmin, Deputy-Director of the Bureau of Shanghai World Expo Co-ordination, details the branding involved in relation to the unique values and characteristics required to win a competition between cities (Gilmore and Dumont 2003). Displaying a sophisticated understanding of branding and of public relations, Zhou positions Shanghai as a traditional part of China that is also open to the West, a window to and from the world, absorbing the best foreign influences. Shanghainese are used to reinventing themselves, and have an entrepreneurial spirit that combines playing 'in accordance with the rules, but with a creative flair', not only leading culture and fashion but also making their city the obligatory place to establish a business in the Chinese market. This approach directly competes with that of Hong Kong, and employs, as essential elements of the brand, positive descriptors such as 'clear sense of roots', 'opportunity to think freely', 'creative drive', 'pioneering spirit of freedom' and 'absorb foreign advancements'. In an interview conducted

---

5   Jeffrey Wasserstrom is a noted historian of Shanghai and his very useful article offer a synoptic view of development and scale on the Bund.

with the project team in 2004, Wang Tianyun remarked that these attributes might be due to Shanghai's actual position, well to the south of Beijing and the seat of imperial power, but close to the opportunities for trade and international commerce:

> Shanghai is a city at the mouth of the Yangtze River, it is in contact with the Yellow Sea and so it has an open consciousness. This isn't just due to the threat of imperialism. It was there before the 1840s and the Opium War. It came through maritime trade. People here have always had a consciousness of naturally standing on one shore and looking across the ocean to the side where the monsters lived, where people have three eyes. So therefore Shanghai people have a special bravery and curiosity. I feel the city has this, a kind of special spirit contained in Shanghai's geographic location and historic crux.[6]

Wang's thoughts and Zhou's plans are, unsurprisingly, in tune with public pronouncements and publications about the city's bid. A series of essays published locally in 2003 as 'Expo 2010 Shanghai' put forward Shanghai's essential brand attributes and underlying characteristics. A professor of urban design, Zhu Yunmao iterates the strong and by now well-accepted mantra that a world city is also a cultural hub. He argues that this is the key area for development, if the Expo is to make sense beyond 2010. A global city is also a creative city, a city with internationally recognized artists and cultural icons, and, crucially, a city where sufficient GDP is generated from education, art, culture and digital industries to support brand energy across the whole spectrum of the industrial, tertiary and service sectors of the economy. This is the standard rationale for creative industries in China. It is reiterated for urban development in creative corridors from Beijing to Chengdu, but Zhu's further emphases on tolerance, diversity and complexity identify a global ambition for the Shanghai version. Zhu sketches the challenge for Shanghai as an issue of depth. The city boasts the trappings of tolerance and diversity, but a matching polyvalent cultural image is still missing, and that is probably because the value system that would support real diversity is not in place.[7] Zhu suggests that this must be developed across institutions, architecture, local attitudes, fashion and lifestyle choices. Without mentioning the concept of brand identity, his program for Shanghai's internationalization is highly perceptive in the range of elements that he identifies as belonging to the image of the city.

Another academic, Kong Yan, proposes 'openness – *kaifeng*, fusion – *ronghe*, safety – *anquan*' as Shanghai brand values, which places the city in direct competition with Hong Kong's contemporaneous brand, in which the cited values include 'free' and 'opportunity', and 'stable'. Of course, 'stability' is not at all the same thing as 'safety', and the translation of *anquan* may reflect a deliberate choice by the brand designers, or else simply be due to a slippage made possible in English. In fact, as a proposition it initially seems at odds with the changes in Hong Kong since

---

6   This and the earlier quotations are taken from the interview conducted in Shanghai in 2004 by the project team with Wang Tianyun. Leicia Petersen was responsible for translating the transcript.

7   The PhD thesis of Julie Lim (a postgraduate student at the University of Technology, Sydney), entitled 'Race and Belonging in an International City: Overseas Chinese in 'new' Shanghai', will examine these issues in more detail.

1997, given the enormity of the shift from colonial rule, via minimal post-colonial democracy, to Mainland sovereignty – all in the space of thirteen years. Some may regard a 'stable Hong Kong' as more of an aspirational promise than a description, requiring its brand steerers to do some political wheeling and dealing in order to ensure that it becomes accepted a description in the future (Virgo and De Chernatony 2006). At the same time, the label is not entirely unjustified, if one compares what has happened in Hong Kong over the past decade with the changes in infrastructure and attitudes effected in Shanghai, rapid but far from complete. 'Stable Hong Kong' codes a message to the world's business audience connoting Hong Kong's comparative advantage in transparency of business dealings, 'law and order' and corporate governance. Nonetheless, Shanghai has safe streets and a low crime rate, and is safely understood as the major port and financial hub in China's southern corridor (Leman 2002). One might even argue that it is *predictable*, given that it is also subject to the leadership of a Party state based in Beijing to the north (although this also entails the environmental and political problems that accompany China's accelerated development).

We have enumerated a number of possible brand values for Shanghai, suggested in the media and by official commentators in the run-up to Expo 2010. These attributes have apparently been chosen to capture and cultivate the city's preferred past, to enhance its current image as a sophisticate in the region, and to explore the underlying strengths of its population base. We also note that the brand is not as coherent as it might be, and that this could be attributed to parochialism and an 'outsiders / insiders' mentality at the heart of a series of migrant villages which make up the city's nodes, as much as to its continued reliance on Beijing's approval for any politically sensitive decision. From the metropolitan government perspective, Shanghai's brand proposition is deliberately pitched towards world-city competitiveness, with, as its main objective, an educated, creative and internationally fluent population. According to Zhou (2003), its competitors are several and, though they all challenge Shanghai's assumed pre-eminence at different geographic and regional levels, none undermine its imaginative hold as a world city on its way up. Within China the competitors for visitors is modern Shenzhen to the south and 'attractive Dalian' to the north. Neither has a film industry and, although Dalian has an international past, including occupation by Britain, Japan and the Soviet Union, it is not a brand competitor on the global-city index. In investment the picture is more complicated given Shanghai's pivotal role in the economic networks of the south and Dalian's heavy-industry infrastructure. Perhaps the Closer Economic Partnership Arrangement (CEPA) of the Pearl River Delta, and the output that flows from there through Shenzhen, potentially constitutes a mighty challenge to Shanghai. The force of that challenge will depend on the way in which the collaboration between Guangzhou and Hong Kong focuses on the services and high-value industries that characterize Shanghai's profile for future development. While a quick browse around the blogs and online top-ten lists (as well as the more sustained research-based work in GaWC) indicates that Hong Kong and Singapore fulfil world-city functions at a level higher than Shanghai, Zhou is less sure. But he is, after all, a local commentator and the only regional city he rates is Tokyo, and even there he cites the Japanese city as a model for Shanghai's future.

Zhou's argument is worth repeating, as it indicates the level of Shanghai's confidence for the long term. Tokyo is the world's leading digital city and, given the creative-industry orientation that we have already remarked on, this is a field in which Shanghai is very likely to compete. As its Expo developments proceed, it will possess both a young city's infrastructure and an educated workforce operating adaptively in a knowledge-based economy. The official analysis put forward for the Expo logo of two colourful circles is explicit in the focus on the jump-started effort to create Shanghai from the prototypes of other, older places on the Rim:

> The changing colors trigger one's imagination. Green whirlpool symbolizes life and nature; purple whirlpool symbolizes space, technology and exploration. A good combination of the two brings out the essence of the city. The two circles swirl at a high speed and gradually merge, indicating the motto of World Expo: A place where the best things are displayed. Learn from others their advantages.[8]

In a similar vein, Wang expounds on the subject of Shanghai's creative superiority. It is a matter of urban class and migrant energy, and a sense of a global city which exceeds the national remit, but which takes the best from its locality and region:

> We have already built the Nanpu Bridge. We've built the Oriental Pearl Tower. We've built the Shanghai Opera. Even though the central Government said that they have never been approved. We created the Shanghai International Film Festival, and the Arts Festival. The central Government didn't approve those either. But then, I think the most outstanding people in China come from Zhejiang [Shanghai's surrounding province]. A Zhejiang *ren* [person] is fiercely competitive. In the day he's the boss, at night he'll sleep rough if necessary. If he has a million, he wants ten million. His thinking is broad and his aspirations are high. He is part of the Shanghai character.[9]

Wayfinding in a World City

Infrastructure development in connection with Expo is unprecedented, and is positioning Shanghai for world competitiveness in several areas. A second airport, a new satellite city built on mud flats, a dock for cruise liners and Lupu Bridge, the world's longest arch bridge are some significant recent projects. The superfast Maglev train from the airport gives international arrivals an immediate sense of Shanghai's speed, while ongoing urban-rail development will see the six or seven lines that were in place in 2006 more than doubled by 2012 (Chen 2005), and the total length of rail-track laid at present increase almost fourfold. The metro systems of London and Tokyo are two world-city benchmarks which Shanghai is seeking to exceed. From an information-design perspective, the London Tube map has for many years provided other cities with an exemplary model. And we have also remarked on its success in creating an idea of the city space for residents, visitors

---

8   An explanation of the logo may be found at http://www.shanghai.gov.cn/shanghai/node8059/node8626/node8634/userobject21ai13791.html. Retrieved on 25 October 2006. The current Expo slogan is 'Better city, better life'.

9   From an interview conducted with Wang Tianyun by the project team in April 2005.

and past sojourners. The tube map is as spatially persuasive on paper as Dietrich and Ruan are emotively affective on film in conjuring city image. Shanghai's rail-lines may currently be manageable by London's type of representation of the city's nodes and flows, where an association between station colours, overground sections, long stretches and bends also provides regular commuters with a kinaesthetic or proprioceptive map for their everyday spatial orientations. Tokyo's is probably the world's most complicated rail system: 'With over 1,000 stations', writes designer Ross Howard (2006), 'even the locals get lost and disoriented.' Howard describes Japan Rail's 'ambient signifiers', subtle information cues that not only form part of the experience of the city, but also contribute to a navigational strategy. Different chime melodies sound at each station – the stop for Tokyo Disneyland plays the theme for 'It's a small world after all' – and regular commuters quickly and effortlessly learn the sequence of melodies leading to their stop. Unfamiliar sounds can signal a missed stop, and awareness of the station before their destination warns passengers to start detaching from their book, game or phone. As an informatized, sensational city that seeks to compete with Tokyo's digital brand, Shanghai has a shape and edges that may in future be understood by different forms of path and wayfinding from those of earlier times. Clearly there are many different possibilities for this type of signage and other information provision and its potential for emotional engagement. This is also critical for commercial legibility and attention-seizing in an increasingly cluttered environment. In *Leaving Me, Loving You*, Leon Lai spots Faye Wong on a superscreen in the city centre. In *Suzhou River*, Mala finds his lost love swimming in a tank in a nightclub, dressed as a mermaid. Both women, already metonyms for the city as Shanghai's new 'modern girls', are also absorbed into the city's informatic commercial and sensual environment. Thus, they achieve visibility on its streets.

The physical experience of the city, however, essentially relies on *all* Shanghai's residents, and urbanization and unsought migration are a challenge to the brand. Will they behave? 'The movement of people into Shanghai needs to be managed well or else there may be resulting damage to our brand' (Zhou 2003, p. 57). Politically speaking, Shanghai is in a position to influence its citizenry, although the new generations of domestic migrants are *not* citizens unless and until they acquire an urban passport and work card. Shanghai is also sufficiently centralized and non-democratic in urban consultation procedures to be able to make large-scale changes to its built appearance. Built in eighteen months between 2002 and 2004, the city's Formula One race track was rapidly achieved in a way that would have been unfeasible elsewhere – by large-scale demolition and the eviction of thousands of residents. As we write, some 18,000 families of existing residents are being relocated to apartments in Pudong's Sanlin Town and other newer areas, as their homes are razed to make way for Expo sites. The municipal government has stated several principles to avoid 'unnecessary social upheaval', including acting transparently, respecting the families' legal rights, paying compensation in line with market value, providing homes, transitional help and a complaints network (Shanghai Municipal Government 2005). But 'necessary' social upheaval will certainly occur and is already commonplace. Migrants with no valid citizenry status in the city are even more vulnerable than 'ordinary residents'. We might see these many maids, construction workers and factory hands as the 'flowers of Shanghai'.

Rewi Alley was not wrong when, referring to the Shanghai he had visited four years earlier, he wrote in 1973: 'Perhaps no place in China changes so rapidly as does Shanghai.' He went on to say that 'in another ten years it [was] certain all [would] have changed again' (pp.79, 86). And just thirty years later, in 2003, Peter Ter-Kulve made the same observation: 'Shanghai is unrecognisable from eight years ago – at that time Pudong did not exist' (quoted by Gilmore and Dumont 2003, p. 219).

It is scarcely surprising, then, that Shanghai should be regarded as 'the fastest city' (Urban Age Project 2005). But speed is not necessarily a positive quality in the context of city branding. Dynamism may not be seen as wholly consonant with other traditional brand categories that look to lay emphasis on consistency of identity and message, reliability of expectations and stabilized, established attributes in the public imagination. As a metonym for China's larger transition to a market economy, Shanghai epitomizes the 'paradox of images' that make a representational model problematic for destination marketing. The research of Xiao Hong-gen and Heather Mair (2006) demonstrates that China's paradoxical image is due to contrasting perceptions of the changing and the unchanged in representational narratives, and that this motivates a different basis for brand conceptualization and imaging. Would other world cities exhibit fighting horse, boxing bears and clowns punching kangaroos in an Animal Olympics such as were held in Shanghai in 2006?

Brand Identity for a New Shanghai

In Shanghai in the late 1990s, the artist Shi Yong (b. 1963) posted images of himself on the Internet and asked people to vote for the one that, in their view, best represented the ideal look for contemporary Shanghai. The most popular 'New Image of Shanghai Today' was a hip-looking businessman wearing sunglasses and a Mao suit (Yong 1999). It referred to Shanghai's sense of self and inter-textually to the pop art movement of the 1980s, in particular to the 1980s image of a young man walking away out of frame, an image which had satirized images of Mao as a young man. Yong's art continues to explore themes of modernization and consumerism, satirizing architecture and image commoditization, and is acutely conscious of the ironies of shaping an identity that is also Western referenced. These motifs, in other words, are ambivalent: they ape Shanghai's entrepreneurial impetus, its trendy culture and yet, at the same time, acknowledge, and possibly critique, its official, dutiful Chineseness.

The difficulty in personifying the Shanghai identity is discussed by Lu Hanchao, who suggests that an interdisciplinary collaboration involving 'historians, sociologists, anthropologists and even psychologists' is required to connect identity with wider Chinese studies. The very criteria for being identified as Shanghainese are vague, in view of the fact that neither by birth or language, yet definite identifications as Shanghainese (or not) can be made (1999, p. 309.) The system of *waiguo*[10] and *waidiren* (i.e. non-Chinese foreigners and Chinese from outside the city more generally) as official excluding categories is symptomatic of the sense

---

10 There are several other words that denote Chinese 'foreigners'.

of self that operates according to principles of exclusion rather than according a positive welcome to the new city strangers. In this Shanghai differs markedly from, say, London, where newcomers declare themselves Londoners within a very few years of taking up residence.

Seen as a collection of personality attributes, Shanghai's history has always been marked by sharp commercial instincts, the sophistication towards both East and West, and the *haipai* spirit (flexible, adaptable, assimilative of diversity), which stands in sharp contrast to the *jingpai* traditionalism of conservative Beijing. Originally signifying distinctive schools of art, the *haipai* style now informs Shanghai's culture more generally and implies aspirationalism. The mercantility is still implied, but framed against a pragmatic nostalgic history, and the drive is confident, knowing, fast and youthful. In that it reflects a range of different eras and diverse national cultures of architecture, Shanghai's built environment can be called *haipai*: the juxtaposition of the postmodern Pearl Tower with much older commercial buildings is characteristic, whereas elsewhere it might seem chaotic. Analyses in terms of the 'East meets West' cliché or of 'regaining its 1930s' glory' simply miss the mark. Shanghai is building a new city, and perhaps even a new idea of a city (see Plate 8).

The 2010 Expo gives both a deadline and a unifying purpose to the city's debut preparations, but these are on a far grander scale than the construction of new stadia and exhibition halls typical of what other cities might produce. The entire city is being reconstructed – literally and metaphorically – and, although the sheer pace of the development may lend it an appearance of gold-rush chaos and despite the fact that the master-plans keep on changing, there is clear evidence of considerable long-term planning. The strategic objectives in the period from around 1990 to 2010 embrace both the machine and the garden as Shanghai targets a 'multi-centre multi-functional megalopolis of about 14 million citizens and 4–5 million floating population … [T]he city … is now orienting towards a tertiary economy based around finance, trade, information exchange and multinationals' (Yeh 1996, p. 276). Shanghai's strong university sector supports its positioning as a major node in a knowledge economy and between 2003 and 2006 the city attracted back over 10,000 overseas Chinese, mostly from developed countries – 98 per cent of these have degrees, including 23 per cent PhDs and over 60 per cent Masters – and it is currently campaigning to attract a further 10,000. Moreover, if Shanghai fails to produce China's first Nobel Prize-winner, 'it will be a big failure for the city' (Zhou 2003, p. 56). Nobel Prize-winners qualify as *Shanghairen*.

'Being experienced and knowledgeable' is a major criterion for qualifying as 'a Shanghai person' (Lu 1999, p. 309) and the emergence of talented people from Shanghai in any field, along with brands originating in Shanghai, are seen as essential to bolster the city's brand identity. At the moment, foreign brands dominate: the imagery in the Shanghai promotional video *Seven Days in Shanghai* (2003) includes Starbucks, Louis Vuitton and Prada. It is well understood that native brands are also required and, though few are as yet global names, brands can emerge very quickly. Many of China's top brands are becoming known, but still do not have the cultural cachet to carry place brand with them. In any case, the top manufacturing brands, such as Lenovo and Hai'er, are based in China and are only vaguely associated with China as a brand, outside the country itself. This is perhaps because the effect of national brand identity and product characteristics is at best a mutual dialectic of reinforcement of the main message. German cars are technologically reliable: *Vorsprung durch Technik!*

A national brand is not easily imagined spatially until this dialectic has matured. Ideas behind national brands are essentially about character and political influence. Germany conjures up technical brilliance and reliability. Britain connotes cool. China conjures up size, endless scope and a few key icons: the dragon, the Party flag, the Great Wall and the colours red and yellow. Brand China is actively working on this conundrum through its nationwide creative-industries strategy, which ideally will bring together China's overall hugeness and a sensibility to its many sub-brands: active in terms of Chinese-named products that are taking over from global names, but still dormant with respect to the features that differentiate one province, city or internal region from another. The first aspect of branding place in China through manufacturing and service brands is already under way. In June 2006 the PRC Ministry of Commerce (MOFCOM) initiated a brand promotion tour of fifty-one cities to extend the popularity of China's own brands for trade and domestic growth. This was seen as representing the nation's image and economic strength. As Minister Bo Xilai said, when opening a brand promotion tour in June 2006, 'Self-made brand is the image of a nation and the sign of its economic strength. Also, self-made brand is the fruitful result of the scientific improvement and a sacred promise to customers' (Beijing International 2006).

Similarly, many Chinese product brands have been overcoming their (domestic and export) market share in several categories and this reflects back to influence country-of-origin perception for the better. 'Made in China', however, currently has the reputation that 'Made in Japan' used to have for poor-quality goods, but that is changing. In recent years Chinese brands have been developing rapidly, and improving in quality, particularly in the consumer appliance and whitegoods markets traditionally dominated by Japan. The growth rate of whitegoods manufacturer Hai'er, for instance, towards 2000 was a remarkable 413 per cent, and Legend (Lenovo), Konka and other indigenous brands have shown similar growth (Tse 2001). TCL Electronics' and Changhong's television sets cost only two-thirds of the price of comparable Japanese models. Traditional domestic-marketing channels are relatively weak; the potential for digital commerce and services is considered much stronger in Chinese markets, and, while most large national brands are based elsewhere, this 'soft' brand power is an area of strength for Shanghai. Shanghai's online gaming and interactive entertainment companies, Shanda and Linktone, have significant consumer uptake,[11] and are both regarded as originators of uniquely Chinese business models in media technology areas (Ramo 2006). Above all, digital technologies will underpin civic life in richer provinces as the nation rolls out its digital capacity on the eastern seaboard. So, with a strong tertiary sector, Shanghai and other cities can be expected to develop and continue innovation.

---

11 According to their website, as of 30 June 2005, Shanda had 'approximately 460 million registered accounts' (SNDA Entertainment 2004).

Central to the perception of Shanghai as a modern tertiary economy is the development of Pudong new area: across the river to the east of the Bund, replete with its own Times Square and skyscrapers designed by both local and international 'starchitects'. Historically, Pudong had always been an area targeted for development, but policy since 1949 meant it remained untouched until in 1986, when State Council moved 'to develop Pudong into a modern district' (Yeh 1996, p. 276). From 1990, 'development' moved very rapidly. Foreign direct investment (FDI) was encouraged and sustained growth occurred through 2005 to the point where 56 per cent of China's trade surplus was due to FDI. As China has toughened its policies, notably with more incentives now in place for service and human-resource than for manufacturing industries, FDI has steadily declined. This is good for Shanghai. Pudong's developmental orientation towards FDI, along with an advanced transport, communications and ICT network infrastructure, is seen as a major step towards becoming a world city. Although growth has slowed down, Shanghai's FDI has continued to rise, and service industry investment is increasingly important to the city's wealth (see Shanghai Vision 2006).

But the situation remains dynamic and *un*stable: Hong Kong is the major contributor of FDI in Shanghai, followed by the Virgin Islands, a situation interpreted by the US-China Business Council (2006) as 'round trip' PRC funds. And, despite a number of victories, Shanghai is not 'the most practical place for MNCs [multinational corporations] to set up their regional headquarters', as Pamela Yatsko (2001) has suggested. Lack of banking sophistication and openness; a restrictive business environment; rules on foreign ownership; approval regimes and a 'capricious' legal system, together with only a small pool of high-quality business leaders, and the situation of all these within a framework of Communist governance means that Shanghai is not there yet, nor especially close. The infrastructure and trust currently enjoyed by Hong Kong will take time for Shanghai to develop.

Perhaps we should admit two anomalies at this point. Film will again become a major industry in Shanghai once the verticalization of television, digital content creation, private studios and animation are mature. At the moment, films from Shanghai are not making the city rich, although they do drip-feed a 'brand identity' into the international imagination. Likewise, tourism is not a major industry in Shanghai. Despite the spectacular sights around the Bund, the handful of festivals and an emergent emphasis on shopping, and even though the MICE market (meetings, incentives, conventions and exhibitions) is well served and promoted, tourism remains no more than a nascent industry. But still, business visitors dominate and for this reason Shanghai's brand is not currently led by destination marketing propositions geared towards casual tourists.[12] Of course, ambition is a factor here, and the overall gearing to be a world city inevitably

---

12 Visitor numbers and occupancy rates, however, dropped in 2006: only one-star hotels increased share, having dropped their average prices from the previous year. This indicates domestic tourists. See http://www.meet-in-shanghai.net/sjtj.htm, retrieved on 25 January 2007.

creates good locational and logistic opportunities for tourism, as indeed it does for film. For example, the North Bund district, currently old warehouses and residential complexes, is being developed as a business centre and an historical tourism area according to a master plan designed by RTKL – a firm for whom creating a sense of place is fundamental their design philosophy. As part of a CBD providing employment around professional services, the plan proposes a subway that is accessible by foot and a central green space. In addition, two important heritage features, a prison and a temple, are to be preserved. Altogether, it is a winning submission that balanced 'the rational with the romantic' (RTKL 2006b). The Shanghai Star, a giant Ferris wheel that is modelled on the London Eye, will dominate the cityscape, a 'landmark structure that matches the city's image as an international metropolis' (quoted by Watts 2005). Not only will Shanghai's wheel – of course – be considerably bigger than London's, but, with capsules holding far more people, it will entertain a veritable community! Or, at least, it would have, had they been able to see past the city's smog and pink skies! The Star plan has now been discarded,[13] but its inspiration to be larger than its UK model, and more attuned to an idea of urban management, is typical of the world-city drive that guides Shanghai's planning decisions.

Shanghai has also taken up the idea, successfully executed in Paris and Brisbane, of bringing the shore to the people, and has opened an artificial beach on Fengxian Bay, with 120,000 tons of golden sand brought from Hainan Island. By a special process, murky water from the East China Sea, shipped into an artificial lagoon – has been turned blue. The Jingsha Blue Sea Resort was opened to the public in July 2006. Related plans include Thames Town, a massive real-estate development in suburban Shanghai designed to recreate a small rural English community. Colleagues from the UK say that it looks like 'a cross between Guildford and somewhere in Kent': it has a pub, a 5-star hotel, a marina, a golf course and a full-scale Gothic church. Tuscan, Dutch and German residential developments are also under construction (see figures 6.1 and 6.2). These European activities will be supplemented by onsite festivals such as an annual Oktoberfest, which, given the German origins of Qingdao beer in Shandong, is not as perverse as it might seem. Or it wouldn't be if Shanghai were in Shandong, which it isn't! But these efforts, however damaging they risk being to one's sensitivities, are by no means irrational: Oktoberfests, beaches and the theme-park residences have proved themselves to be highly successful tourism business models. Its golden sand and blue sky have successfully branded Queensland's Gold Coast and its Oktoberfest has worked for modern Olympic Munich. But –and it is a vitally important 'but' – these were born and grew naturally from the respective culture and topography of each of these places, and the experience of those places identifies them as 'home'. Shanghai's current tourism proposition follows well-learnt, but not indigenous, models. They are inauthentic, and 'untrue', to an even greater degree than is usual for tourism development elsewhere.

---

13 According to an Associated Press report (Bodeen 2007), the Ferris-wheel project has been cancelled amid allegations that government-held pension funds had been illicitly invested by city officials.

Figure 6.1   Songjian, Shanghai 1975
(courtesy David S.G. Goodman)

Figure 6.2   Thamestown, Shanghai 2006
(courtesy David S.G. Goodman)

What has been 'true' for us on our visits to China has been the pleasure of meeting people, the privilege of witnessing another's everyday life and the chance to experience and come to appreciate a different, energetic, future-oriented possibility of being. Exploring the alleys, buying food from street vendors, being helped when lost and being smiled at by real people are the kinds of experience that delight in ways that overpriced tourist traps simply cannot. While this may be understood intellectually, it seems not to have informed the investment-oriented agenda of global cities that squander their social, historical and affective capital. Shanghai is working on its global-city status, the measurable aspects of which are infrastructure, financial networks and investment figures. The city's organic history and particular formations of Chineseness are not currently as valued as they may be in the future by more mature generations of culturally aware urban planners. The Gold Coast is an iconic beach destination, but Shanghai will not depend on its beach, or even its tourism. Its brand, while imageable, will not depend on its icons. Shanghai's Oriental Pearl Tower and its conventional high-rises are finally dispensable. The image of development is more important than what exactly is being developed, and why. The ongoing changes proposed for the skyline over the years leading up to 2010 confirm Shanghai's reputation as 'the fastest city'. Permanent buildings are less important than permanent building.

Tourism, which is expected to account of 7 per cent of China's economy by 2010, is not a pillar industry for Shanghai: heavy industry is. The travels in the China of the Mao era were carefully managed tours showcasing factories and industrial advances. Tourist phrase-books of the period included useful phrases such as 'I would like to see a watch factory / visit a commune' and 'Tell me about your industrial relations' (Cheng 1981). Although the world's advanced global cities are measured by tertiary achievement, graduation through substantial, sedimented economic development is required first. Shanghai and sister cities in Zhejiang are visibly accelerating this process. The vision is magnificent. Two hours south of Shanghai, the Ningbo Municipal Authority has built a combined campus of technical and comprehensive universities for 60,000 students. They share resources and have access to affordable accommodation. What remains untested is the degree to which these new collaborations will produce the creative energy and industry that is mooted to be the brand's driver.

The structure of employment across the manufacturing sector will also rely to a very large extent on the viability and docility of the interior. A more labour-intensive growth mode is indicated (Chinese Ministry of Finance 2003), but this has the potential to create a greater polarization of wealth than currently exists, with a much more clearly defined poor urban underclass. Already the prices of Shanghai property have reached unaffordable levels. No stability seems imminent in that area. Already too, Shanghai has proven itself a political city where migrants become activists and activists become revolutionaries. The age of revolutions may be gone, and the urban proletariat is uprooted and spread across the new production zones, but we would hazard a guess that the urban poor in Shanghai would still put up a fight if pragmatic nostalgia edges too close to 1930s levels of exploitation. Over the many years of living memory it was Shanghai that serviced the interior, whereas earlier it was the interior that serviced Shanghai (Alley 1973). The peripheral edge of Shanghai is increasingly defined by its political positioning with respect to its surrounds. Historically, outward from the city was an edge of market gardens leading towards bigger farms. The extent of land ownership created stratified interactions, organized according to proximity to the city. Though still evident as one travels into the city from the airport, rapid urbanization and property-price excesses are engaging with this historical dynamic, with some edge farmers looking to develop land for privileged communities, while others are being dispossessed of their land. These are the 'edges' of the contemporary metropolis. They define not merely space and land, but are also indicators of the political undercurrents which are caused by Shanghai's reach into the countryside. It is upon these farmers that the Shanghairen depend for food, and it is they who drive through the polluted pink skies in the early morning to deliver it.

Senses of the Old City

Shanghai's perpetually changing nature means that whole buildings and areas change their form, and those that don't disappear become recontextualized. The Peace (formerly the Cathay) Hotel was perhaps the most luxurious hotel in the world when it opened in 1929. Though it has lost none of its celebrity, it is now, however, an anachronism of both size and style: its 'mere' 17 storeys are dwarfed by tall buildings across the river and up the Nanjing Road. Guests' complaints of pervasive 'musty smells', 'dilapidated furniture' and a problem with rats and cockroaches prompted the owners to undertake a major face-lift in 2006. It is rumoured that the refurbishment is to be in the style of the Waldorf Astoria in Manhattan (Coonan 2007). The hotel's unique selling proposition is a combination of location, history and style – the band still plays old-time jazz (Faehnders 2006). But rather more is involved than retaining the original layout and the ageing jazz band, and the hotel that has cosseted international celebrities from Charlie Chaplin to Chiang Kai-shek, from Noel Coward to Muhammad Ali, risks losing irretrievably some of the more sensuous aspects of its history. To feel oneself in the room where Noel Coward finished *Private Lives* (Room 314, incidentally), perhaps looking at the same curtains and chairs, even sniffing the smells and textures of those days in 1930, is a sensational tourism proposition. It is something that cannot be replicated: the hotel rooms of a glass and steel skyscraper are unlikely to attract stars with the iconic status of Chaplin, or, indeed, to inspire any affectionate visitation by their fans.

The 1930s Shanghai that Chaplin and Coward knew has been recreated in a documentary soundtrack and 'audio film' entitled *Metropolis Shanghai: Showboat to China*. The CD is described as mixing city sounds with Asian folk, European classical and salon music, traditional Jewish and Klezmer styles, and American jazz. Sounds of the time and place contrive to immerse the listener into a sound story: foghorns and ships, hotel bars and market bustle, marching soldiers, temple bells and chants of monks, and old women playing Mah Jong (Funk 2006). The Peace Hotel bar, Long Hua temple, the harbour and Little Vienna are some of the specific locations that the music commemorates. Bubbling Well Street (now Nanjing Road West) is another and its original name is grounded in Buddhism and mythology'. The

Bubbling Well, along with other scenic spots, was finally filled in and disappeared without trace in 1919, when the paving of the road towards the Jing'an Temple, a project begun by the British over fifty years earlier, was completed (Shi 2000).

Hypermodern narratives that blend the genres of film and print draw strongly on the city as a modern character, and on the modern woman as an avatar within and of that space. Again, this pattern allows narrative patterns of the old city to breach the new with nostalgic tropes of male voyeurism and female vulnerability. On Shanghai-ed.com ('Shanghai's home on the web') there is a real-time cyber-saga that 'breaks the limits of time and space and the rules of reality' (Shanghai-ed 2006). *20 Nanjing Road* is a novel told from the viewpoint of the male protagonist, Swiss journalist Tom Wildt, and, simultaneously, as a blog on Shanghai-story.net, from the viewpoint of the lead female, E-Wa, who is part-human and part-android. Moreover, there are two E-Was, one of whom lays false trails to protect the other, who for various reasons is being chased. The blog enters a fictional, unstable Shanghai 'which is continually changing from the past to the present, and vice versa' (Shanghai-story 2006). Photos of a possible E-Wa are proposed by contributors and, while the story suggests particular characteristics, 'authentic' representations remain intangible. The implication of all these physical representations is of a mysterious, exotic and erotic Oriental female Other (Teo and Leong 2006), both subject to and yet also exploiting that trope, as she performs the 'new' role of the *modeng nüxing* (modern woman: a 1930s term in film, literature and commerce), playing a serious game of *flânerie* and pathmaking in the 'new' modern Shanghai.

Environmental Shanghai

[It has been said] that cityness as historically understood and produced is simply no longer operative. But it is quite possible that cityness continues to be a dimension. It is a particular kind of space in a geographic terrain where there are also other spaces and they are overlapping and so we do indeed need to rethink our tools for analysis, for representation. I believe that cityness is still there, it is just how do we capture it; and then comes a question of design and architecture (Saskia Sassen).[14]

Environmental protection is an officially stated aspiration in Shanghai and environmental credibility has been a political objective for some time. In 1998 afforestation and environment was the top issue area in state/political advertising, four times more common than the leader thoughts of Deng and Jiang (Lewis 2002). Since 1990 green groups have emerged in many Chinese universities (the cradle of future leaders), and these are often supported materially (Lu 2006). Many other specific efforts are ongoing in targeting a 'green city' image in the medium term. A recent issue of the Shanghai *Airport Journal* (Shanghai Airport 2003) carried an analysis of the Shanghai Airport Authority logo in which the English letters SAA are so stylized as to reflect the 'One city two airports' idea. One airport is blue and the other green, to both suggest sky and land, and make symbolic reference to environmental protection awareness. The analysis describes how the design reflects SAA's values

14 http://www.urban-age.net/10_cities/01_newYork/newYork_PL+US_quotes.html.

– big scale, big conglomerate, standardization of its operations – and also an airflow suggesting 'circling, vitality, continuous progress and sustained growth'. The Hong Kong airport logo also has a highly sophisticated design reflecting considerable consultation and consideration of its communication to various stakeholders and different target markets. As a part of what he calls 'getting the right message to the right people', Conway Morgan (1999) has outlined four different levels on which this logo can be read. These show the intentional positioning of brand messages in global contexts and, incidentally, the competitiveness between Hong Kong and Shanghai.

Green, '[enriching] vitality and liveliness', is the keynote colour of the Shanghai Expo design palette: the emblem 'expresses the Chinese people's strong aspiration to stage a multicultural world expo' (Shanghai Municipal Government 2006a). In fact, the only other colour in the emblem is a blob of dusky pink / orange, a colour used for some time in Shanghai's branding and marketing and, as we noticed when discussing pink on film, one that risks creating another ambivalence, given that pink skies are caused by pollution. The Expo theme of 'Better city, better life' is aspirational and green is the antidote to fouler colours. The Shanghai Suzhou Creek Rehabilitation and Construction Company is currently executing a twelve-year project to remove 'foul-smelling and discoloured' water from untreated agricultural, industrial and municipal waste in Suzhou Creek, which flows through Shanghai. Part of the plan is to install greenbelts along both banks of the waterway, and the idea of ReBAM (recreational belt around metropolis) has become critical to an understanding of Shanghai's tourism boundaries and ongoing development (Wu and Cai 2006). Wealthier urban residents on day trips to the suburbs contribute significantly to China's domestic tourism, and analysis of ReBAM suggests a distinctive contribution to the urban and village model of understanding urban space in Shanghai. The ReBAM gives city-wide coherence to the 'district' typology common in identifying suburbs and other urban organizational forms. This supports the local logic of environmentalism, as these better-off members of society (*xiaokang*, *xingui*) seek a harmonious balance between their newly gained spending power and a decent environment for their families to enjoy. One should be aware that the context for choices of life-style, expenditure and development both at individual and governmental levels is affected by influential political discourse. The current political slogan for managing problems in Reform China is the creation of a harmonious society (*hexie shehui*) that will build bridges between rich and poor, development and the environment and so on. The notion of harmony can never be thought of without some reference to this rhetoric. Harmonious society is very much about Brand China, and vice versa, as an internal realization of the Government's agenda, seeking to create minimal political damage to social relations on the one hand, and maximum management of its external image on the other.

External image, however, rather than environment, seems to be driving much of Shanghai's decision making. The city's scenic lights used to be switched off so as to save power on hot days, but this will no longer happen, since dark nights might discourage international tourists and investors (English.eastday.com 2005a). The harmonious compromise which characterizes a great deal of contemporary social and environmental policy is in evidence here too. Recognizing that lit billboards signal prosperity, but also degrade the nocturnal environment, Shanghai has developed a standard for environmental and decorative lighting that gives high priority to issues of night safety and security, but also to light pollution and artistic effects. Urban lighting is required to express the character of the city and its different areas by ensuring harmony with surrounding buildings and facilities (Li 2005). 'In recognition of the increasing number of lamps imported from China', write Mark Ellis and Shane Holt (2005), of the Australian Greenhouse Office, 'Australasian policy makers have recently been working towards harmonising efficiency standards with China.'

Shanghai's urban development also officially espouses environmental values and is planned for sustainability. Solar energy is used in rural areas of the city, while green space development along Suzhou Creek reflects a political will to exploit the waterfront. The green space cover, which helps reduce urban heat islands, was 38 per cent in 2005, despite the fact that the cost of green space had tripled since 2000: it is estimated that by 2010 no resident within the outer ring road will live more than half a kilometre from an open space (English.eastday.com 2005). In 1993, Shanghai's per-capita green area was 1 square metre; by 2003 it was 7.2 and by 2005 it was around 11 square metres. A ratio such as this permits the city to qualify for official designation as a 'garden city', and in 2004 central government accorded Shanghai the title of 'National Garden City'. Garden City, however, is the current brand of Singapore, thanks to former Prime Minister Lee Kuan Yew's vision for the greening of Singapore, a project aimed at both lifting the spirits of residents and persuading potential investors of sustained development (United Nations 2003). Singapore's attraction for investors and positioning as a 'model green city' have not gone unnoticed by Asian city planners, and many are following this lead. By comparison, Hong Kong's historic tendency to build, which requires extensive land reclamation, has reduced its Victoria Harbour by 3,200 hectares, half its original size, and a high-level coalition supported by most residents is now mobilizing to stave off further threats. As the young Mainland prostitute in *A Night in Mongkok* (*Wong gok hak yau*, dir. Tung-shing Yee, 2004) asks, as she wanders through a desolate Mongkok at night, 'Why is Hong Kong called Hong Kong (*xiang gang* / Fragrant Harbour)?' She is finally told by a voice-over that the name refers to the scent of spices and herbs, that were once packed and shipped in the colony, and that used to waft over the Harbour. They are long gone and much of the Harbour is disappearing too. Although Hong Kong's tourism promotion has increased awareness that most of the SAR is green space, and used the green colour in the dragonhead logo to emphasize this, the dominant visual perception of the city is of tall buildings packed tightly into the downtown area. There are advantages to this density, however: businesses and services are within walking distance of one another, and there are efficient connections to port, airport and factories, as well as to parkland and coast. But the competition for height and urban bravura comes at the expense of other, more sensual, qualities.

In 1985 Shanghai had just one skyscraper, but by 2003 it had nearly 5,000 buildings over 8-storeys high, over 2,800 of which were above 18-storeys high. The density of skyscrapers in the city centre was eventually considered excessive and detrimental to living standards, so the authorities moved to restrict the number of tall buildings. Wenhui Mansion, built in 1990 to a height of 25 storeys, was demolished in 2006, as it was judged to be 'disharmonious' with its surroundings (ShanghaiDaily.com 2006). Moreover, in certain circumstances the glass curtain walls on skyscrapers are liable to explode and in August 2006 a campaign to check these began (Expo2010China.com 2006), further suggesting impermanence and change in the built environment.

As is made evident by the scale model on display in its urban planning exhibition hall, Shanghai's form is of spatially distributed urban islands, with extreme verticality centred in Pudong and some outlying satellites. Although subletting arrangements have often caused urban density to often be higher than it would appear, the model gives the impression of an efficient business machine married to a natural garden. This echoes the historical development of Shanghai, with its mix of crowded shantytowns of rural migrants, the gardened courtyards of more upmarket habitation, and suburban market gardens between purely urban and rural areas.

Shanghai's ambiguous absorption and assimilation of Western typologies have led Christopher Choa (2004) to ask, 'Is there an appropriate urbanism for contemporary Shanghai?' Identifying a mismatch between Western urban design models and traditional Chinese notions of cities and public space, Choa notes that the codes for 'green space' are not understood in China in the same way as in the West, and include small and hard ground spaces. Moreover, urban design that favours the car, as Shanghai's recent codes have, engenders 'automobile dependency' (Newman and Kenworthy 1989) and has spawned other social and energy problems in developed societies. Shanghai's arbitrary codes for green space reflect an emphasis on economic, rather than on social or environmental, capital. For example, *lilong*, or *longtang*, interior neighbourhood lanes, are distinctively Chinese, and have high-density but low-rise characteristics, suited to social interaction. In recent years they have been *un*systematically destroyed to make way for skyscrapers and high-rise apartments. This destruction, however, is discouraged in Shanghai's recent building codes, which are considered out of touch with what people actually need, based on a scale inimical to human life. These codes are not only ruining considerable urban heritage (albeit meeting some popular resistance), but actually preventing the design of *lilong* and residential courtyards in modern iterations. While some current residents may prefer relocation to Pudong high-rises, these are neither an exotic tourist proposition nor a link with a deep social history.

An authoritative gathering in Beijing in 2000 has also considered preservation issues of China's modernization and urban development. At any event, an assessment by MIT's Dennis Frenchman (a former student of Kevin Lynch's and a cultural heritage expert who has spent much time in China) has described Shanghai's Pudong skyline as driven by the need for 'new and progressive urban images' in an information age characterized by visual images and symbols (2000). His response to the (generic) problem of 'marrying [the] old and [the] new' is to assert that one mustn't 'widen old roads', that 'the city is a garden' in which different forms relate to one another in a harmonious whole, and that the 'old can inspire the new'. Running through Frenchman's thinking is a clear message: buildings should be thought of as stories, 'together making up a unique character and narrative [for the city]'. Noting that good narratives are valuable in an information economy, decisions to tear buildings down and put new ones up should be made carefully. These are often irreversible actions and are crucially beneficial (or destructive) with respect to the contribution that each might make to the story of the city.

A description in the *Daily Telegraph* of the making of Sydney's Wentworth Avenue in 1911 – marked by the racism of the day – is not irrelevant to the present discussion:

> Dirty hovels have been razed flat, narrow lanes have been wiped out, branch streets have been widened, and corners have been rounded off … The buildings were mainly old and small, and often tumbledown. The Chinese in them … built partitions across rooms and ran up sheds in their back yards, to take in paying guests. A little room, meant to contain one bed, you would find packed full of bunks … full of filthy Chinese, smoking opium.

As Sydney before it did for the suburb of Surry Hills, Shanghai has worked vigorously to replace its slum areas and, again like Sydney, it has been by edict and with little regard for residents. Between 1992 and 2000, helped by some international investment from overseas developers, the '365 Project' demolished 3.65 million square metres of crowded slums and shacks. One 'beneficiary' of this construction project, Wang Jilin (now relocated to a Pudong high-rise) could not locate his old family home, which, like other slum sites, was now covered by avenues, public greens, elevated highways or tall buildings (Yongzhe 2000). Like many more, this man's former neighbours had been dispersed and, while some seem happier, others resented being moved. Indeed, elsewhere the forced displacement of slum residents has occasionally resulted in community protest. In Beijing, this has taken the ultimate form of self-immolation and public suicide, as, in the lead-up to the 2008 Olympics, the historic city's historic *hutongs* have been cleared (Hawthorne 2004).[15] Meanwhile, most household continue to be overcrowded, and the city's central areas continue to grow ever denser, creating ever more severe quality of life problems (Urban Age Project 2005). And – need it be said? – many do not want to be moved: one writer finds that the 'near slum' environment with alleys full of character in which he now lives to be infinitely preferable to his previous sterile yuppie suburban complex. Along with laundry hanging outside of windows to dry on poles, street hawkers and outdoor cooking constitute a characteristic feature of a fast-disappearing neighbourhood, one that most tourists are not encouraged to see.[16] Without being of particular heritage interest, it 'preserves a harmonious way of life that is uniquely Shanghai' (Liang 2006, p. 4). The use of the word 'harmonious' in this critical context is a direct snub to the implementation of national policies at a municipal level. The social fabric, in which long-time neighbours supply each other with vegetables and eggs, is clearly under serious threat, as is the possibility of ever being able to experience a 'true place'.

---

15 Similar to Shanghai's *longtangs*, Beijang's *hutongs*, small streets or lanes between courtyards with an associated community, were mostly built during the Yuan, Ming and Qing dynasties (1271–1911). See TravelChinaGuide.com 2007.

16 In 2006, in an attempt to sanitize the city's image, Shanghai Municipal Government censors tried to cut from the film *Mission Impossible III* (dir. J.J. Abrams) scenes which did not exemplify a cosmopolitan Shanghai. One of these showed laundry being dried publicly on outside poles.

In 2004 and 2005 Shanghai was often described by our respondents in terms of the pragmatic nostalgia which characterizes the city's contemporary film and tourism industries: 'an old-world city with nostalgic style' or 'bright but sad, almost wanting to forget the [immediate] past'. They also noticed its obvious antitheses: the blend of old, cultured, 'calligraphic' architectural styles, bustling streets and diverse, 'almost frenzied', 'Disneyland-type' new development. When asked to give a few words to describe the city's visual characteristics, many referred to its social texture as much as to its style: 'extreme wealth alongside great poverty', 'international history recovering from oppression', 'over-polluted clash of East meets West'. It seemed that for some visitors Shanghai represented a China outside China itself, a place that was at once emblematic of the new China's economic clout, and yet in recovery from its 'hot nationalism' of Liberation and the Maoist era. Yet, of course, Shanghai is as much a part of that continuing regime as it is a landmark of capitalism and Reform, albeit in a phase of banal national branding, as the country reaches out for global power based on economic success. Perhaps those critical visitors are picking up on an instinct of 'true place', or maybe they sense a trace of the old Orientalisms, or the denigrations of 1950s Party propaganda: a version of Shanghai firing 'sugar-coated bullets', a red city with a polluted pink underbelly of pragmatic, bourgeois self-interest.

Chapter 7

The Future of City Branding

[M]odern branding as a discipline is only 50+ years old ... [A]lmost all the theories and methodologies regarding branding are derived from that period. This means that nothing is set in stone, and in fact it's quite likely that branding as a discipline is still in the 'flat earth' stage. (Long 2006, p.1)

In this book we have been concerned to expand the idea of branding into a richer theoretical frame applicable to the complex entity of the city. We hope that this can be used, not to replace existing commercial systems of thought and praxis-derived theoretical models, which are already brilliantly adaptive and challenging (Thrift 1998), but to provide us with a fresh way of thinking about film, image and space in the urban context. In short, we want to appropriate the idea of branding as a theoretical premise, from which to make a cinematic evaluation of 'places that matter' in the contemporary world, and, equally, to use film for a visual analysis of why and how city brands work. And, as academics, we want to pull together political, cultural and commercial perspectives, in order to produce an informed, interdisciplinary narrative regarding key cities in the West Pacific region in a period ('*another* period', perhaps we should say!) of extraordinary change.

The preceding chapters have discussed three cities, all of which are spatially and temporally meaningful in ways too complex for 'flat earth' media-advertising to exhaust. Indeed, they are both complex and contradictory: cinematic, industrial, pragmatic, political, parochial, cosmopolitan, and expansive. Media responses must therefore also be imaginative and multi-faceted in taking up the challenge of making an idea of the city legible to the outside world and to itself. The city 'itself' comprises a great deal, but here we refer particularly to its residents, cultures, and structures of local atttention. We have suggested that cinema is ideally suited to take up the visuality of place and make it intersect emotionally and aesthetically with narratives of belonging. Branding has a comparable opportunity, as long as its exponents are able to grasp that, while the city's future is its most motivational dynamic, the contradictions of the past cannot, and should not, be easily brushed away. Residents and visitors want to get to know a place rather as they would a person. It is very much like love: it can strike as suddenly as lightning, but be slow to mature. And feelings grow stronger as details of a loved one's past bubble unexpectedly to the surface at moments of much looked-for intimacy. The passion of Hong Kongers for their home was born at a disastrous moment in the country's history, and the films that explored that passion dwelt on other trials of the past in order to bring this patriotism to life onscreen. Sydney is hedonistic and young; and whilst Kevin Lynch described 'paths' as the mainstay of how the city is navigated, Sydney is a one-'path' town in the opinion of new arrivals, suggesting that, for them at least, the city's diversity is *not* navigated by visitors. But, the long-term Sydneysiders with whom we spoke did know that this is a city of historical and topographical depth and breadth. They, for instance, invariably rated sandstone amongst the city's finest qualities. Not only does the natural stone recall the early days of European settlement, but it is also a metonym for the land itself, and so brings to mind the original owners and their continuing presence in Eora.

So, how might these passions be realized in branding a city, and why should we make a link between this emotional 'paying of attention' and the art of cinema? Briefly, a film presents an idea of place, a series of snapshots, a sequence of celluloid images, all of which are framed by the narrative and couched visually in tonal and chromatic intensity. The cinematic image is stylised and partial, and does not replicate the city as such, but it does present a cumulative version of what it might look and feel like. The suggestive power of the film image is allied to the passion and emotive power of a city to attract loyalty and love from its residents and visitors. We might describe branding in a not dissimilar way. A city brand is not a city, but it does offer a convenient and suggestive idea of one, something that can be used in place of complexity in order to convey the power and attraction of place. Like cinema, branding is deceitful in so far as it makes highly strategic decisions about which face to show the world. As the Brand Hong Kong website puts it, 'Every world-class city has a personality – attributes that make it distinctive, memorable and instantly identifiable. In the case of the Hong Kong brand, these … are reflected in … core values … best described by the words progressive, free, stable, opportunity, high quality' (Brand Hong Kong n.d.). These values, or qualities as we have termed them elsewhere, are neither mandatory nor chosen at random. What is important is that they add up to an comprehensive, popular 'feel' of the city as a place, and work for the specific interests of their market (in this case they need to attract financial investors from overseas). Thus, 'free' and 'progressive' are a somewhat loose translation of the city's well-known high energy levels and very limited democratic rights! In cinema, these same attributes are explored in genres as diverse as anarchic comedy (for example, *McDull, The Alumni*) and gangster films (for example, *Infernal Affairs*). In the latter, there is a sense of controlled violence, offset by a stable, generic balance between hero and anti-hero in the structure of the plot. In *McDull, The Alumni*, the anarchism is propelled by ever more ridiculous references to Hong Kongers' habit of talking about food, which is as noticeable a cultural tic as the Australians discussing sport, or the English the weather. In both films, narrative and narration depend on, and maintain, a connection between place identity, people, belonging and cinema.

Clearly, then, there are several aspects to the process of communicating the complexity of a city by referring to a nebulous but nonetheless shared idea, in which one recognized aspect of city life – a predilection to talk about food, a particular level of energy, a landmark phrase, acts as a metonym for the whole experience. Tourism-led, destination-branding campaigns provide one dimension of the public projection of a place. They are directed at end-users and target populations, they select the most attractive parts of the city, and they tend to avoid conflictual or difficult narrative. Filmmakers use urban locations and an imagined 'idea of a city' to motivate the narrative energy in a plot, and to underpin the movement and the poesis of its story ('story' is understood in formalist film theory as the details and narrational tones which locate the 'plot' in time and space). Their audiences are determined by a film's genre and its distribution capacity. Urban planners and politicians create new spaces or re-invigorate (or shut down) older ones as they inscribe identity on place. Their concerns tend to be local and political in the first instance, with a wider remit to attract foreign investment and talent as a secondary but very important outcome for the city's future. All of these activities happen without benefit of branding as such, but branding gives them a different edge. It pulls discrete images into alignment, but, crucially, it requires that there is consensus and unity of purpose amongst the various people involved. The Brand Hong Kong endeavour was, for instance, flawed and frustrated because key players were not working under the same roof, nor to the same political agendas: the brand team were in a different branch of local government from the town-planning department, the tourism bureaux, and the leisure and culture departments. These latter were literally, or at least geographically, in competition with the former, which were in turn briefed to make tourism and planning policies the objects of their attentions.

Nigel Thrift (1998) has written that the value of theoretical thinking is not confined to academic disciplines, and that business problem solving over the centuries of capital growth has been the real engine of economic development and innovation. Capital itself has also been the cause and site of 'chronic uncertainty and instability' (p. 162), thus necessitating further innovation or damage control. Globalism, argues Thrift, has not deracinated capitalism, nor has money (in and of itself) corroded the social worlds of actual people (p. 162 ff). Rather, the world's networks of money, capital and business produce anomalies of time and space which bring past and present (and future) into competition with one another, mix up trans-national, national and regional interests and priorities, and make complexity a feature of everyday life. It is in this world context, so shrewdly acknowledged in Thrift's analysis, that world cities seek to explain themselves, sell their qualities and manage their populations. City brands might be understood as a product of the clashing 'raucous conglomeration' (p. 163) of modern economies. They aim to streamline, quieten and focus the attention on *their* place, *their* ambitions and *their* presumed character in an otherwise untameable present. The rise of place branding is therefore attributable to much more than the escalation of modern tourism.

Place branding, still – but only just – a sub-category of branding, is rapidly becoming, at both national and regional levels, a well-known theoretical and methodological field in its own right. There is a short A-list of exponents, of which Wally Olins and Simon Anholt are clearly the most prominent in terms of market respect and visibility. Both propound practical, long-sighted aims and means for the process of making places into 'magnets' (Anholt 2006) for investment, tourism interest, and success in their export markets. Indeed, the whole field is one that they have to a degree invented. Anholt has been particularly persuasive in his thinking on the relationship between democracy, economic development and national branding, the difference between product advertisement and a long-term, cultured[1] branding strategy, and the absolute ascendancy of reputation over spin (Anholt 2003 and 2006). As he points out in his foreword to the inaugural issue of *Place Branding*, 'Place branding is the consequence of a realisation that public opinion is an essential component of achieving a political end' (2004, p. 9). Indeed, he is somewhat visionary in his suggestion that a brand can be not so much a statement of place as that place is at present, but a laying-out of what a nation, or region, 'wants to be' in the future (2006). This is very much in line with our own observations at the level of the city. Shanghai, for example, may be future-oriented and non-democratic now, but historically it was a radical and tortured city. Its image is a combination of its past and future: a city of hectic growth, industrial energy, cinematic decadence and inherent cosmopolitanism. Arguably, the outside world's perception of Shanghai's international status outstrips its present reality, in terms of its people's autonomy, its management of energy and the environment, its little parochialisms in day-to-day human relationships, and the need to reform its service and financial sectors. Even its colour-scape of brown, dusky-pink and orange is paradoxically muddy and unclear for a city that wants to be seen as the model of capitalism with Chinese characteristics and a beacon of Asian development in the region.

Yet, perhaps this is why the city 'works' in the world's imagination: it tells us what it 'wants to be' – internationally relevant, cosmopolitan and thriving – even though living there, in Shanghai, one is also aware of confusion, intensely local networks, and an ambition that outstrips the political weight it carries in Beijing. The combination exemplifies Thrift's 'raucous conglomeration' thesis of the effects of capital on human society. Furthermore, the city's strategic choices as to which qualities best capture its particular *mélange* of past and future styles are assertive. The city's emphasis on its women's intelligence and glamour, its commitment to change, and what we have termed its pragmatic nostalgia in certain aspects of history and architecture produces a *jolie-laide* appearance which proves as powerfully attractive to the outside world as do Sydney's physical beauty and Hong Kong's harbour.

Shanghai certainly has more buzz than Singapore, a city-state perfectly attuned to its economic development and its principles of national integration, but which was once described as 'Disneyland with the death penalty' (Gibson 1993). This is a problem that smaller states can have with brand perception: both positive and negative aspects can play off each other in a neat capsule of irony and critique. It is vital that the gap between real complexity and a true image exists in order to allow brand and cinema to capture the imaginative uncertainties, and produce affect, of a city idea. But when the brand 'clean, organized, managerial' can be applied to every feature of a city's life, producing a literalism that leaves no space for the imagination to work, or for hopes to emerge, then that gap disappears. Meanwhile, of course, China's use of the death penalty far outstrips that of Singapore, but that doesn't seem to matter for its major sub-brands: Hong Kong, Shanghai and Beijing. In any case, Shanghai is somehow untouched by the grimness of the Chinese criminal system,

---

1   Anholt's use of the word derives from the culturing of pearls: putting the cultural 'grit' in the oyster to create something new in a place's sense of self, and in the perception of that place by others.

suggesting once again that, while Beijing is *jingpai*, a responsible villain, both scary and respectable, Shanghai remains largely unaffected by China's bad image and draws attention to only the better aspects of modernization and economic reform.

What Branding Can't Do

Shanghai attracts workers and students from all over China and the region, and most global brands and larger companies feel the need to be 'in' Shanghai in some form. The city's 'magnetism' pre-dates a branding portfolio. Like Sydney, New York and Hong Kong, Shanghai has always been a city of migrants, where a sense of belonging is hard won, but – once achieved – invigorates the place and the people. New York and Hong Kong have thrived, as does Shanghai now, on local versions of capitalism and enterprise. These capitalisms are not necessarily rooted in democratic principles, and they flout any expectation that the market needs a particular form of liberalism to grow, but the debate is open on whether they may need something closer to open, responsive government if they are to sustain cities of character. People arrive in these cities and work hard to make their way in whatever manner available to them. In Sydney, one meets recent migrants with arts degrees from key universities in the region, who are starting their new lives by driving taxis, and selling and making new ideas and new products, not one of them a job for which their educational training prepared them. Migrancy means sacrificing one possible life in order to try and live another. Eventually, migrants expect to settle down and enjoy what they have worked to achieve. The move from the accumulation of wealth to the enjoyment of a particular lifestyle is typical. In contemporary China, surveys suggest that the new rich and those who are simply 'richer than before' are ready to go beyond the activity of building wealth.[2] In 1994, 68 per cent of respondents (urban residents in key cities) prioritized 'getting rich' as their main aim in life. By 2004, that number had dropped to 53 per cent. A rising number, from 10 to 26 per cent, felt that their objective was to live a life of their own devising and taste (McEwen et al. 2006, p. 70). This might be read as a statement on taste structures, on personal consumerism, or as a broader wish for autonomy and influence within the remit of one's daily existence. The latter tends to require devolved power structures, collaborative decision-making, and – for a city brand – a willingness to invite the population to be the 'grit' in their own oysters.[3] Anholt (2006) has argued in this regard that a democratic approach to place branding needs to be 'harmonious'. Harmony, he argues, should be established and maintained between how people live and how they are perceived to live; between the city as it is externally perceived and the city as it actually operates as a site of residence, development and political cohesion. Given the PRC's current emphasis on the need for a harmonious society as a model for reconciling contradictions in the social sphere, Anholt's approach – which is also premised on a democratic system

---

2 Stephanie Hemelryk Donald has discussed this issue in two unpublished papers: see 'Richer than Before', a public lecture given jointly by herself and Yi Zheng at Renmin University, Beijing on 3 July 2006 and 'Richer than Before – A Social Semiotic Approach', a presentation given at the University of Wollongong, New South Wales, on 11 August 2006.

3 See note 1.

of governance – seems apposite and yet at the same time contradictory. Perhaps harmony is a concept that would make rhetorical and political sense in Shanghai, but not in terms that are reconcilable with the idea of a working, participatory system in a city under democratic rule.

As Zhou Hanmin (2003) reiterates for us in relation to the branding of Shanghai, branding a city is always more challenging than branding a product. Products have designed attributes, which can be modified as long as the company concerned has the necessary creative or technical skills. Cities are organic and diffuse; they have various features and capacities, positive or otherwise, many of which are constantly exposed in various public media, on the streets and in every aspect of daily life. The paths, nodes and landmarks of a city – including the phrases and accents that we have remarked in Sydney's case, or the linguistic exclusions made possible by Shanghai's dialect and Hong Kong's Cantonese – are performed, deployed and modified by millions of users and speakers, walkers and travellers, as they traverse the spaces of everyday urban life. While these habits may be highly local, nonetheless the visitation and movement of tourists and business travellers through these same spaces entails the recognition of ordinary speech habits, landmark phrases, and patterns of movement as a daily authentication of a city's publicized image. Authentication is not a matter of demonstrating that a place is exactly like its image – an impossible and unreasonable task, anyway – but rather a reasonably acceptable, a 'good enough', substantiation of the structures of attention which have been brought to bear on it in film, online media, news, long term reputation and deliberate marketing. In Shanghai's case, the official presentation might seem to accord easily with a highly managed population in an authoritarian state. Yet, for Shanghai there is also an expectation that the future orientation of the city's architecture will be supplemented by an historical glamour, which will be evident in the way in which people shop, dress, interrelate, think and behave politically (very differently from the *jingpai* manner of Beijing) and present themselves in media. This added dimension of Shanghai's character is the point of 'pragmatic nostalgia', in itself a managed commodification of the past, but there is more to the future imaginary of Shanghai than a few preserved laneways and the 1920s' teahouses (although they also matter). Shanghai has demonstrated that it possesses the cinematic potential to transform itself from night to day, and from visit to visit, from regime to regime. Indeed, we would suggest that it is precisely in this versatility that its enduring strength as a city resides. Consider Filip de Boeck's 'visible and invisible city' (see below) in his recasting of paradigms of urbanism and modernity:

> ... a city that not only by its size but by its very shape-shifting nature resists objectification, colonization, synthesis and summary. It constantly remains out of focus. It is a city difficult to tame, and impossible to capture in one master narrative. It eludes any order which one imposes upon its realities. Its constant energy and movement refuse to be frozen in static images, in linear text. Its sum is always more than its parts.[4]

---

4   From an interview conducted by Vincent Lombume Kalimasi with De Boeck about his book (De Boeck and Plissart 2004) at Kinshasa in February 2004; see Kalimasi 2004.

De Boeck is actually talking about Kinshasa here, but he could very easily be describing Shanghai.

Hong Kong, whose LegCo (legislative council) comes as close to being democratic as any of those in the special regions in the PRC are allowed to get, also has a strong identity based on attributes of 'speed' and 'energy'. Its predominant film narrative is of 'small potatoes' who 'get rich quick' and its touristic attraction to Chinese visitors is as a cosmopolitan alternative to the Mainland. Anholt's idea of harmony is problematic for Hong Kong, particularly as Beijing's 'harmonious society' model will entail a capitulation to Mainland ways of doing the things that make the Special Autonomous Region special: politics, film, cultural and linguistic exceptionalism and the accumulation of wealth. The patriotism of the *1:99* films, the ghost stories that reveal Hong Kong's fascination with the layers of the past, and its website claim to be 'Asia's world city' – none of these quite fit with the Beijing model of harmony and social cohesion. Patriotism should be national and Chinese, not sub-national and located in Hong Kong. Ghosts are deemed superstitious, and ghost films are usually banned by state censors for that reason, while the ongoing status of 'Asia's world city' will be determined in negotiation with the ambitions of Beijing in 2008 and Shanghai in 2010.

What Branding Does

Building democracy through harmony is, we would politely suggest, beyond the capacity of a branding initiative, however sophisticated. A distinctive public image is, however, a brand requirement, and there the West Pacific Rim has few problems. Our three cities are visually stunning, with strong, distinctive imagery and iconic buildings, and structures both exotic and indigenous. These allow instantaneous brand recognition worldwide through connotative designs, which are immediately – and *visibly* – substantiated by the city itself. The *invisible* cities of residence and belonging, historical awareness and cultural interaction can benefit from the impact of these topographies. The apparent dichotomy between real and virtual experiences may be viewed as an emerging *rapprochement* in which the functional concerns of civic life are increasingly enacted in public and through the built environment's response to nature (Papacharissi 2005).

Meanwhile, new concepts of urbanity propose a sensory urbanism in which the sounds, smells, textures and ambience provide other dimensions to the visual impact of place. These additional 'data of the everyday', as we might call them, suggest a bridge between the seen and the unseen, the visible and the invisible. The sensorium beyond visuality is harder to mediate, of course, and, for tourists seeking an authentic experience, these modes traditionally require the dimensionality of a physical visit, when smells, poor air quality and cacophony become immediately evident. Developments in the fuller imaging of places, by means of virtual reality and communication technologies, allow selective, vicarious and mediated experiences,[5]

---

5 Something future generations may well prefer, though it be, as observers like Doheny-Farina (1996) have observed, at the expense of real community.

and permit the introduction of new tourism modes and means of access based on the economic principle of staying at home.

The structures of attention through which the city is made and perceived are both temporal and spatial, both sensory and imaginary, and these tensions provide a common framework for understanding the variously experienced city. The image of the city is liberated from a singular physical realization, with the result that the projection of its brand, with its values, offers and aspirations, becomes unbound from the tightly defined outcomes of a marketing campaign or advertising brief. It is here that the theory of branding can be reconceptualized beyond attributes and the impossible requirements of mandated character and consistency, to include constructs powerful enough to handle at least *an idea of* complexity, contradiction, evolutionary trajectories and visual metamorphoses. Constructs from film – narrative, palette, mediated interactivity and intersecting plotlines, for example – offer a metaphorical way of thinking about city character as a dynamic force, as well as an actual repository of images and affects for branding cities.

In viewing cities through the restrictive lens of traditional branding there is a problem around the notion of identity – and the applicability of a singular 'personality' to a multidimensional entity. We have therefore sought to characterize our three cities with reference to saliencies evident in a wide range of stakeholders and media products. While necessarily selective, these sets of indicators suggested that each had a particular combination of distinctive propositions that qualify them as brands. These discrete identities do not lie in functional attributes, since each city is manifestly capable of hosting events, servicing visitors, managing finance and infrastructure projects and maintaining viable commerce, trade and nightlife. Unsurprisingly perhaps, our analysis of the repertory grid ratings of each city on relevant attributes ('progressive', 'global, 'free' and so on) revealed no significant differences between the cities.[6]

Instead, the essence of an urban brand springs from deeper qualities of greater substance and permanence than merely cosmetic superficialities. These necessarily come from the place, from its people and their stories, and from particular forms of everyday life as these become established and reinforced. Ultimately, a sustainable place brand can only be an approximation of the 'true' spirit of the place, but that truth is utterly necessary to its success. Over time, a substantiated identity emerges: and in each case their distinctive identities are the key to the three cities' brands, their reputations and their future. As some of our respondents observed, world cities are world cities 'because they are' and their brand is effectively whatever position they hold in the public imagination. For example, the conclusion that Chris Choa reaches regarding Shanghai's urban development activity is that within twenty years Shanghai will not be 'just another city', but distinctively Shanghai (2004, p. 26).

---

6 A series of comparative t-tests on the repertory grid constructs showed, as we expected, that a large number of respondents did not differentiate the cities in terms of functional attributes and that individual perceptions varied in assessing this. A more finely grained demographic analysis was not possible for our particular sample, but whether a city is seen as 'cool' or 'stagnant' is likely to vary according to both demographic and access to the city's specific possibilities, rather than to the city brand itself.

Despite its famous past, Shanghai is becoming what it wants to be now, and on its own terms. Its past will not go away, but it will re-emerge and re-activate its qualities, not just through 'pragmatic nostalgia', but through new radicalisms, new migrations and new explosions of creative activity. Shanghai is determined to build its profile as a creative city, a hub of China's knowledge economy, and a leader of service industries in the southern region. If it can achieve this, Shanghai will have found another way to be a Chinese city with sufficient local power to describe its own identity by means of its products and creative workforce. Yet it will also have deployed another strategy in its bid for an element of leadership in China's future as a modern, global, nation-brand.

Sydney, a young city on old land, seems also now to be maturing into itself but, we argue, it has yet to cultivate a depth of character, or at least one that outsiders can easily perceive. As perception is fundamental to branding, this is a real challenge, although not inconsistent with a young, naturally favoured city with many first-generation migrants. Like those of many Shanghainese and Hong Kongers, the ethnic roots of many Sydneysiders lie elsewhere and some at least of their memories and motivations remain detached from everyday Sydney life. The 'face of Sydney' art project representing 1,400 of the real, everyday characters of the true Sydney (see Chapter 4) eliminated their multicultural back stories in an artwork which represented their present. This seems both symbolically appropriate and socially intelligent. The image of Sydney reflected in the drawings made by participants in our study appears to have been prompted by notions of the city as a tourist destination, with a particular lifestyle: structures of everyday life and present moment. Though apparently superficial, the character of place as it is manifest in the timelessness of the ocean, beach and harbour, and the universally popular human aspirations – in the main to 'better homes and gardens', but, more recently, as New South Wales suffers its most severe drought, to the quantity and quality of our water – seems trustworthy, true to itself and not just understandable within any culture but constitutive of contemporary Sydney's values. Such a proposition does not imply that Sydney does not have clever, cultured, hard-working people, capable of putting on 'the best Olympics ever', nor that it will not in time fully appreciate its tapestry of villages and become reconciled to its deeper history and the tragedies of its past. If we want to access that history in a cinematic moment, we could return, uncomfortably, to nineteenth-century Sydney and the unnamed and unmourned shrunken head in Hitchcock's *Under Capricorn*, a token of the failure of settlers past and present to reconcile Indigenous Australian pasts with the present in which we are all actors. For Sydney to be fully itself, such horrors as the head of an Aboriginal person in a 1940s British film need to be named, and atoned for. The hedonism of contemporary Sydney is not necessarily a bad thing either for the image of the city or for those who live there, but it cannot be maintained as a brand image at the expense of the invisible history of its construction.

Hong Kong's brand is also 'itself': the city has its currently understood role in the world, and in twenty years' time many of its attributes may be different as it adapts its identity in an uncertain context. Given its recent turns of fortune, nostalgia is already strongly developed both in film and in the way in which the city presents itself on postcards, and in tourism activities which stress the past – such as walks around the site of the old Kowloon Walled City. Hong Kong's consciously undertaken brand activity emerged around the time of the identity crisis following Handover in 1997. The newly established SAR required repositioning in the context of a re-emerging China, and in particular, a surging Shanghai. The high-level, government-led approach to what is typically a commercial activity, along with the establishment of a dedicated unit, showed the kind of serious commitment that has only been matched, in Sydney's case, by the 2000 Olympics and, in Shanghai's, by its current World Expo 2010 activity. As we have pointed out, however, Hong Kong's commitment was also in opposition to the work of other government offices and a symptom of the CEO top-down mentality of Hong Kong's struggling democratic apparatus.

Hong Kong has been required to draw more deeply than Sydney in identifying its underlying qualities and in adapting to the external environment. Its extraordinary political situation means it that it cannot help but change: as its identity evolves, more layers will be added and others peeled away. This in turn will engender more nostalgia for those who were happiest in earlier days – just as the current 45-plus age group admit to a bizarre nostalgia for British Hong Kong (if only it had not entailed the British!).

Hong Kong's sustainable identity was seriously questioned in the period between 1997 and 2003, and its resilience and depth of character were sorely tested by the SARS outbreak in 2003. In their city profile, published just before SARS, University of Hong Kong academics Sharon and Kevin Cullinane (2003) expressed concern at the state of the city's social structure; development, lack of community spaces and structural unemployment having dislocated many traditional communities. Pollution, of both air and water, and littering are cited as environmental impacts that are only taken seriously when they adversely impact on tourism or inward investment. These social and environmental factors are raised in the context of how a place branded as a world city 'should behave'. Noting Beijing's intention that Shanghai should become Asia's leading commercial city, the Cullinanes argue that Hong Kong is blending with the greater area of the Pearl River Delta. Eventually, they suggest, it will move into a regional sphere, with a 'South China' identification, in which the similarly populous Shenzhen will play 'factory' to Hong Kong's 'showroom', and in which Hong Kong may disappear to 'become just another city in China' (p. 279).

Mega-cities are indeed the next 'big thing' in urban theory and, as Nigel Thrift points out, they invented themselves from necessity before academic theorizing brought them into being. For branding on the West Pacific Rim, then, the next move will be sub-national, or *regional*, which in the case of China means a region involving several European nations. Our observations of Hong Kongers' ability to imagine their cohesion as a city within and in opposition to the larger entity of China were based on contemporary comments and on the strength of filmic responses to external threats such as SARS. They suggested that Hong Kong can withstand the regional impulse at present, and our own nostalgia for Hong Kong as a symbol of something different and ultimately approachable in the wider region of Asia, make us wish this were so. The realities of economic networks and population growth may not allow Hong Kong to survive as an idea, however. If not, then it is likely that the region will subsume Hong Kong, and that Shanghai will remain in the ascendant. Likewise, the southern China corridor will either produce a challenge to the concept of China or else will be tempered into offering itself as a contribution to Brand China's much larger ambition of economic power in the Asia pacific region.

Sydney is sprawling, but with a population of fewer than 5 million it can lay little claim to be called a megacity. It is, however, 'mega' in the sense that it operates as a metonym for Brand Australia, and thus bears a burden of representation that obscures some of its own nuance. Undoubtedly, Sydney's brand perception has remained positive since the 2000 Olympics. In 2005 the Anholt-GMI City Brands Index rated Sydney the third-best city in the world.[7] On several criteria – welcome extended to visitors, climate, cleanliness and physical attractiveness, for example – Sydney came first. The same qualities featured strongly in our own surveys and interviews. The over-determined association with the nation was apparent in mid-2006, when the Anholt Nation Brands Index rated Australia the world's Number 1 tourist destination. Again, it appeared that the perceived friendliness of the people and the physical image of Australia necessarily derived in large measure from films, books and advertisements, since relatively few have visited. On the other hand, we gained from our own surveys, no sense of a future orientation, or, indeed, of a past that might provide insights and dynamics that might help shape the Australia and the Sydney of tomorrow. In Anholt's view, both brands are 'stagnant' (Anholt-NBI 2007). The conundrum for those marketing Australia and some of its cities is that campaigns that fail to reinforce the dominant perception run the risk of diluting the brand, but, without invigoration and an 'idea of complexity', there is little to say that is new. Campaigns from Paul Hogan's mid-1980s' 'I'll slip an extra shrimp on the barbie for you' to Lara Bingle's 2006 'Where the bloody hell are you?' paint a picture of friendliness, outdoors living and irreverence, but not much else. Campaigns such as these can even appear damagingly incongruent with the professionalism required for conducting international business. One Sydney marketer noted that the successful organization and delivery of the 2000 Olympics surprised many observers, for whom Sydney's reputation lay in being laid-back, with a casual 'No worries, she'll be right' attitude.

In closing this discussion, we should like to share a few thoughts on what branding and cinema might usefully do to keep us in touch with the urban environments we inhabit and visit. Shanghai and Hong Kong are brands within a national brand that has a rising and phenomenally powerful aspect. Brand China is as much about the balance of regional power as it is about inward investment and whether the merest reference to their origin can make Chinese products attractive overseas. Shanghai is a major player in Brand China and has a good basic strategy to distinguish itself. The city is looking seriously to forge a convergence of lifestyle (garden-city) and economic power (knowledge-based), these features being 'like-characters' in its clever, green, urban personality (Ure 2001, p. 149). It is also a regional leader and a trans-national lodestar for investors and educated migrants. It uses film as a vehicle of pragmatic nostalgia to romanticize its pasts – exalting in a wayward, feisty, but ultimately unthreatening, femininity and emasculating or ridiculing its radical

---

7   A poll of over 17,000 consumers rated 30 major cities worldwide according to criteria such as international presence, potential, people and opportunities.

affronts to Beijing. Hong Kong is still on the cusp of the Mainland, but the processes of its incorporation are steady and only lightly contested in the mainstream of the political world. Brand Hong Kong's progressive, and free, attributes may be the saving of its economic souls, but its films and Cantonese distinctiveness are certainly threatened by the national brand and the political power which fuels it. And Sydney? It is the most powerful and iconic element in the idea of Australia, and for that reason it needs to breathe new life into its image and establish itself independently – and film could play a significant role in this. There is so much more about the place that could be put on show to the world, but so much more courage is needed to do it. For this conundrum, we offer a quote from Stephen Muecke's treatise on the most distinctive of all modernities and all modern histories which Australia possesses, but which is still not incorporated in the structures of attention that are brought to bear on its past, present and future:

> [B]eing modern means having a range of inventive responses to the contemporary world. In Europe this meant rapid industrialisation and urbanisation. In Australia, for Aborigines, it meant adaptation to a highly dangerous invader, for instance, as labourers in market-based industries. Survival has meant a lot of creative work, not only of a modernist sort in culture, but also in the technological, bureaucratic and economic systems that are usually associated with modernity (2004a, p.145).

This inclusive description of survival against the odds is meant here to emphasize just how much creative work is put by ordinary people into living and adapting to the modern world. The effort has been especially daunting for Australian Indigenous peoples since a rough and ready European modernity was visited upon them in the early eighteenth century. The great modernist task of invention, self-invention and survival continues today. Australia still seeks to manage the ghosts of the past into a coherent future, and still needs to harness the power of image and narrative to make that happen sooner and better rather than later. China's re-emergence into a technologized sphere of production and consumption entails re-invention of lifestyle and – crucially – of the urban experience. The great new urban centres that support and grow from these adventures into the future-present are on the West Pacific Rim. They are all global cities, and some are megacities. They are the hubs of regional power and enterprise, which drive forward both national economies and trans-national understandings of space, time and money. They are the national brand leaders of major trading nations on the Rim, yet also competitors for status and leadership in Asia Pacific, a region that now challenges the US/European North in global politics. They are also home to many millions of people. We trust that this discussion has indicated the degree to which the idea of the city as a geopolitical entity, the image of the city as a cinematic presence and a global brand, and the sense of knowing the city as a life's companion are all connected. Once such a connection is appreciated, perhaps we might cautiously suggest that cities, people and politics will move a step closer to something like a happy ending.

References

Aaker, D.A. (1991), *Managing Brand Equity: Capitalizing on the Value of a Brand Name* (New York: Free Press).

Aaker, D.A. and Joachimsthaler, E. (2000), *Brand Leadership* (New York: Free Press).

Aaker, J.L. (1997), 'Dimensions of Brand Personality', *Journal of Marketing Research* 34, 347–56.

Abbas, A. (1997), *Hong Kong: Culture and the Politics of Disappearance* (Hong Kong: Hong Kong University Press).

ABC (2000), *In the Mind of the Architect*: Episode 2, *The Public Good*. Retrieved 19 November 2006, from http://www.abc.net.au/arts/architecture/ep_trn2.htm.

ABC (2006), 'Comment Sought on Brisbane Planning Changes', 18 September 2006. Retrieved 17 October 2006, from http://www.abc.net.au/news/newsitems/200609/s1743896.htm.

Abrahamyan, G. (2005), 'New Plan for Old Yerevan: Aram Street to become Center of History and Nostalgia', Armenia: Special Features, News and Events. Retrieved 12 October 2006, from www.armeniainfo.am/news/view.php?news_id=160.

Ackerman, F. and Eden, C. (2001), 'SODA: Journey Making and Mapping in Practice', in J. Rosenhead and J. Mingers (eds), *Rational Analysis for a Problematic World Revisited: Problem-Structuring Methods for Complexity, Uncertainty and Conflict* (Chichester: John Wiley), pp. 43–60.

Adams, F. (1997), 'Re-reading the Space(s) of the City, Sydney 1948', in L. Finch and C. McConville (eds) (1997), *Images of the Urban* (Maroochydore South: Sunshine Coast University College).

ARF (2006), 'Marketers Mulling ARF's "Engagement" Definition', 4 April 2006. Retrieved 22 November 2006, from http://www.thearf.org/about/news/2006-04-04clickz.html.

Alexander, C. (1977), A *Pattern Language: Towns, Building, Construction* (New York: Oxford University Press).

Alford, D.M. (2002), 'The Great Whorf Hypothesis Hoax: Sin, Suffering and Redemption in Academe' (Chapter 7 from *The Secret Life of Language*, 17 October 2002: draft). Retrieved 19 November 2006, from http://www.enformy.com/dma-Chap7.htm>.

Alley, R. (1973), *Travels in China, 1966–71* (Peking: New World Press).

Anderson, J.R. (1983), *The Architecture of Cognition* (Cambridge, MA: Harvard University Press).

Anderson, N.R. (1990), 'Repertory Grid Technique in Employee Selection', *Personnel Review* 19:3, 9–15.

Anholt, S. (2003), *Brand New Justice: The Upside of Global* Branding (Oxford: Butterworth Heinemann).

Anholt, S. (2004), 'Editor's Foreword to the First Issue', *Place Branding* 1:1, 5–11.

Anholt, S. (2005), 'Editorial', *Place Branding* 1:4, 333–46.

Anholt, S. (2006), 'Interviews with Simon Anholt', *Baltic Development Forum 2006*, Cadenabbia (Italy) colloquium. Retrieved 20 January 2007, from http://www.bdforum.org/sideinhold.asp?sideid=565.

Anholt-NBI (2007), 'It's Official – Australia is the World's Dream Destination', *Anholt-Nation Brands Index*. Retrieved 1 February 2007, from www.nationbrandindex.com/nbi_q206-australia-press-release.phtml.

Anon. (2006), 'What's Love Got to Do with It?', *Australian*, Shanghai Business Review, 4 October.

Appadurai, A. (1996), *Modernity at Large: Cultural Dimensions of Globalization* (Minneapolis: University of Minnesota Press).

Arteallarte.com (2003), *Wang Du- san gimignano*. Retrieved 30 December 2006, from http://www.arteallarte.org/aap/english/2003/du/index.html.

Ashton, P. (1988), 'Place', *Parallax 1: The Rocks* no. 1, 23–6.

Aslam, M.M. (2006), '"Are You Selling the Right Colour?": A Cross-Cultural Review of Colour as a Marketing Cue', *Journal of Marketing Communications* 12:1, 15–30.

ATC (2001), Australian Tourism Commission, Brand Stocktake Research, August 2001. Retrieved 28 November 2006, from http://www.tourism.australia.com/content/Research/olypres2.pdf.

Baidu (Chinese-language blog), Retrieved 19 March 2006, from http://post.baidu.com/f?kz=89101321.

Balnaves, M. and O'Regan, T. (2002), 'Governing Audiences', in Balnaves, O'Regan and Sternberg (eds), pp. 10–28.

Balnaves, M. and O'Regan, T. (2002), 'The Ratings in Transition: The Politics and Technologies of Counting', in Balnaves, O'Regan and Sternberg (eds), pp. 29–64.

Balnaves, M., O'Regan, T. and Sternberg, J. (eds) (2002), *Mobilising the Audience* (St Lucia, Qld: University of Queensland Press).

Barsalou, L.W. (1987), 'The Instability of Graded Structure: Implications for the Nature of Concepts', in Neisser (ed.), pp. 101–40.

Bateson, G. (1979), *Mind and Nature: A Necessary Unity* (New York: Dutton).

Beaverstock, J.V., Smith, R.G. and Taylor, P. (1999), 'A Roster of World Cities', *Cities* 16:6, 445–58.

Beaverstock, J.V. et al. (2000), 'Globalization and World Cities: Some Measurement Methodologies', *Applied Geography* 20, 43–63.

Beerli, A. and Martin, J.D. (2004), 'Factors Influencing Destination Image', *Annals of Tourism Research* 31:3, 657–81.

Beerli, A. and Martin, M.D. (2004a), 'Tourists' Characteristics and Perceived Image of Tourist Destinations: A Quantitave Analysis – A Case Study of Lanzarote, Spain', *Tourism Management* 25, 623–36.

Beeton, S. (2004), 'The More Things Change ... A Legacy of Film-Induced Tourism', in W. Frost, G. Croy and S. Beeton (eds), *International Tourism and Media Conference Proceedings* (Melbourne: Tourism Research Unit, Monash University), pp. 4–14.

Beeton, S. (2005), *Film-Induced Tourism* (Clevedon: Channel View Publications).

Beijing International (2006), 'China Embarks on "Brand Promotion" Tour', *China Daily*. Retrieved on 22 October 2006, from http://www.ebeijing.gov.cn/News/LocalNews/t629767.htm.

Belhassen, Y. and Caton, K. (2006), 'Authenticity Matters', *Annals of Tourism Research* 33:3, 853–6.

Benjamin, A. (2006), 'Urbanity and Aesthetics (Richard Goodwin's Sydney)', paper presented at *Branding Cities and Urban Borders: Cosmopolitanisms and Parochialisms in Europe and Asia-Pacific*, conference 12–14 January 2006, Australia House and the Australia Centre, London.

Benjamin, W. (1992), 'The Work of Art in the Age of Mechanical Reproduction', in Mast, Cohen and Braudy (eds), pp. 665–81.

Beretta, G. and Nonaka, Y. (1999), 'House Painting with NCS in the USA', *Inter-Society Color Council's 68th Annual Meeting*, Vancouver, B.C., 5–7 May 1999. Retrieved 24 October 2006, from http://www.inventoland.net/pdf/Reports/iscc2rev.pdf.

Berlin, B. and Kay, P. (1969), *Basic Color Terms: Their Universality and Evolution* (Berkeley: University of California Press).

Berry, C. (1988), 'The Sublimative Text: Sex and Revolution in *Big Road [The Highway]*', *East-West Film Journal* 2:2, 66–86.

Berry, C. and Farquhar, M. (2006), *China on Screen: Cinema and Nation* (New York: Columbia University Press).

Berry, J. and McGreal, S. (eds) (1999), *Cities in the Pacific Rim: Planning Systems and Property Markets* (London: E. and F.N. Spon).

Berthon, J.P. et al. (2001), 'Organizational and Customer Perspectives on Brand Equity: Issues for Managers and Researchers', paper presented at *Australian and New Zealand Marketing Academy Conference (ANZMAC)*, Massey University, Auckland. Retrieved 22 November 2006, from http://smib.vuw.ac.nz:8081/WWW/ANZMAC2001/anzmac/AUTHORS/pdfs/Berthon1.pdf.

Best, S. (2000), 'Public Art in the Olympic City', *Architecture Australia*, September/October 2000. Retrieved 25 October 2006, from http://www.architectureaustralia.com/aa/aaissue.php?issueid=200009andarticle=10andtypeon=2.

Billig, M. (1995), *Banal Nationalism* (London: Sage).

Blain, C., Levy, S. and Ritchie, J.R. Brent (2005), 'Destination Branding: Insights and Practices from Destination Management Organizations', *Journal of Travel Research* 43:4, 328–38.

Blichfeldt, B.S. (2005), 'Unmanageable Place Brands?', *Place Branding* 1:4, 338–401.

Blum, A. (2003), *The Imaginative Structure of the City* (Montreal: McGill-Queen's University Press).

Bock, T., Davis, T., Freeman, L. and Garlin, F. (2001), 'Towards a Taxonomy of Brand Association Statements: The Ignorance of Measurement or a Measurement of Ignorance', paper presented at *Australian and New Zealand Marketing Academy Conference (ANZMAC)*, Massey University, Auckland. Retrieved 22 November 2006, from http://smib.vuw.ac.nz:8081/WWW/ANZMAC2001/anzmac/AUTHORS/pdfs/Bock1.pdf.

Bodeen, C. (2007), 'Shanghai Cancels Plans to Build Massive Ferris Wheel', *Associated Press / Taiwan News*, 12 January 2007. Retrieved 14 January 2007, from http://www.taiwannews.com.tw/etn/news_content.php?id=365292andlang+eng_newsandcate_img=35.jpgandcate_rss=news_Business.

Bordwell, D. (2000), *Planet Hong Kong: Popular Cinema and the Art of Entertainment* (Cambridge, MA: Harvard University Press).

Bottomley, P. and Doyle, J. (2006), 'The Interactive Effects of Colors and Products on Perceptions of Brand Logo Appropriateness', *Marketing Theory* 6:1, 63–83.

Bounds, J. (2006), 'Birmingham: It's not Shit', newsletter. Retrieved 25 October 2006, from http://www.jonbounds.pwp.blueyonder.co.uk/jon/brum/brum.php.

Boundy, K. (2003), 'Marketing Australia: Meeting the Challenges of a Turbulent Global Market', paper presented at *AMI National Conference*, October 2003. Retrieved 1 November 2006, from <http://www.atc.net.au/cms/pdf/KB%20AMI%20Speech.pdf>.

Braester, Y. (2005), '"A Big Dying Vat": The Vilifying of Shanghai during the Good Eighth Company Campaign', *Modern China* 31, 411–47.

Bramley, R. (2000), 'Cultural Tourism: Will it Work for You?: The Use of Cultural Resources as a Catalyst for Regional Tourism Development', paper offered to *CRC Tourism*, Brisbane, 2000. Retrieved 1 December 2006, from http://www.pc.gov.au/inquiry/heritage/subs/sun004.rtf.

Brand Hong Kong (n.d.), 'Hong Kong: Asia's World City'. Retrieved on 29 January 2007, from http://www.brandhk.gov.hk/brandhk/emesstop.htm.

Brown, G.P. (1990), 'Tourism and Place-Identity' PhD thesis, Texas A&M University.

Brown, R. (2006), '2006 Florida Splendid China'. Retrieved 5 October 2006, from http://www.lostparks.com/china.html.

Brunovs, N. (2006), 'Palettes for Perth', blog post, 15 May 2006. Retrieved 19 November 2006, from http://journals.concrete.org.au/nat/archives/inspiration/.

Burgmann, V. (1993), 'A Perspective on Sydney's Green Ban Campaign, 1970–74'. Retrieved 17 October 2006, from http://www.teachingheritage.nsw.edu.au/d_reshaping/wd2_burgman.html.

Burnham, C. (2006), 'What Shanghai has Razed', *Vancouver Sun*, 30 September 2006. Retrieved 20 November 2006, from www.canada.com/vancouversun/news/arts/story.html?id=d227fbaf-14c3-4d23-beb8-fd2647d9ca9a.

Burson-Marsteller, Landor Associates and Wirthlin Worldwide (2001), 'Perceptions of Hong Kong: Branding and Positioning Considerations Based on Research in Hong Kong and Internationally'. Report for the Information Services Department of the Hong Kong Government (May 2001).

Butler, T. and Robson, G. (2003), *London Calling: The Middle Classes and the Re-making of Inner London* (Oxford: Berg).

Buzan, T. (1974), *Use Your Head* (London: BBC Books).

Cai, F. (2003), 'China's Employment Situation and Forecast for the Next Few Years', *China and World Economy* no. 4, 38–43.

Caldwell, N. and Friere, J.R. (2004), 'The Differences between Branding a Country, a Region and a City: Applying the Brand Box Model', *Journal of Brand Management* 12:1, 50–61.

Callahan, W.A. (2004), 'Remembering the Future – Utopia, Empire and Harmony in 21st-Century International Theory', *European Journal of International Relations* 10, 569–601.

Cameron, D. (2006), 'Bloody Well not Here, That's for Sure', *Sydney Morning Herald* 25 August.

Cannane, S. (2004), 'Beauty is Skin-deep in Our Overpriced, Overrated Hype City', *Sydney Morning Herald* 28 January.

Caprara, G.V., Barbaranelli, C. and Guido, G. (2001), 'Brand Personality: How to Make the Metaphor Fit?', *Journal of Economic Psychology* 22:3, 377–95.

Carmel, E. and Eisenberg, J. (2006), 'Narratives that Software Nations Tell Themselves: An Exploration and Taxonomy', *Communications of the Association for Information Systems* 17, 851–72.

Carroll, M. (2006), 'The Urban Sensorium' (exhibition review), *The Senses and Society* 1:2, 283–8.

Cartier, C. (2005), 'Seductions of Place / Touristed Landscapes', in Cartier and Lew (eds), pp. 1–19.

Cartier, C. and Lew, A. (eds) (2005), *Seductions of Place: Geographical Perspectives on Globalization and Touristed Landscapes* (London: Routledge).

Castells, M. (1989), *The Informational City: Information Technology, Economic Restructuring and the Urban-regional Process* (Oxford: Basil Blackwell).

Castells, M. (1999), 'Setting the Context', in D.A. Schön, B. Sanyal and W.J. Mitchell (eds), *High Technology and Low-income Communities: Prospects for the Positive Use of Advanced Information Technology* (Boston, MA: MIT Press).

Chalip, L. (2000), 'An Interview with Maggie White, Business Manager Olympic Games for the Australian Tourist Commission', *International Journal of Sports Marketing and Sponsorship* 2:3, 187–98.

Chen, D. (2003), 'View from Shanghai: Darryl Chen's Shanghai is more a Process than a Static Cityscape: An Explosion of Object Buildings is Tempered by New Infrastructure, Parks and Conservation', *Architecture Review* February, 30–1.

Chen, J. (2005), 'City Gears up Development of Metro', *Shanghai Daily News* 27 December.

Chen, P.P-S. (1976), 'The Entity-Relationship Model: Towards a Unified View of Data, *ACM Transactions on Database Systems* 1:1, 9–36.

Chen and Wang (2005), *Chengdu shenghuo* (Happy Living in Chengdu) (Chengdu: Sichuan People's Press).

Cheng, F. (1981), *Say It in Chinese* (Beijing: Foreign Languages Press).

Cheung, A.B.L. (2000), 'New Interventionism in the Making: Interpreting State Interventions in Hong Kong after the Change of Sovereignty', *Journal of Contemporary China* 9, no. 24, 291–309.

Cheung, A.B.L. (2004), 'Another Massive Turnout: The Message of the July 1st March 2004', *Synergynet Bulletin* no. 32, 5 July.

Chinese Ministry of Finance (2003), 'China's Employment Situation and Forecast for the Next Five Years', *China and World Economy* no. 4, 38–43.

Chiu, T.-H. (Beryl) (2005), 'Public Secrets: Geopolitical Aesthetics in Zhang Yimou's *Hero*', *E-ASPAC: An Electronic Journal in Asian Studies*, n.d. Retrieved 5 February 2007, from < http://mcel.pacificu.edu/easpac/2005/tzuchiu.php3>.

Choa, C. (2004), 'One Modernism, Two Systems: Is there an Appropriate Urbanism for Contemporary Shanghai?', presentation at 4th Annual Forum on City Informatization in the Asia-Pacific Region, 20–22 May, Shanghai. Retrieved 28

January 2007, from http://unpan1.un.org/intradoc/groups/public/documentds/ APCITY/UNPAN016967.pdf.

Chow, R. (1998), 'King Kong in Hong Kong: Watching the "Handover" from the USA', *Social Text 55* 16:2, 93–108.

Chow, R. (1998a), *Ethics after Idealism: Theory-Culture-Ethnicity-Reading* (Bloomington: Indiana University Press).

Chu, Y. (2000), 'Hong Kong Cinema and National Cinema: Coloniser, Motherland and Self', PhD thesis, Murdoch University.

Chu, Y.C. (2003), *Hong Kong Cinema: Coloniser, Motherland and Self* (London: Routledge Curzon).

Churchill, E.F. and Bly, S. (2000), 'Culture Vultures: Considering Culture and Communication in Virtual Environments', *SIGGroup Bulletin* 21:1, 6–11.

Cicada (2006), 'Nick Ritar's Free Artist Portfolio'. Retrieved 14 October 2006, from http://www.absolutearts.com/portfolios/c/cicada/.

City of Melbourne (2004), 'Places for People'. Retrieved 20 November 2006, from http://www.melbourne.vic.gov.au/info.cfm?top=202andpg=2602.

City of Sydney (2002), 'Barani: Indigenous History of Sydney City'. Retrieved 17 October 2006, from http://www.cityofsydney.nsw.gov.au/barani/timeline/ timeline.htm.

City of Sydney (2006), 'The Face of Sydney'. Retrieved 17 October 2006, from http:// www.cityofsydney.nsw.gov.au/artandabout/ExhibitionsEvents/CircularQuay/ TheFaceofSydney.asp.

Clark, J.O.E. (ed.) (2005), *Remarkable Maps: 100 Examples of How Cartography Defined, Changed and Stole the World* (Sydney: ABC Publishing).

Cler, M. (2004), 'Against Colour Globalisation. Colour Trends and Colour Collections: Their Use as a Vocabulary and Effect upon Colour Culture', AIC 2004 Color and Paints, Interim Meeting of the International Color Association, Porto Alegre, Brazil. Retireved 20 November 2006, from www.fadu.uba.ar/sitios/ sicyt/color/aic2004/208-210.pdf.

Clode, J. (2002), 'Review of *Suzhou River*', *Intersections: Journal of Gender, History and Culture in Asia* Issue 7, March. Retrieved 27 January 2007, from http://wwwsshe.murdoch.edu.au/intersections/issue 7/clode_review.html.

Cohen, E. (1979), 'A Phenomenology of Tourist Experiences Sociology', *The Journal of the British Sociological Association* 13:2, 179–201.

Color Kinetics (2006), 'Color Kinetics Showcase: The Westin, Shanghai'. Retrieved 20 November 2006, from http://www.colorkinetics.com/showcase/installs/print. html?id=66.

Coomaraswamy, A.K. (1956), *Christian and Oriental Philosophy of Art* (New York: Dover Publications).

Coonan, C. (2007), 'Monument to All that Jazz: Shanghai's Peace Hotel, a Piece of Old Europe in New China', *Guardian* 13 January.

Coshall, J.T. (2000), 'Measurement of Tourists' Images: The Repertory Grid Approach', *Journal of Travel Research* 39, 85–9.

Council of the City of Sydney (2006), 'Government and Developers to Bulldoze Sydney's Heritage'. Retrieved 17 October 2006, from http://www.sydneymedia. com.au/html/2979-government-and-developers-to-bulldoze-sydneys-heritage.asp.

Cowan, G. (n.d.), 'Nomadic Resistance: Tent Embassies and Collapsible Architecture: Illegal Architecture and Protest'. Retrieved 17 October 2006, from the Koori History Website at http://www.kooriweb.org/foley/images/history/1970s/emb72/embarchit.htm.

Coward, L.A. and Salingaros, N.A. (2004), 'The Information Architecture of Cities', *Journal of Information Science* 30:2, 107–18.

Craik, J. (1995), 'Are there Cultural Limits to Tourism?', *Journal of Sustainable Tourism* 3, 87–98.

Craik J. (2001), 'Tourism, Culture and National Identity', in T. Bennett and D. Carter (eds), *Culture in Australia: Policies, Publics and Programs* (Cambridge: Cambridge University Press), pp. 89–113.

Crary, J. (1999), *Suspensions of Perception: Attention, Spectacle and Modern Culture* (Cambridge: MIT Press).

Craven, J. (2005), 'The Sydney Olympic Stadium'. Retrieved 13 October 2006, from http://en.sportnet.cn/news/view.asp?id=241.

Crozier, W.R. (1999), 'The Meanings of Colour: Preferences among Hues', *Pigment and Resin Technology* 28:1, 6–14.

Cugley, J. (2001), 'Seeing and Sensing Place', poster presentation at *9th International Colour Association Conference*. Retrieved 19 November 2006, from http://www.iscc.org/aic2001/abstracts/poster/Cugley.doc.

Cullinane, S. and Cullinane, K. (2003), 'City Profile: Hong Kong', *Cities* 20:4, 279–88.

Curtis, J. (2001), 'Branding a State: The Evolution of Brand Oregon', *Journal of Vacation Marketing* 7:1, 75–81.

Damasio, A.R. (1994), *Descartes' Error: Emotion, Reason, and the Human Brain* (New York: Penguin Putnam).

Davey, P. (1998), 'True Colours: The Glorious Polychromy of the Past Suggests a Strong Historical Need for Colour, despite Current Reductive Fashions: Color in Architecture, *Architectural Review* November 1998, pp. 34–6.

Davies, A. (2006), 'Part of the City will be Hungry again', *Sydney Morning Herald* 26 September 2006. Retrieved 14 January 2007, from www.smh.com.au/news/national/part-of-the-city-will-be-hungry-again/2006/25/09/25/1159036472164.html/.

De Boeck, F. and Plissart, M.-F. (2004), *Kinshasa: Tales of the Invisible City* (Ghent-Amsterdam: Ludion).

De Certeau, M. (1984), *The Practice of Everyday Life*, trans. Steven Rendall (Berkeley: University of California Press).

De Chernatony, L. and McDonald, M.H.B. (1998), *Creating Powerful Brands in Consumer, Service and Industrial Markets* (Oxford: Butterworth-Heinemann).

Delong, M. et al. (2004), 'Perception of US Branded Apparel in Shanghai', *Journal of Fashion Marketing and Management* 8:2, 141–53.

Desser, D. (2001), 'New Kids on the Digital Block: The Post-colonial, Post-industrial, Post-modern Situation in Korean, Chinese and Japanese Youth Films', paper presented at *International Conference on Media and Culture Development in the Digital Era*, Taipei.

Doheny-Farina, S. (1996), *The Wired Neighborhood* (New Haven, Conn.: Yale University Press).

Donald, J. (1999), *Imagining the Modern City* (London: Athlone).

Donald, S.H. (2006), 'The Idea of Hong Kong, Structures of Attention in the City of Life', in C. Lindner (ed.), *Urban Space and Cityscapes* (London: Routledge), pp. 63–74.

Donald, S.H. (2007), 'Out on a Limb: Urban Traumas on the Pacific Rim', in A. Marcus (ed.), *Visualising the City* (London: Routledge) (forthcoming).

Donald, S.H. and Gammack, J. (2005), 'Drawing Sydney: Flatlands, Chromatics and the Cinematic Contours of a World's Global City', *SCAN: Journal of Media Arts Culture*, 2:1. Retrieved 24 October 2006, from www.scan.net.au/scan/journal/.

Donald, S.H. and Zheng, Y. (2008), 'A Taste of Class: Manuals for Becoming Woman', in *Positions: East Asia Cultures Critique* (forthcoming).

Dong. S. (2001), *Shanghai 1842–1941: The Rise and Fall of a Decadent City* (New York: Harper Collins).

Dovey, K. (1999), *Framing Places: Mediating Power in Built Form* (London: Routledge).

Downs R.M. and Stea, D. (eds) (1973), *Image and Environment* (Chicago: Aldine).

Du, Y. (1988), *Zhonghua minguo dianying shi* (History of Film in the Republic of China), 2 vols (Taipei: Committee for Cultural Construction of the Administrative Yuan).

English.eastday.com (2005), Shanghai Municipal Government Press Conference Memo (15 November 2005). Retrieved 18 January 2007, from http://english.eastday/englishedition/specials/node20817/uerobject1ai1680810.html.

Eberhard, W. (1986), *A Dictionary of Chinese Symbols: Hidden Symbols in Chinese Life and Thought* (London: Routledge).

Eden, C. (2004), 'Analyzing Cognitive Maps to Help Structure Issues or Problems', *European Journal of Operational Research* 159, 673–86.

Eden, C., Jones, S. and Sims, D. (1979), *Thinking in Organizations* (London: Macmillan).

Elkins, J. (2002), *Stories of Art* (New York: Routledge).

Elliott, C. (2005),'Colour™: Law and the Sensory Scan', *M/C Journal* 8.4. Retrieved2 October 2006, from http://journal.media-culture.org.au/0508/06-elliott.php.

Ellis, M. and Holt, S. (2005), 'Experiences in Harmonising Lighting Efficiency Standards between China and Australia', paper delivered at 6th International Conference on Energy-Efficient Lighting, Shanghai, 9–11 May 2005. Retrieved 22 October 2006, from http://www.rightlight6.org/english/proceedings/session_13/Experiences_in_Harmonising_Standards/f022ellis.doc.

English.eastday.com (2005a), 'Lights to Stay on During the Summer'. Retrieved 24 October 2006, from http://english.eastday.com/eastday/englishedition/node20676/userobject1ai1288802.html.

English.eastday.com. (2005b), 'City to Create More Green Space', *Shanghai Daily*, 31 October. Retrieved 19 November 2006, from http://english.eastday.com/eastday/englishedition/specials/node20816/userobject1ai1596067.html.

Enticknap, L. (2001), 'Postwar Urban Redevelopment, the British Film Industry and *The Way We Live*', in M. Shiel, and T. Fitzmaurice (eds), *Cinema and the City* (Oxford: Blackwell), pp. 233–44.

Evans, H. and Donald, S.H. (eds) (1999), *Picturing Power in the People's Republic of China: Posters of the Cultural Revolution* (Boulder, Col.: Rowan and Littlefield).

Expo2010China.com (2006), 'City to Scrutinize Glass Walls'. Retrieved 24 October 2006, from http://www.expo2010china.com/expo/english/eu/nc/ct/userobject1ai34449.html.

Faehnders, T. (2006), 'Shanghai's Famous Peace Hotel Looks to the Future'. Retrieved 22 October 2006, from http://travel.monstersandcritics.com/features/printer_1202901.php.

Faircloth, J.B., Capella, L.M. and Alford, B.L. (2001), 'The Effect of Brand Attitude and Brand Image on Brand Equity', *Journal of Marketing Theory and Practice* 9:3, 61–75.

Feng Min (1985), '*Malu tianshi yu xinxianshizhuyi*' (*Street Angels* and Neorealism) *Dangdai dianying* no. 5, 95–100.

Finlay, V. (2002) *Colour: Travels through the Paintbox* (London: Hodder and Stoughton).

Flannery, T. (ed.) (1999), *The Birth of Sydney* (Melbourne: Text Publishing).

Florian, B. (2002), 'The City as a Brand: Orchestrating a Unique Experience', in B. Hauben, M. Vermeulen and V. Patteeuw (eds), *City Branding: Image Building and Building Images* (Rotterdam: NAI Uitgevers).

Foley, D. (2001), *Repossession of our Spirit: Traditional Owners of Northern Sydney*, Aboriginal History Monograph no 7. (Canberra, ANU: Aboriginal History Inc.).

Fontana, A.M. and Matías, N. (2004), 'Color and Patrimony in La Plata City, Argentina', in AIC Interim Meeting, Porto Alegre, Brazil, November. Retrieved 19 November 2006, from http://www.fadu.uba.ar/sitios/sicyt/color/abstract.pdf.

Friedman, J. (1986), 'The World City Hypothesis', *Development and Change* 17:1, 69–84.

Franzen, G. and Bouwman, M. (2001), *The Mental World of Brands: Mind, Memory and Brand Success* (Washington: World Advertising Research Center).

Frenchman, D. (2000), 'The 6 Secrets of a Happy Marriage – Between the Old and the New', paper delivered at *China-Cultural Heritage Management and Urban Development: Challenge and Opportunity*, UNESCO-World Bank Conference, Beijing, 5–7 July. Retrieved 14 January 2007, from http://www.worldbank.org.cn/Chinese/content/culture.pdf.

Friedman, J. (1986), 'The World City Hypothesis', *Development and Change* no. 17, 69–83.

Frisby, D. (2001), *Cityscapes of Modernity: Critical Explorations* (London: Polity).

Fu, M. (2006), 'Shanghai *longtong* (Shanghai lanes)'. Retrieved 17 January 2007, from http://www.5151abd.com/Article/ShowArticle.asp?ArticleID=39550.

Fu, P. (2003), *Between Shanghai and Hong Kong: The Politics of Chinese Cinemas* (Stanford: Stanford University Press).

Fu, P. and Desser D. (eds) (2000), *The Cinema of Hong Kong* (Cambridge: Cambridge University Press).

Funk, S.V. (2006), 'CD Review: Metropolis Shanghai - Showboat to China'. Retrieved 22 October 2006, from http://blogcritics.org/archives/2006/02/08/093740.php.

Gallarza, M.G., Saura, I.G. and Garca, H.C. (2002), 'Destination Image: Towards a Conceptual Framework', *Annals of Tourism Research* 29:1, 56–78.

Gammack, J.G. (2002), 'Synaesthesia and Knowing', in P. McKevitt, S.Ó. Nualláin and C. Mulvihill (eds), *Language, Vision and Music: Selected Papers from the 8th International Workshop on the Cognitive Science of Natural Language Processing*, Galway, 1999 (Amsterdam: John Benjamins), pp. 157–70.

Gammack, J.G. and Donald, S.H. (2006), 'Collaborative Methods in Researching City Branding: Studies from Hong Kong, Shanghai and Sydney', *Tourism, Culture and Communication* 6:3, 171–80.

Gammack, J.G., Goulding, P. and Seow, H.H. (2002), 'Communicating Regional Identity: The Hong Kong Tourism Board Website', in F. Sudweeks and C. Ess (eds), *Proceedings CATAC 02*, Montreal, July, pp. 237–58.

Gammack, J.G. and Hodkinson, C. (2003), 'Virtual Reality, Involvement and the Consumer Interface', *Journal of End User Computing* 15:4, 80–98.

Gammack, J.G. and Young, R.M. (1984), 'Psychological Techniques for Knowledge Elicitation', in T. O'Shea (ed.), *Proceedings of the European Conference on Artificial Intelligence* (North Holland: Elsevier).

Gates, C. (2004), 'Image/Transformation' Master of Fine Arts Print Media thesis, College of Fine Arts, University of New South Wales. Retrieved 22 November 2006, from <http://vuspace.vu.edu.au/archives/cgates/CGatesThesis.pdf>.

Gencay, O.A. et al. (2005), 'Colors and Cultural Interactions in the Turkish Sport Clubs', *Sport Journal* 8:2. Retrieved 22 October 2006, from <http://www.thesportjournal.org/2005Journal/Vol8-No2/Okkes-Gencay.asp>.

Gerritsen, F. (1975), *Theory and Practice of Color: A Colour Theory based on Laws of Perception* (London: Studio Vista).

Gibbons, M. et al. (1994), *The New Production of Knowledge: The Dynamics of Science and Research in Contemporary Societies* (London: Sage).

Gibson, W. (1993), 'Disneyland with the Death Penalty', *Wired* 1.04, September/October. Retrieved 20 January 2007, from http://www.wired.com/wired/archive/1.04/gibson.html.

Gilbert, J. and Santilli, P. (2000), 'Stadium Australia: Where the Games Begin and End'. Retrieved 13 October 2006, from http://olympics.ballparks.com/2000Sydney/index.htm.

Gilmore, F. (2004), 'Shanghai: Unleashing Creative Potential', *Journal of Brand Management* 11:6, 442–8.

Gilmore, F. and Dumont, S. (2003), *Brand Warriors China: Creating Sustainable Brand Capital* (London: Profile Books).

Given, J. (2003), *America's Pie: Trade and Culture after 9/11* (Sydney: UNSW Press).

Glaser, M. (1991), 'The Business Psyche: Exploring Relationships between Local Quality of Life and City Image', *Public Administration Quarterly* 15:3, 287–303.

Goldberg, K. (ed.) (2001), *The Robot in the Garden: Telerobotics and Telepistemology in the Age of the Internet* (Cambridge, MA: MIT Press).

Goldsmith, B. and O'Regan, T. (2005), *The Film Studio: Film Production in the Global Economy* (Lanham: Rowman and Littlefield).

Goodman, B. (1995), *Native Place, City and Nation: Regional Networks and Identities in Shanghai, 1853–1937* (Berkeley: University of California Press).

Goodman, D.S.G. (1981), 'The Shanghai Connection: Shanghai's Role in National Politics during the 1970s', in C. Howe (ed.), *Shanghai: Revolution and Development in an Asian Metropolis* (Cambridge: Cambridge University Press), pp. 125–52.

Goodyear, M. (1996), 'Divided by a Common Language: Diversity and Deception in the World of Global Marketing', *Journal of the Market Research Society* 38:2, 105–22.

Gordon, M. and Tan, F. (2002), 'The Repertory Grid Technique: A Method for the Study of Cognition in Information Systems', *MIS Quarterly* 26:1, 39–57.

Gorn, G.J., Chattopadhyay, A. and Dahl, D.W. (1999), 'The Use of Visual Mental Imagery in New Product Design', *Journal of Marketing Research* 36:1, 18–28.

Graburn, N. with Bartliet-Bouchier, D. (2001), 'Relocating the Tourist', *International Sociology*, 16:2, 147–58.

Graham, S. and Marvin, S. (1996), *Telecommunications and the City* (London: Routledge).

Grau, O. (2001), 'The History of Telepresence: Automata, Illusion, and the Rejection of the Body', in Goldberg (ed.), pp. 226–43.

Green, B.C. (2002), 'Marketing the Host City: Analyzing Exposure Generated by a Sport Event', *International Journal of Sports Marketing and Sponsorship* 4:4, 335–54.

Green Building Council Australia (2006), 'The Dollars and Sense of Green Buildings, 2006'. Retrieved 17 October 2006, from <http://www.gbcaus.org/download.asp?file=%5CDocuments%5CDollars+and+Sense+of+Green+Buildings%2Epdf>.

Guangzhou Daily (2006), '"Cartoon and Animation City" Opens', 22 August 2006. Retrieved 17 November 2006, from http://www.lifeofguangzhou.com/node_10/node_37/node_85/2006/08/22/11562165537248.shtml.

Gunn, C.A. (1988), *Vacationscape: Designing Tourist Regions* 2nd edn (New York: Van Nostrand Reinhold).

Guzmán, F. (2005), 'A Brand Building Literature Review', excerpt from 'Brand Building Towards Social Values: Associating to Public Goods', PhD thesis, Esade Business School. Retrieved 17 November 2006, from http://www.brandchannel.com/images/papers/257_A_Brand_Building_Literature_Review.pdf.

Habbo (2006), 'Habbo Home Page'. Retrieved 17 October 2006, from www.habbo.com.au/.

Habbo.com (2006), 'The Veronicas in Habbo Hotel'. Retrieved 17 October 2006, from http://www.habbo.com.au/entertainment/veronicas.

Hall, R. (1988), *Home: A Journey through Australia* (Melbourne: Minerva).

Hamilton, G.G. (1999), 'Hong Kong and the Rise of Capitalism in Asia', in G.G. Hamilton (ed.), *Cosmopolitan Capitalists: Hong Kong and the Chinese Diaspora at the End of the Twentieth Century* (Seattle: University of Washington Press), pp. 14–34.

Hankinson, G. (2004), 'Relational Network Brands: Towards a Conceptual Model of Place Brands', *Journal of Vacation Marketing* 10:2, 109–21.

Hård, A. (1969), 'Qualitative Aspects of Colour Perception', *Colour 69: Proceedings of 1st AIC Congress*, Stockholm, pp. 1–26.

Hari, J. (2006), 'Woody's London is a Star Turn', *Evening Standard* (London), 13 January.

Harris, C. (1997), 'The New Woman Incident: Cinema, Scandal and Spectacle in 1935 Shanghai', in Lu, S.H. (ed.), *Transnational Chinese Cinemas: Identity, Nationhood, Gender* (Honolulu: University of Hawaii Press), pp. 277–302.

Harrison, J. (2001), 'Thinking about Tourists', *International Sociology* 16:2, 159–74.

Harvey, S. (n.d.), 'Shanghai: On the Cutting Edge of China's Economic Miracle'. Retrieved 21 October 2006, from http://www.gonomad.com/destinations/0601/shanghai.html.

Hatch, M.J. and Schultz, M. (2003), 'Bringing the Corporation into Corporate Branding', *European Journal of Marketing* 37:7/8, 1041–64.

Hauben T., Vermeulen, M. and Patteeuw, V. (eds), (2002), *City Branding: Image Building and Building Images* (Rotterdam: NAI Vitgevers).

Häussermann, H. and Colomb, C. (2003), 'The New Berlin: Marketing the City of Dreams', in L.M. Hoffman, S.S. Fainstein and D.R. Judd (eds), *Cities and Visitors: Regulating People, Markets and City Space* (London: Blackwell), pp. 200–18.

Hawthorne, C. (2004), 'China Pulls up the Drawbridge', *New York Times*, Arts and Leisure section 19 September.

Henderson, J.C. (2000), 'Selling Places: The New Asia-Singapore Brand', *Journal of Tourism Studies* 11:1, 36–44.

Henderson, P.W. and Cote, J.A. (1998), 'Guidelines for Selecting or Modifying Logos', *Journal of Marketing* 62:2, 14–30.

Henderson, P.W., Cote, J.A., Leong, S.M. and Schmitt, B.H. (2003), 'Building Strong Brands in Asia: Selecting the Visual Components of Image to Maximize Brand Strength', *International Journal of Research in Marketing* 20:4, 297–313.

Hill, B., Arthurson, T., and Chalip, L. (2001), *Kangaroos in the marketing of Australia*, Wildlife Tourism Research Report Series (Gold Coast, Qld: Co-operative Research Centre for Sustainable Tourism).

Holt, R. (2002), 'Faces of The "New China": A Comparison of Touristic Web Sites in the Chinese and English Languages', *Information Technology and Tourism* 5:2, 105–19.

Horan T.A. (2000), *Digital Places: Building Our City of Bits* (Washington, DC: Urban Land Institute).

Howard, R. (2006), 'Ambient Signifiers: How I Learned to Stop Getting Lost and Love Tokyo Rail'. Retrieved 22 October 2006, from http://www.boxesandarrows.com/view/ambient_signifi.

Hudson, S. and Ritchie, J.R. Brent (2006), 'Promoting Destinations via Film Tourism: An Empirical Identification of Supporting Marketing Initiatives', *Journal of Travel Research* 44:4, 387–96.

Huppatz, D.J. (2005), 'Globalizing Corporate Identity in Hong Kong: Rebranding Two Banks', *Journal of Design History* 18:4, 357–69.

IIASA (1999), International Institute for Applied Systems Analysis website, 'Arguments – Prediction Error'. Retrieved 17 October 2006, from http://www.iiasa.ac.at/Research/LUC/ChinaFood/argu/error/err_33.htm.

Invest HK (2006), 'Invest Hong Kong (InvestHK)'. Retrieved 30 October 2006, from http://www.investhk.gov.hk/pages/1/329.aspx.

Jackson, K.M. and Trochim, W.M.K. (2002), 'Concept Mapping as an Alternative Approach for the Analysis of Open-Ended Survey Responses', *Organizational Research Methods* 5:4, 307–36.

Keller, K.L. (1993), 'Conceptualizing, Measuring, and Managing Customer-Based Brand Equity', *Journal of Marketing* 57, 1–22.

Keller, K.L. (2003), *Strategic Brand Management: Building, Measuring and Managing Brand Equity* (Upper Saddle River, NJ: Prentice Hall).

Keller, P. (2001), 'Conclusions from Tourism Summit 2001, Chamonix-Mon-Blanc'. Retrieved 17 November 2006, from http://www.sommets-tourisme.org/e/sommetsG/troisieme-sommet/actes/keller2.html.

Kelly, G.A. (1955), *The Psychology of Personal Constructs* 2 vols (New York: Norton).

Kengo, K. (1999), 'Color to Make Architectural Forms Stand Out or Fade Away', *Nipponia* 4. Retrieved 25 October 2006, from www.inventoland.net/pdf/Reports/nipponia4-p6.pdf.

Kerr, G. (2006), 'From Destination Brand to Location Brand', *Journal of Brand Management* 13:4/5, 276–83.

Kheng-Lian, K. (n.d.), 'Garden City to Model Green City'. Retrieved 25 October 2006, from http://www.unescap.org/DRPAD/VC/conference/bg_sg_14_gcm.htm.

Kim, H. and Richardson, S.L. (2003), 'Motion Picture Impacts on Destination Images', *Annals of Tourism Research* 30:1, 216–37.

King, J. (2002), 'Destination Marketing Organisations – Connecting the Experience rather than Promoting the Pace', *Journal of Vacation Marketing* 8:2, 105–8.

Kobayashi, S. (1990), *Color, Image, Scale* (Tokyo: Nippon Color and Design Research Institute).

Komar, V. and Melamid, A. (1997), *Painting by Numbers: Komar and Melamid's Scientific Guide to Art* ed. J. Wypijewski (New York: Farrar, Straus and Giroux).

Koolhaas, R., Foster, N. and Mendini, A. (2001), *Colours* (Basel: Birkhäuser).

Kotler, P. et al. (2001), *Marketing Asian Places* (Chichester: Wiley).

Kotler, P. and Gertner, D. (2002), 'Country as Brand, Product and Beyond: A Place Marketing and Brand Management Perspective', *Journal of Brand Management* 9:4/5, 249–61.

Kotler, P., Gertner, D. and Rein, I. (2006), *Marketing Places: Latin America* (New York: Pearson Education).

Krätke, S. (2003), 'Global Media Cities in a Worldwide Urban Network', *European Planning Studies* 11:6, 605–28.

Kristeva, J. (1980), *Desire in Language : A Semiotic Approach to Literature and Art* ed. L.S. Roudiez (New York: Columbia University Press).

Kuhn, A. (2002), *An Everyday Magic: Cinema and Cultural Memory* (London and New York: Tauris).

Kunstler, J.H. and Salingaros, N.A. (2001), 'The End of Tall Buildings', Op-Ed, 17 September 2001. Retrieved 25 October 2006, from http://www.planetizen.com/node/27.

Lange, B. (1995) *The Colours of Rome* (Copenhagen: Royal Danish Academy of Fine Arts, School of Architecture).

Lange, B. (1997), *The Colours of Copenhagen* (Copenhagen: Royal Danish Academy of Fine Arts, School of Architecture).

Lee, L.O. (1999), *Shanghai Modem: The Flowering of a New Urban Culture in China, 1930–1945* (Cambridge, MA: Harvard University Press).

Lee and Leung (2003), 'City of Turmoil', *South China Morning Post*, 7 August.

Leece, B. (2001), 'Sydney: The Results Olympic Games and Architecture: The Future for Host Cities', paper presented at *Joint Conference IOC / IUA*, May 2001. Retrieved 25 November 2006, from http://multimedia.olympic.org/pdf/en_report_641.pdf.

Leman, E. (2002), 'Can Shanghai Compete as a Global City?', *China Business Review*, September-October, 7–15.

Lenclos, J.-P. and Lenclos, D. (2004), *Colors of the World: A Geography of Color* (New York: W.W. Norton).

LePla, F.J. and Parker, L.M. (1999), *Integrated Branding: Becoming Brand-Driven through Companywide Action* (London: Quorum).

Levy, A. (2003), *Small Island* (London: Hodder Headline).

Levy, S. (2002), *Ready, Steady, Go!: Swinging London and the Invention of Cool* (London: Fourth Estate).

Lewis, J.W. (1965), 'Revolutionary Struggle and the Second Generation in Communist China', *China Quarterly* no. 2, 126–47.

Lewis, S.W. (2002), 'What Can I Do For Shanghai?: Selling Spiritual Civilization in Chinese Cities', in S.H. Donald, M. Keane and Y. Hong (eds), *Media in China: Consumption, Content and Crisis* (London: Routledge Curzon), pp. 139–51.

Leyda, J. (1972), *Dianying: An Account of Films and the Film Audience in China* (Cambridge, Mass.: MIT Press).

Li, D. (2005), *Zhongguo dianying wenhua shi* (History of Chinese Film Culture) (Beijing: Beijing daxue chubanshi).

Li, Q. (2005), 'Constitution of the Standard for the Urban Area Environment and Decorative Lighting in Shanghai', *6th International Conference on Energy-Efficient Lighting*, 9–11 May 2005, Shanghai, China.

Liang, H. (2006), 'Don't Look Down on City's "Slums"', *China Daily* 27 June 2006. Retrieved 29 January 2007, from http://www.chinadaily.com.cn/2006-06/27/content_628279.htm.

Lindner, C. (ed.) (2006), *Urban Space and Cityscapes: Perspectives from Modern and Contemporary Culture* (London: Routledge).

Lindstrom, M. (2005), *Brand Sense: Build Powerful Brands through Touch, Taste, Smell, Sight and Sound* (New York: Free Press).

Liu, C. (2002), 'Light Branding', MA design and Branding Strategy, Brunel University. Retrieved 20 November 2006, from dea.brunel.ac.uk/downloads/courses/desbrandstrat/dissertations/c_liu.pdf.

Liu, Y. (2003), 'The Importance of the Chinese Connection: The Origin of the English Garden', *Eighteenth-Century Life* 27:3, 70–98.

Liu, Z. (2005), 'Shanghai's Urban Sculptures: Don't Sit on us!' Retrieved 25 October 2006, from http://www.shanghaiist.com/archives/2005/11/28/shanghai_needs.php.

Lo, K. (2001), 'Transnationalization of the Local in Hong Kong Cinema of the 1990s', in E. Yau, E. (ed.), *At Full Speed: Hong Kong Cinema in a Borderless*

World (London: University of Minnesota Press), pp. 261–76.

Long, K. (2006), 'Brief History of Branding' (blog: posted 15 June 2006). Retrieved 25 January 2007, from http://blog.experiencecurves.com/archives/brief-history-of-branding.

Lu, H. (1999), *Beyond the Neon Lights: Everyday Shanghai in the Early Twentieth Century* (Berkeley: University of California Press).

Lu, H. (2006), 'Bamboo Sprouts After the Rain: The History of University Student Environmental Associations in China', *China Environment Series*, no. 6. Retrieved 22 October 2006, from http://www.wilsoncenter.org/topics/pubs/ACFF6.pdf.

Lü, X. (2000), *Cadres and Corruption: The Organizational Involution of the Chinese Communist Party* (Stanford: Stanford University Press).

Luo, X. (2006), '*Longtongs* in Shanghai', *Resource Centres Network Magazine*, Beijing Modern Teaching Institute. Retrieved 17 January 2007, from http://www.bjmti.com/resource/ShowArticle.Asp?ArticleID=3693/.

Lury, C. (2005), '"Contemplating a Self-portrait as a Pharmacist": A Trade Mark Style of Doing Art and Science', *Theory, Culture and Society* 22:1, 93–110.

Lutron.com (2006), 'Case Study / Lighting Control Systems: JW Marriott Hotel, Shanghai, China'. Retrieved 19 November 2006, from http://www.lutron.com/CLC/PDFs/JW_Marriott_%2015_8.pdf.

Lynch, K. (1960), *The Image of the City* (Cambridge, MA: MIT Press).

Ma, Y.-J. (2001), 'Building a Cybercity: The Taipei Experience'. Retrieved 3 February 2007, from http://www.taipei.gov.tw.

MacCannell, D. (1999), *The Tourist: A New Theory of the Leisure Class* (Berkeley: University of California Press).

Mack, L. (2002), 'Searching for Shanghai'. Retrieved 25 October 2006, from http://www.shanghaiexpat.com/modules.php?op=modloadandname=Newsandfile=articleandsid=44.

Mackay, S. (1999), 'City Life Beckons on Net', *Sunday Times* (Perth), 12 December.

Madden, T.J., Hewett, K. and Roth, M.S. (2000), 'Managing Images in Different Cultures: A Cross-National Study of Color Meanings and Preferences', *Journal of International Marketing* 8:4, 90–107.

Madriz, E. (2000), 'Focus Groups in Feminist Research', in N.K. Denzin and Y.S. Lincoln (eds), pp. 835–850.

Manovich, L. (2001), *The Language of New Media* (Cambridge, MA: MIT Press).

Mao, Z. (1949), 'Report to the Second Plenary Session of the Seventh Central Committee of the Communist Party of China', *Selected Works of Mao Tse-tung*, Vol. IV. Retrieved on 18 January 2007, from <http://marxists.org/reference/archive/mao/selected-works/volume-4/index.htm>.

Marcus, A. (ed.) (2007), *Visualizing the City* (London: Routledge).

Martin.com (2001, 'CyberExpress Taking Retailing into the 21st Century'. Retrieved 21 November 2006, from http://www.martin.com/casestory/casestory.asp?id=382.

Maslow, A. (1954), *Motivation and Personality* (New York: Harper).

Mast, G., Cohen, M. and Braudy, L. (eds) (1992), *Film Theory and Criticism: Introductory Readings*, 4th edition (New York: Oxford University Press).

Mason, K. (2004), 'Sound and Meaning in Aboriginal Tourism', *Annals of Tourism Research* 31:4, 837–54.

McEwen, W. et al. (2006), 'Inside the Mind of the Chinese Consumer', *Harvard Business Review* 83:3, 68–76.

McKercher, B. and Chow, B. (2001), 'Cultural Distance and Cultural Tourism Participation', *Pacific Tourism Review* 5:1/2, 21–30.

Medin, D.L. and Coley, J.D. (1998), 'Concepts and Categorization', in J. Hochberg (ed.), *Perception and Cognition at Century's End: History, Philosophy, Theory* (San Diego: Academic Press), pp. 403–39.

Metcalfe, P. (2001), 'Gender, Colour and the Domestic Sphere', *Proceedings of the 9th Congress of the International Colour Association*, 24–29 June 2001, Rochester, NY. Retrieved 21 November 2006, from http://www.iscc.org/aic2001/abstracts/oral/Metcalfe.doc.

Meyer, R.J. (2005), *Ruan Ling-yu: The Goddess of Shanghai* (Seattle: University of Washington Press).

Millard, K. (1994), 'Beyond the Pale: Colour and the Suburb', in S. Ferber, C. Healy and C. McAuliffe (eds), *Beasts of Suburbia: Reinterpreting Cultures in Australian Suburbs* (Melbourne: Melbourne University Press).

Miller, M. (1997), 'Adrian Rifkin: *Street Noises: Parisian Pleasure, 1900–1940*' (review), *H-France, H-Net Reviews.* Retrieved 6 February 2007, from http://www.h-net.org/reviews/showrev.cgi?path=30806864998288.

Mills, B. (2005), 'Canadian City Brands – A Statistical Survey', September 2005. Retrieved 19 November 2006 from http://www.pier8group.com/pdf/Canadian_City_brands.pdf.

Mimura, K.U. (1994), 'Soetsu Yanagi and the Legacy of the Unknown Craftsman', *Journal of Decorative and Propaganda Arts* 20, 208–23.

Min, A. (2000), *Becoming Madame Mao* (New York: Houghton Mifflin).

Mishra, P. (2006), 'Getting Rich', *London Review of Books* 28:23, 3–7.

Mitchell, W.J. (1995), *City of Bits: Space, Place and the Infobahn* (Cambridge, MA: MIT Press).

Mitchell, W.J. (1999), 'The City of Bits Hypothesis', in D.A. Schön, B. Sanyal and M.J. Mitchell (eds), *High Technology and Low-income Communities: Prospects for the Positive Use of Advanced Information Technology* (Boston, Mass. MIT Press).

Moberly, J., Morrison, F. and Neville, T. (1997), *Sydney: A Guide to Recent Architecture* (Cologne: Konemann).

Morgan, C.L. (1999), *Logos: Logo, Identity, Brand, Culture* (Hove, UK: Rotovision).

Morgan, D.L. (1998), *The Focus Group Guidebook* (Thousand Oaks, CA: Sage Publications).

Morgan, N., Pritchard, A. and Pride, R. (eds) (2004), *Destination Branding: Creating the Unique Destination Proposition*, 2nd edn (Amsterdam: Elsevier Butterworth-Heinemann).

Morrison, F. (1997), *Sydney: A Guide to Recent Architecture* (London: Ellipsis).

Morse, J. (2001), 'The Sydney 2000 Olympic Games: How the Australian Tourist Commission Leveraged the Games for Tourism', *Journal of Vacation Marketing* 7:2, 101–7.

Mould, O. (2006), 'Sydney: A World City of Cultural Connections', PhD thesis, University of Leicester.

Muecke, S. (2004a), *Ancient and Modern: Time, Culture and Indigenous Philosophy* (Sydney: UNSW Press).

Muecke, S. (2004b), '"I Don't Think They Invented the Wheel": The Case for Aboriginal Modernity', *Angelaki: Journal of Theoretical Humanities* 9:2, 155–63.

Nachmanovitch, S. (1990), *Free Play: Improvisation in Life and Art* (New York: Penguin-Putnam).

Napack, J. (2001), 'The Selling of Shanghai: Art in America'. Retrieved 25 October 2006, from http://www.findarticles.com/p/articles/mi_m1248/is_7_89/ai_ 76332992.

NBI (2006), National Brands Index website. 'It's Official – Australia is the World's Dream Destination'. Retrieved 25 October 2006, from http://www. nationbrandindex.com/nbi_q206-australia-press-release.phtml.

Naughton, B. (1999), 'Between China and the World: Hong Kong's Economy before and after 1997', in Hamilton (ed.), pp. 80–99.

Naveh, Z. (2001), 'Ten Major Premises for a Holistic Conception of Multifunctional Landscapes', *Landscape and Urban Planning* 57:3, 209–84.

Naveh, Z. (2005), 'Epilogue: Toward a Transdisciplinary Science of Ecological and Cultural Landscape Restoration', *Restoration Ecology* 13:1, 228–34.

Neisser, U. (ed.) (1987), *Concepts and Conceptual Development: Ecological and Intellectual Factors in Categorization* (Cambridge: Cambridge University Press).

New London Architecture (2007), 'Legible London: 28 September 2006–3 March 2007'. Retrieved 17 October 2006, from http://www.newlondonarchitecture.org/ exhibitions.php#legible.

Newman, P.W.G. and Kenworthy, J.R. (1989), *Cities and Automobile Dependence: An International Sourcebook* (Aldershot: Gower).

Nixon, S. (2006), 'High-rise Residents Big Energy Guzzlers', *Sydney Morning Herald*, 30 May 2006.

Novak, J.D. (1998), *Learning, Creating and Using Knowledge: Concept Maps as Facilitative Tools in Schools and Corporations* (Mahwah, NJ: Lawrence Erlbaum Associates).

O'Brien, D. (2006), 'Event Business Leveraging the Sydney 2000 Olympic Games', *Annals of Tourism Research* 33:1, 240–61.

O'Connor, Z. (2006), 'Environmental Colour Mapping Using Digital Technology: A Case Study', *Urban Design International* 11:1, p. 21.

O'Leary, S. and Deegan, J. (2003), 'People, Pace, Place: Qualitative and Quantitative Images of Ireland as a Tourism Destination in France', *Journal of Vacation Marketing* 9:3, 213–26.

O'Regan, T. (1996), *Australian National Cinema* (London: Routledge).

OIEPR (2006), Office of International Exchange and Public Relations (China). 'Brand Promotion Program was Launched in Shanghai, Jiaotong University'. Retrieved 25 October 2006, from http://www.asom.sjtu.edu.cn/enedtion/publish/ viewNode.jsp?OID=2-36788.

Olins, W. (1999), *Trading Identities: Why Countries and Companies Are Taking on Each Others' Roles* (London: Foreign Policy Centre).

Olins, W. (2004), *On B®and* (London: Thames and Hudson).

Olympic Games (2005), 'Introduction of the Colours: The Great Wall Grey'. Retrieved on 20 November 2006, from http://en.beijing2008.com/43/71/article211987143.shtml.

Open University (2006), 'Canary Wharf'. Retrieved on 17 October 2006, from <http://www.open2.net/modernity/3_17.htm>.

Overy, P. (2001), 'Colour in the Work of Norman Foster', in Koolhaas, Foster and Mendini.

Pang, L. (2002a), *Building a New China in Cinema: The Chinese Left-Wing Cinema Movement, 1932–1937* (Lanham, NY: Rowman and Littlefield).

Papadopoulos, N. and Heslop, L. (2002), 'Country Equity and Country Branding: Problems and Prospects', *Journal of Brand Management* 9:4/5, 294–314.

Papacharissi, Z. (2005), 'The Real/Virtual Dichotomy in Online Interaction: New Media Uses and Consequences Revisited', *Communication Yearbook* 29:1, 215–38.

Park, R. (1948), *Fishing in the Styx* (Ringwood, Vic.: Penguin).

Park, R. (1980), *Playing Beatie Bow* (Ringwood, Vic.: Puffin).

Passow, T., Fehlmann, R. and Grahlow, H. (2005), 'Country Reputation – From Measurement to Management: The Case of Liechtenstein', *Corporate Reputation Review* 7:4, 309–26.

Pastoureau, M. (2000), *Blue: The History of a Color* (Princeton, NJ: Princeton University Press).

Perry, E.J. (1994), 'Shanghai's Strike Wave of 1957', *China Quarterly* no. 137, 1–27.

Petty, S. (2005), 'Where the Misfits Find they Still Fit in', *Australian Financial Review*, 14–16 October.

Planning.nsw.gov (n.d.), 'Walking Sydney Harbour', NSW Department of Planning. Retrieved on 16 January 2007, from http://www.planning.nsw.gov.au/harbour/walking.asp.

Plummer, J. (2006), 'Re:Think! Engagement', talk given at *ARF 52nd Annual Convention*, New York, March 2006, New York, in *Reach and Response: A Proven Model* (Ipsos, 2006). Retrieved 19 November 2006, from http://www.ipsos-ideas.com/article.cfm?id=3161.

Porter, T. (1997), 'Environmental Colour Mapping', *Urban Design International* 2:1, 23–31.

Powerhouse Museum (2000), 'Green Games 2000'. Retrieved 13 October 2006, from http://www.powerhousemuseum.com/sydney2000games/statements.php?themeId=21.

Priester G.W. (2006), 'Consistent Colors for Your Site - All You Need to Know about Web Safe Colors', *Web Developers Journal* (online). Retrieved 19 November 2006, from http://www.webdevelopersjournal.com/articles/websafe1/websafe_colors.html.

Queensland Government (2006), 'State Colour'. Retrieved on 20 November 2006, from www.premiers.qld.gov.au/Government/emblems/State_colour/.

Rabuini, E. (2004), 'Color as a Key Factor in the Cultural Inheritance of La Boca District, Buenos Aires. *AIC Interim Meeting*, Porto Alegre, Brazil, November 2004. Retrieved 19 November 2006, from http://web.archive.org/web/20050803075300/http://www.fadu.uba.ar/sicyt/color/aic2004oral.htm.

Rao, A.R. and Ruekert, R.W. (1994), 'Brand Alliances as Signals of Product Quality', *Sloan Management Review* September, 1994: 87–97.

Ramo, J.C. (2006), *Brand China* (London: Foreign Policy Centre).

Ratnatunga, J. and Muthaly, S. (2000), 'Lessons from the Atlanta Olympics: Marketing and Organisational Considerations for Sydney 2000', *Journal of Sports Marketing and Sponsorship*, September-October, pp. 239–57.

Reay, C. (1990), 'Add Colour to Lift Brand Appeal', *Marketing Week* 13:10, p. 27.

Reisinger, Y. and Steiner, C. (2006), 'Reconceptualising Object Authenticity', *Annals of Tourism Research* 33:1, 65–86.

Restall, C. and Gordon, W. (1993), 'Brands – The Missing Link: Understanding the Emotional Relationship', *Marketing and Research Today* 21:2, 59–67.

Richards, G. (2002), 'Marketing China Overseas: The Role of Theme Parks and Tourist Attractions', *Journal of Vacation Marketing* 8:1, 28–38.

Rieber, R.W. (1989), 'A Cross-Cultural Study of Language Universals: The Emotional Meaning of Iconic and Graphic Stimuli', in R.W. Rieber (ed.), *The Individual, Communication, and Society* (Cambridge: Cambridge University Press) pp. 170–90.

Rifkin, A. (1995), *Street Noises: Parisian Pleasure, 1900–1940* (New York: St Martin's Press).

Riley, C.A. II (1995), *Color Codes: Modern Theories of Color in Philosophy, Painting and Architecture, Literature, Music, and Psychology* (Lebanon, NH: University Press of New England).

Rittel, H. and Webber, M. (1973), 'Dilemmas in a General Theory of Planning', *Policy Sciences* 4, 155–69.

Roberts, H. (2006), 'What's Love Got to Do with It?', *Shanghai Business Review*, July 2006. Retrieved 4 October 2006, from http://www.lovemarks.com/?pageID=20022and_fr_collectionid=9and_fr_collection1id=59>.

Roberts, K. (2005), *Lovemarks: The Future Beyond Brands* (New York: PowerHouse Books).

Robertson-Friend, B. (2004), 'Aboriginal Tourism', *Year Book Australia, 2004*. Retrieved 17 October 2006, from http://www.abs.gov.au/Ausstats/abs@.nsf/94713ad445ff1425ca25682000192af2/b8038bd7df52a8b0ca256dea00053968!OpenDocument#.

Robins, K. (1999), 'Foreclosing on the City? The Bad Idea of Virtual Urbanism', in J. Downey and J. McGuigan (eds), *Technocities* (London: Sage), pp. 34–59.

Rodriguez-Ortega, V. (2004), 'An Interview with Christopher Doyle', Linklater Symposium, *Reverse Shot Online*. Retrieved on 12 December 2006, from http://www.reverseshot.com/legacy/summer04/doyle.html>.

Rohdie, S. (2001), *Promised Lands: Cinema, Geography, Modernism* (London: BFI Publishing).

Rolls, E. (1993), *From Forest to Sea: Australia's Changing Environment* (St Lucia, Qld: University of Queensland Press).

Roodhouse, S. (2006), *Cultural Quarters: Principles and Practices* (London: Intellect).

Room, A. (ed.) (2000), *Brewer's Dictionary of Modern Phrase and Fable* 16th edition (London: Cassell).

Rosch, E. and Lloyd, B.B. (eds) (1978), *Cognition and Categorization* (Hillsdale, NJ: Erlbaum).

Rowden, M. (2000), *The Art of Identity: Creating and Managing a Successful Corporate Identity* (Aldershot: Gower).

RTKL.com (2006a), 'Great Places Need to be Planned'. Retrieved 22 October 2006, from http://www.rtkl.com/docs/brochures/rtkl_urban_design.pdf.

RTKL.com (2006b), 'Create a Sense of Place', in *A New Heartbeat for the City*. Retrieved 17 October 2006, from http://www.rtkl.com/docs/brochures/rtkl_retailmini.pdf.

Ruíz, F.J.M. (2000), 'The Supplier-Retailer Relationship in the Context of Strategic Groups', *International Journal of Retail and Distribution Management* 28:2, 93–106.

Rushkoff, D. (2003), 'Coercion', *M/C: A Journal of Media and Culture* no. 6. Retrieved 21 November 2006, from <http://www.media-culture.org.au/0306/06-coercion.php>.

Rusinek, S. 'Does the Emotional Context Influence the Recollection of Color?', PSYART: An Online Journal for the Psychological Study of the Arts, article 040212. Retrieved 12 October 2006, from http://www.clas.ufl.edu/ipsa/journal/articles/psyart/2004_rusinek01.shtml.

Rutherford, D. (2001), 'Intimacy and Alienation: Money and the Foreign in Biak', *Public Culture: Society for Transnational Cultural Studies* 13:2, 299–324.

Said, E. (1993), *Culture and Imperialism* (New York: Knopf).

Salingaros, N.A. (2002), 'Development of the Urban Superorganism', *Katarxis* no. 3. Retrieved 26 October 2006, from http://www.katarxis3.com/Salingaros-Urban_Superorganism.htm.

Sandin, E.-L. and Äkäslompolo, N. (2004), 'Developing Advertising Messages: Examples from the Swedish Print Media', Bachelor's thesis, International Business and Economics Programme, Luleå University of Technology, Sweden. Retrieved 21 November 2006, from http://epubl.ltu.se/1404-5508/2004/195/LTU-SHU-EX-04195-SE.pdf.

Sassen, S. (1991), *The Global City* (New York: Princeton University Press).

Sassen, S. (ed.) (2002a), *Global Networks, Linked Cities* (London: Routledge).

Sassen, S. (2002b), 'Locating Cities on Global Circuits', *Environment and Urbanization* 14:1, 13–30.

Sassen, S. (2005), 'Urban Age – A Worldwide Series of Conferences Investigating the Future of Cities'. Retrieved 22 October 2006, from http://www.urban-age.net/10_cities/01_newYork/newYork_PL+US_quotes.html.

Saunders, B.A.C. and Van Brakel, J. (1997), 'Are there Non-Trivial Constraints on Colour Categorization?', *Behavioral and Brain Sciences* 20, 167–228.

Scannell, P. (1996), *Radio, Television and Modern Life* (Oxford: Blackwell).

Scannell, P. (2000), 'For Anyone as Someone Structures', *Media Culture and Society*, 22, 5–24.

Schachter, R.D. (1986), 'Evaluating Influence Diagrams', *Operations Research* 34: 871–82.

Schindler, V.M. (2004a), 'Colour as Vocation: Werner Spillmann's Contribution to Environmental Colour Design', *Color Research and Application*, 30:1, 53–65.

Schindler, V.M. (2004b), 'Prefabricated Rolls of Oil Paint: Le Corbusier's 1931 *Colour Keyboards*', AIC 2004 Color and Paints, Interim Meeting of the International Color Association, Proceedings, Porto Alegre, Brazil.

Schlosser, A.E. (2003), 'Experiencing Products in the Virtual World: The Role of Goals and Imagery in Influencing Attitudes versus Intentions', *Journal of Consumer Research* 30, 184–98.

Schmitt, B. (2006), 'Closing Remarks: The Changing Face of Marketing', *2006 Corante Innovative Marketing Conference*, June. Retrieved 29 December 2006, from http://corante.com/skypecasts/marketing.BerndSchmitt.05-12-061.mp3.

Schnabel, M. A. and Kvan, T. (2001), 'Design Communication in Immersive Virtual Environments: An Initial Exploration; *Architectural Information Management.* 19th eCAADe Conference, Helsinki, 29–31 August 2001, pp. 472–8. Retrieved 20 November 2006, from http://www.arch.hku.hk/~marcaurel/phd/initialveds. html.

Schöpflin, G. (2000), *Nation, Identity, Power: The New Politics of Europe* (London: Hurst).

Scott, A.J. (2005), *On Hollywood: The Place, The Industry* (Princeton, NJ: Princeton University Press).

Shanghai Airport (2003), 'Back Cover', *Airport Journal*, 2003/6, no 51.

ShanghaiDaily.com (2006), 'XVII. Future Objectives: Shanghai's Middle- and Long-Term Development Goals'. Retrieved 24 October 2006, from http://www1. shanghaidaily.com/bf_17_future.php.

Shanghai Daily (2006), 'Eyesore Building in Shanghai to be Demolished', *Shanghai Daily*, 23 April 2006. Retrieved 18 November 2006, from http://english.sina.com/ china/1/2006/0423/73661.html.

Shanghai-ed.com (2006), '20 Nanjing Rd'. Retrieved 30 September 2006, from http://www.shanghai-ed.com/nanjinglu/.

Shanghai Municipal Government (2005), 'Press Conference Memo', 16 November 2005. Retrieved 24 January 2007, from http://www.shanghai.gov.cn/shanghai/ node8059/node10470/node10475/userobject22ai19347.html.

Shanghai Municipal Government (2006a), 'Shanghai Prospects'. Retrieved 13 January 2007, from http://www.shanghai.gov.cn/shanghai/node8059/ShanghaiProspects/ userobject22ai22060.htm.

Shanghai Municipal Government (2006b), 'Shanghai – Chinese Bright Pearl to Bring World Expo Pleasant Surprise'. Retrieved 18 January 2007, from http:// www.shanghai.gov.cn/shanghai/node8059/node8631/userobject2113851.html.

Shanghai Star (2005), 'Skin-deep Meanings', *Shanghai Star*, 17 March 2005. Retrieved 25 October 2006, from http://app1.chinadaily.com.cn/star/2005/0317/ cu14-1.html.

Shanghai-story.net (2006), 'Chasing E-Wa'. Retrieved 30 September 2006, from http://www.shanghai-story.net/ewa/?page_id=2.

Shanghai Vision (2006), 'Shanghai Vision: Feb 2006'. Retrieved 22 October 2006, from http://www.shanghaivision.com/files/feb2006_research.pdf.

Shaw, S.-M. (2003), 'A Steady Rot?', *South China Morning Post*. Retrieved 19 November 2006, from http://sinmingshaw.com/docs/html/a_steady_rot_scmp_2003.ht ml.

Shi, H. (2000), 'Well's Spiritual Tale Bubbles Over', *Shanghai Star*, 29 February.

Retrieved 28 January 2007, from http://app1.chinadaily.com.cn/star/history/00-02-29/c14-tale.html.

Shi, Y. and Hamnett, C. (2002), 'The Potential and Prospect for Global Cities in China: in the Context of the World System', *Geoforum* 33, 121–35.

Shiel, M. (2001), 'Cinema and the City in History and Theory', in M. Shiel and T. Fitzmaurice (eds), *Cinema and the City: Film and Urban Societies in a Global Context* (Oxford: Blackwell), pp. 1–18.

Shiel, M. (2006), *Italian Neorealism: Rebuilding the Cinematic City* (London: Wallflower Press).

Shocker, A.D. and Weitz, B. (1988), 'A Perspective on Brand Equity Principles and Issues', report no. 91–124 (Cambridge, MA: Marketing Science Institute).

Siguaw, J.A, Mattila, A. and Austin, J.R. (1999), 'The Brand-Personality Scale', *Cornell Hotel and Restaurant Administration Quarterly* 40:3, 48–55.

Sikkens Foundation (n.d.). 'Special Projects: Maastricht – Colors of the City'. Retrieved 12 October 2006, from www.sikkens.com/Colours/CaseStudies/MaastrichtColorsCity.htm.

Sikkens Foundation (n.d.), 'Special Projects: Barcelona – Rambla'. Retrieved 20 November 2006), from www.sikkens.com/Colours/CaseStudies/BarcelonaRambla.htm.

Silverstone, R. (1994), *Television and Everyday Life* (London: Routledge).

Simpson, C. and Lambert, A. (2005), '"The Glittering Tart": Imaging Sydney', *Scan: Journal of Media Arts Culture*. Retrieved 17 October 2006, from http://scan.net.au/scan/journal/display_synopsis.php?j_id=4.

Singh, S. (2006), 'Impact of Color on Marketing', *Management Decision* 44:6, 783–9.

Siu, S.K.W. (1999), 'The Escalator: A Conveyor of Hong Kong's Culture', *Human Relations* 52:5, 665–81.

Skaggs, S. (1994), *Logos: The Development of Visual Symbols* (Menlo Park, CA: Crisp Publications).

Skrbina, D. (2001), 'Participation, Organization and Mind: Toward a Participatory Worldview', PhD thesis, University of Bath. Retrieved 20 November 2006, from http://www.bath.ac.uk/carpp/davidskrbina/summarycontents.htm.

Smyth, R. (1998), 'From the Empire's Second Greatest White City to the Multicultural Metropolis: The Marketing of Sydney on Film in the 20th Century', *Historical Journal of Film, Radio and Television*, 18:2, 237–63.

SNDA Entertainment (2004), 'Overview'. Retrieved 1 February 2007, from http://www.snda.com/en/about/overview.htm.

Spearritt, P. (1999), *Sydney's Century: A History* (Sydney: UNSW Press).

Spearritt, P. (2002), 'Marketing Cities: Icons, Brands and Slogans', 12 June 2002. Retrieved 17 October 2006, from http://www.brisinst.org.au/resources/spearritt_peter_cities.html.

SPG Media Limited (2006), 'Shanghai Pudong Development Bank, Shanghai, China'. Retrieved 17 October 2006, from http://www.designbuild-network.com/projects/shanghhai-pudong/.

Stamps, A. E. III (1990), 'Use of Photographs to Simulate Environments: A Meta-analysis', *Perceptual and Motor Skills* 71, 907–13.

Swirnoff, L. (2000), *The Color of Cities: An International Perspective* (New York: McGraw-Hill).

Sydney Media (2006), 'Government and Developers to Bulldoze Sydney's Heritage', Media release (22 June 2006). Retrieved 21 October 2006, from <http://www.sydneymedia.com.au/html/2979-government-and-developers-to-bulldoze-sydneys-heritage.asp>.

Tallack, D. (2005), *New York Sights: Visualizing Old and New* (Oxford: Berg).

Tavassoli, N.T. (2001), 'Color Memory and Evaluation for Alphabetic and Logographic Brand Names', *Journal of Experimental Psychology* 7:2, 104–11.

Tavassoli, N.T. and Han, J.K. (2000), 'Branding with Logographic and Phonetic Scripts: Memory for Relations among Brand Names, Logos and Auditory Icons', MIT Sloan School of Management, Cambridge, MA.

Tavassoli, N.T. and Han, J.K. (2001), 'Scripted Thought: Processing Korean Hancha and Hangul in a Multimedia Context', *Journal of Consumer Research* 28, 482–93.

Tavassoli, N.T. and Han, J.K. (2002), 'Auditory and Visual Brand Identifiers in Chinese and English', *Journal of International Marketing* 10:2, 13–28.

Temporal, P. (2000), *Branding in Asia: The Creation, Development and Management of Asian Brands for the Global Market* (Singapore: John Wiley).

Teo, P. and Leong, S. (2006), 'A Postcolonial Analysis of Backpacking', *Annals of Tourism Research* 33:1, 109–31.

Teo, S. (2001), 'Wong Kar-wai's *In the Mood for Love*: Like a Ritual in Transfigured Time', *Senses of Cinema*, March-April. Retrieved 11 December 2006, from http://www.sensesofcinema.comtents/01/13/mood.html.

Tewary, A. (2006), 'Think of Pink' *Deccan Herald*, 8 November 2006 (Internet edition). Retrieved 20 November 2006, from http://www.deccanherald.com/deccanherald/Nov82006/panorama212202006117.asp.

Theroux, P. (1989), *Riding the Iron Rooster: By Train through China* (London: Penguin).

Thompson, E.R. (2004), 'The Political Economy of National Competitiveness: "One Country, Two Systems" and Hong Kong's Diminished International Business Reputation', *Review of International Political Economy* 11:1, 62–97.

Thrift, N. (1998), Virtual Capitalism: The Globalisation of Reflexive Business Knowledge', in J.G. Carrier and D. Miller (eds), *Virtualism: A New Political Economy* (Oxford: Berg), pp. 161–86.

Tianyaclub.com (Forum post) (2006), 'Product Placement in *Mission Impossible III*'. Retrieved 25 October 2006, from http://www.zonaeuropa.com/culture/c20060614_1.htm.

Tischler, L. (2006), 'The Gucci Killers', *Fast Company* no. 102, 42.

Toffler, A. (1970), *Future Shock* (New York: Random House).

Tourism Australia (2001), 'Impact of Sydney 2000 Olympic Games on Brand Australia'. Retrieved 21 October 2006, from http://www.tourism.australia.com/content/Research/olypres2.pdf.

TravelChinaGuide.com (2007), 'Beijing's *Hutong* and Courtyard'. Retrieved 25 October 2006, from http://www.travelchinaguide.com/cityguides/beijing/hutong/yard.htm.

Tress, B., Tress, G. and Fry, G. (2004), 'Defining Concepts and the Process of Knowledge Production in Integrative Research', in E. Tress, G. Tress, G. Fry and P. Opdam (eds), *From Landscape Research to Landscape Planning: Aspects of Integration, Education and Application* (Netherlands: Frontis Wageningen). Retrieved 21 November 2006, from http://library.wur.nl/frontis/landscape_research/02_tress.pdf.

Trueman, M., Klemm, M. and Giroud, A. (2004), 'Can a City Communicate?: Bradford as a Corporate Brand', *Corporate Communications* 9:4, 317.

Tse, D.K.C. (2001), *Singular Characteristics of the China Market*, Hong Kong University School of Business Paper. no 63463 (Hong Kong: Chinese Management Centre, UHK).

Tse, R.Y.C. and Ganesan, S., (1999), 'Hong Kong', in J. Berry and S. McGreal (eds) *Cities in the Pacific Rim: Planning Systems and Property Markets* (London: E. and F.N. Spon), pp. 67–88.

Tufte, E.R. (1990), *Envisioning Information* (Cheshire, CT: Graphics Press).

Tufte, E.R. (1997), *Visual Explanations* (Cheshire, CT: Graphics Press).

Turner, K. (1999), 'The Criminal Body and the Body Politic: Punishments in Early Imperial China', *Cultural Dynamics* 11:2, 237–56.

Turner, T. (1996), *City as Landscape - A Post-postmodern View of Design and Planning* (London: E. and F.N. Spon).

United Nations (2003), 'Garden City to Model Green City', *ESCAP Virtual Conference: Integrating Environmental Considerations into Economic Policy-Making Processes*, Singapore. Retrieved 29 December 2006, from http://www.unescap.org/drpad/vc/conference/bg_sg_14_gcm.htm.

UPI (2006), 'China Cities to Get Half the Population'. Retrieved 20 November 2006, from http://www.newsdaily.com/TopNews/UPI-1-20061107-11030400-bc-china-urbanization.xml.

Urban Age Project (2005), 'Trading City for Space: Does More Personal Living Space Lead to Urban Sprawl in Shanghai?', panel of *Urban Age: A Worldwide Series of Conferences Investigating the Future of Cities*, Shanghai, July. Retrieved on 29 January 2007, from http://www.urban-age.net/03_conferences/programmeShanghai.html.

Ure, J. (2000), 'Convergence in Hong Kong', in M. Hukill, R. Ono and C. Vallath (eds), *Electronic Communication Convergence: Policy Challenges in Asia* (New Delhi: Sage), pp. 148–76.

Urry, J. (1990), *The Tourist Gaze: Leisure and Travel in Contemporary Societies* London: Sage Publications).

US-China Business Council (2006), 'Foreign Investment in China'. Retrieved 22 October 2006, from http://www.uschina.org/info/chops/2006/fdi.html.

Valdez, P. and Mehrabian, A. (1994), 'Effects of Colors on Emotions', *Journal of Experimental Psychology* 123:4, 394–409.

Van den Berg-Weitzel, L. and Van de Laar, G. (2001), 'Relation between Culture and Communication in Packaging Design', *Brand Management* 8:3, 171–184.

Van de Ven, A.M. and Cox, P. (2000), Interview with Jonathan Nolan (8 November 2000). Retrieved 13 October 2006, from http://www.powerhousemuseum.com/sydney2000games/interviews.php?interviewId=5.

Van Ham, P. (2001), 'The Rise of the Brand State: The Postmodern Politics of Image and Reputation', *Foreign Affairs* 80:5, 2–4.

Varey, R.J. (1999), 'Marketing, Media and McLuhan: Rereading the Prophet at Century's End', *Journal of Marketing* 63:3, 148–53.

Veres, C. and Hitchman, S. (2002), 'Using Psychology to Understand Conceptual Modelling', in S. Wrycza et al. (ed.), *Proceedings of the 10th European Conference on Information Systems*, 6–8 June 2002, Gdansk, Poland (Gdansk: Wydawnictwo Uniwersytetu Gdanskiego), pp. 473–81.

Verhoeven, D. and Morris, B. (2004), *Proceedings of the Passionate Cities Symposium* (Melbourne: RMIT Publishing).

Virgo, B. and de Chernatony, L. (2006), 'Delphic Brand Visioning to Align Stakeholder Buy-in to the City of Birmingham Brand', *Journal of Brand Management* 13:6, 379–92.

Vivian, P. (2006), 'Deutsche Bank Place', *Architecture Australia*, July-August. Retrieved 2 February 2007, from http://www.archmedia.com.au//aa/aaissue.php?issueid=200607andarticle=12andtrpeon=2.

Wahlqvist, S. and Larsson, T. (2006), 'Brand New City: A Place Marketing Study on Jönköping', Undergraduate thesis, Jönköping University, Sweden. Retrieved 25 October 2006, from http://www.diva-portal.org/diva/getDocument?urn_nbn_se_hj_diva-413-1__fulltext.pdf.

Wakeman, F. Jr (1996), *Shanghai Badlands: Wartime Terrorism and Urban Crime* (Cambridge: Cambridge University Press).

Wand, Y., Storey, V.C. and Weber, R. (1999), 'An Ontological Analysis of the Relationship Construct in Conceptual Modeling', *ACM Transactions on Database Systems* 24:4, 494–528.

Wark, M. (1997), *The Virtual Republic: Australia's Culture Wars of the 1990s* (St Leonards, NSW: Allen and Unwin).

Wasserstrom, J.N. (2006), 'A Big Ben with Chinese Characteristics: The Customs House as Urban Icon in Old and New Shanghai', *Urban History* 33:1, 65–84.

Watts, J. (2005), 'Shanghai Star to Top London's Eye', *Age* (Beijing). Retrieved 30 January 2007, from http://www.tiscali.co.uk/news/newswire.php/news/reuters/2005/05/12/topnews/shanghaiferris.

Watts, J. (2006), 'Shanghai Opens Shelter for Young Internet Addicts', *Guardian*, 25 August 2006. Retrieved 20 November 2006, from http://www.guardian.co.uk/china/story/0185778300.html.

Wei, X. (2006). 'A Nostalgia for Another Time'. Retrieved 22 October 2006, from http://www.shanghaidaily.com/art/2006/08/15/289180/A nostalgia for another time.htm.

Whitfield, P. (2005), *Cities of the World: A History in Maps* (London: British Library).

Whitfield, P. (2006), *London: A Life in Maps* (London: British Library).

Williams, R. (1977), *Marxism and Literature* (Oxford: Oxford University Press).

Wilson, B. (2006),'Fountain Furore Overshadows World Cup'. Retrieved 22 November 2006, from http://news.bbc.co.uk/2/hi/business/4771933.stm.

Windsor-Liscombe, R. (2005), *The Ideal City* (Vancouver: Vancouver Working Group, 2005). Retrieved 22 October 2006, from http://www.finearts.ubc.ca/faculty/rhodri/The_Ideal_City.pdf.

Winfield-Pfefferkorn, J. (2005), 'The Branding of Cities: Exploring City Branding and the Importance of Brand Image', MA thesis, Graduate School of Syracuse University. Retrieved 30 December 2006, from http://www.brandchannel.com/images/papers/245_Branding_of_Cities.pdf.

Wong, A.-L. (2003), *The Shaw Screen: A Preliminary Study* (Hong Kong: Hong Kong Film Archive).

Wong, S.-L. (1996), 'The Entrepreneurial Spirit: Shanghai and Hong Kong Compared', in Y.M. Yeung and Y-W. Sung (eds), *Shanghai: Transformations and Modernization under China's Open Policy*, pp. 25–48.

Wood, L. (2000), 'Brands and Brand Equity: Definition and Management', *Management Decision* 38:9, 662–9.

Wood, N. (1999), *Vectors of Memory: Legacies of Trauma in Postwar Europe* (Oxford: Berg).

World Bank (2000), *China-Cultural Heritage Management and Urban Development: Challenge and Opportunity* (Beijing: UNESCO World Bank).

World Expo (2003), 'Shanghai Tourism and Enterprise Committee: Policy and Regulation Section', *World Expo and the New Development in Shanghai: 2010 Expo and Shanghai Tourism*.

Wright, R. (1994), 'Developing our Own Space: Place and Identity in Australian Cinema', Working Papers in Australian Studies, no. 97 (London: Sir Robert Menzies Centre for Australian Studies).

Wu, F. (2000), 'Global and Local Dimensions of Place-Making: Remaking Shanghai as a World City', *Urban Studies* 37:8, 1359–77.

Wu, B. and Cai, L.A. (2006), 'Spatial Modeling: Suburban Leisure in Shanghai', *Annals of Tourism Research* 33:1, 179–98.

Wu, F. (2006), 'Globalization, the Changing State and Local Governance in Shanghai', in Xiangming, C. (ed.), *Local Transformations in Global Cities: Shanghai in Comparative Perspective* (Minneapolis: University of Minnesota Press), pp. 296–321.

Wu, J. (2006), 'Nostalgia as Content Creativity: Cultural Industries and Popular Sentiment', *International Journal of Cultural Studies* 93:3, 359–68.

Xiao, H. and Mair, H.L. (2006), 'A Paradox of Images: Representation of China as a Tourist Destination', *Journal of Travel and Tourism Marketing* 20:2, 1–14.

Xing, X. and Chalip, L. (2006), 'Effects of Hosting a Sport Event on Destination Brand: A Test of Co-branding and Match-up Models', *Sport Management Review* 9, 49–78.

Yang, D.L. (2006), 'Economic Transformation and its Political Discontents in China: Authoritarianism, Unequal Growth and the Dilemmas of Political Development', *Annual Review of Political Science* 9, 143–64.

Yatsko, P. (n.d.), 'Now for a Reality Check: A Reborn Shanghai Needs to Grow beyond just its Glittering Skyline'. Retrieved 22 October 2006, from http://www.asiaweek.com/asiaweek/magazine/nations/0,8782,103434,00.html.

Yau, E.C.M. (2001), 'Hong Kong Cinema in a Borderless World', in E.C.M. Yau (ed.), *At Full Speed: Hong Kong Cinema in a Borderless World* (Minneapolis: University of Minnesota Press), pp. 1–28.

Yeh, A.G.O. (1996), 'Pudong – Remaking Shanghai as a World City', in Y.M. Yeung and Y.-W. Sung (eds), *Shanghai: Transformation and Modernization under China's Open Policy* (Hong Kong: Chinese University Press), pp. 273–89.

Yeung, C. (2003), 'One of a Kind', *South China Morning Post*, 8 October.

Yeung, Y.M. and Sung, Y.-W. (eds) (1996), *Shanghai: Transformation and Modernization under China's Open Policy* (Hong Kong: Chinese National University).

Yong, S. (1999), shangART Gallery website. Retrieved 22 October 2006, from http://china.shanghartgallery.com/galleryarchive/archives/detail/code/sy01;jsessionid=52BF67BCA603E6F64B43EFEC837D1283.

Yongzhe, H. (2000), '"365" Project for Better Housing', *Shanghai Star*, 29 February. Retrieved 6 February 2007, from <http://app1.chinadaily.com.cn/star/history/00-02-29/c13-365.html.

Zavrski-Makaric, D. (n.d.), 'Where to go in Sydney?' Retrieved 21 October 2006, from http://www.challengingdirections.com/pages2/Articles_WhereToGoSydney.html.

Zhang, T. (2004), 'New Urban Garbage: Color Pollution' (China.org.cn, 25 May 2004). Retrieved on 19 November 2006, from http://www.10thnpc.org.cn/english/2004/May/96405.htm.

Zhang, W. (2006), 'City Focuses on Creative Industry', Shanghai Daily News, 17 January 2006. Retrieved 9 November 2006, from http://english.eastday.com/eastday/englishedition/metro/userobject1ai1798448.html.

Zhang, Z. (2001), 'An Amorous History of the Silver Screen: The Actress as Vernacular Embodiment in Early Chinese Film Culture', *Camera Obscura* 16:3, 229–63.

Zheng, S. (2005), 'Shanghai – The Fastest City?', paper delivered at *Urban Age: A Worldwide Series of Conferences Investigating the Future of Cities*, Shanghai, July 2005. Retrieved 30 December 2006, from http://www.urban-age.net/03_conferences/conf_shanghai.html.

Zhou, H. (2003), 'Shanghai City: Spectacular Shanghai', in Gilmore and Dumont (eds).

Zviran, M., Te'eni, D. and Gross, Y. (2006), 'Does Color in Email make a Difference?', *Communications of the ACM* 49:4, 94–9.

Filmography

A Night in Mongkok / *Wong gok hak yau* (2004). Dir. Tung-shing Yee. HK.

Apocalypse Now (1979). Dir. Francis Ford Coppola. USA.

Awakening Spring (*1:99* project) (2003). Dir. Peter Chan. HK.

Before Sunrise (1995). Dir. Richard Linklater. USA.

Billy Connolly's World Tour (TV film: 1996). Dir. Nobby Clark. UK.

Blade Runner (1982). Dir. Ridley Scott. USA.

Braveheart (1995). Dir. Mel Gibson. USA.

Brief Encounter (1945). Dir. David Lean. UK.

Centre Stage / *Yuen ling yuk* / *Yuan ling wang* (1992). Dir. Stanley Kwan. HK.

C'est la vie, mon chérie / *Xin buliao qing* (1994). Dir Yee Tung-shing. HK.

Chungking Express / *Chung hing sam lam* (1994). Dir. Wong Kar Wai. HK.

City of Glass / *Boli zhi cheng* (1998). Dir. Mabel Cheung. HK.

The Deer Hunter (1978). Dir. Michael Cimino. USA.

Deng Xiaoping in 1928 (2004). Dir. Li Xiepu. China.

Le fabuleux destin d'Amélie (2001). Dir. Jean-Pierre Jeannet. France.

Finding Nemo (2003). Dir. Andrew Stanton and Lee Unkrich. USA.

Flowers of Shanghai / *Hai shang hua* (1998). Dir. Hou Hsiao-hsien. Taiwan.

Golden Chicken / *Gam gai* (2002). Dir. Leung Chun 'Samson' Chiu. HK.

Hell has Harbour Views (TV film: 2005). Dir. Peter Duncan. Australia.

Hero / *Ying xiong* (2002). Dir. Zhang Yimou. China.

The Hungry Mile (1953). MUA Film Unit. Australia.

Infernal Affairs / *Mou gaan dou* (2002). Dir. Wai Keung Lau and Siu Fai Mak. HK.

In the Mood for Love / *Fa yeung nin wa* (2000). Dir. Wong Kar-wai. HK / France.

It's a Wonderful Life (1946). Dir. Frank Capra. USA.

Ju Dou (1990). Dir. Zhang Yimou and Yang Fengliang. Japan / China.

Lantana (2001). Dir. Ray Lawrence. Australia / Germany.

Lai Man-Wai Father of Hong Kong Cinema (documentary: 2005). Dir. Choi Kai-kwong. HK.

Leaving Me, Loving You / *Dai sing siu si* (2004). Dir. Wilson Yip. HK/China.

Little Fish (2005). Dir. Rowan Woods. Australia

Lock, Stock and Two Smoking Barrels (1998). Dir. Guy Ritchie. UK.

London (1994). Dir. Patrick Keiller. UK.

The Long Good Friday (1980). Dir. John Mackenzie. UK.

Looking for Alibrandi (2000). Dir. Kate Woods. Australia.

The Lord of the Rings (trilogy) (2001–2003). Dir. Peter Jackson. New Zealand / USA/ Germany.

Marnie (1964). Dir. Alfred Hitchcock. USA.

The Matrix (1999). Dir. Andy Wachowski and Larry Wachowski. USA.

McDull, The Alumni / Chun tian hua hua tong xue hui (2006). Dir Leung Chun 'Samson' Chiu. HK.

McDull, Prince de la Bun (2004). Dir. Toe Yuen Kin-to. HK.

Mission Impossible II (2000). Dir. John Woo. USA / Germany.

Mission Impossible III (2006). Dir. J.J. Abrams. USA / Germany.

Muriel's Wedding (1994). Dir. P.J. Hogan. Australia / France.

My Life as McDull / Maidou Gushi (2001). Dir. Toe Yuen Kin-to. HK.

Napoléon (1927). Dir. Abel Gance. France.

The Natural (1984). Dir. Barry Levinson. USA.

On the Town (1949). Dir. Stanlet Donen. USA.

Once upon a Time in Shanghai / Shanghai jishi (1998). Dir. Xiaolian Peng. China.

Ordinary Heroes / Qian yan wan yu (1999). Dir. Ann Hui. HK.

Playing Beatie Bow (1986). Dir. Donald Crombie. Australia.

Police Story / Ging chaat goo si (1985). Dir. Jackie Chan. HK.

PTU (2003). Dir. Johnny To. HK.

Rabbit-Proof Fence (2002). Dir. Philip Noyce. Australia.

Radiance (1998). Dir. Rachel Perkins. Australia.

Rambo (1982). Dir. Ted Kotcheff. USA.

Rouge / Yin ji kau (1987). Dir. Stanley Kwan. HK.

Sanmao (The Adventures of) / Sanmao liuliang ji, (1949) Dir. Zhao Ming, Yan Gong. China.

Sanmao Joins the Army / San mao cun jun ji (1993). Dir. Zhang Jianya. China.

Shanghai Express (1932). Dir. Josef von Sternberg. USA.

Shanghai Triad / Yao a yao yao dao waipo qiao (1995). Dir. Zhang Yimou. France / China.

Superman (1978). Dir. Richard Donner. UK.

Suzhou River / Suzhou he (2000). Dir. Germany / China.

Temptress Moon / Feng yue (1996). Dir. Chen Kaige. China / HK.

They're a Weird Mob (1966). Dir. Michael Powell. Australia / UK.

Under Capricorn (1949). Dir. Alfred Hitchcock. USA.

Walkabout (1971). Dir. Nicolas Roeg. UK.

Who is Miss Hong Kong? (1:99 project) (2003). Dir. Joe Ma. HK.

The Wild, Wild Rose / Ye mei gui zhi lian (1960). Dir. Wang Tian-lin. HK.

The World of Suzie Wong (1960). Dir. Richard Quine. UK.

Index

Tourism and the Branded City